S0-FEO-675
OF
ARMAGEDDON
by Daniel Brookshier

BOYS BOOK OF ARMAGEDDON

A book of apocalyptic visions, doomsayers, bad puns, and fun facts, to make the end-times delightful and profitable.

By Daniel Brookshier

BOYS BOOKS PUBLISHING™

Making Fun of Making Fun of Everything™

Published by: Boys Books Publishing ®

This is the Print edition 1.0202

Editor: Kevin Gingrich

Cover Design & Illustration: Kathryn Yingling

Persnickety Mistake Seekers: Becky Winslow, Rene Marston, and Charles Akin

This book is a work of parody, satire, puns, pontification and editorial commentary. Do not assume any facts are correct nor that advise is viable. This book should not be read by anyone for any reason — especially not for its entertainment value. Do not read as a cure for insomnia without first consulting your doctor.

Some of the sections may have been published at http://boysbookofarmageddon.blogspot.com/, but in most cases the content has been expanded and the English corrected by a professional editor who had a prior job correcting grammatical errors on license plates.

For citation purposes, please refer to this document as:

Boys Book of Armageddon (2011) by Brookshier, Daniel L. (1960 - 2322) Executive Summary: A book of apocalyptic visions, doomsayers, bad puns, and fun facts, to make the end-times both delightful and profitable.

Dedications

Special thanks to all the people who believe in the end of the world. Without your beliefs, this book would just be about the Sun turning into a red giant in a few million years.

Of course, to Becky, who survived the birth of the book!

Jennifer, who has always said I should
write humor books.

Daniel Byrne, David Lewis and Chris Cook-Sussan,
who helped me sharpen wicked puns in high school.

My brother, Luke (the Skywalker) Brookshier,
who proved our family's awkward humor was comedy by
becoming a writer for *SpongeBob SquarePants*.

Mom and Dad — just send money, okay?

You don't have the God you want.
You have the God that you've got.
Not that there's anything wrong with that.

Blessed is the one who reads the words of this prophecy, and blessed are those who hear it and take to heart what is written in it, because the time is near.

— *Revelation 1:3*

WARNING

By reading this book you are absolving the authors, editors, artists, publisher, book sellers, libraries, and well-meaning friends who lent this book to you, of all responsibility for its contents, advice, predictions, warnings, comfort, completeness, accuracy, fear-mongering, importance, truthiness, interpretations of religions, and its recommendations about zombie defense, fetishes, mind control, aliens, salvation, and marketing.

Every sentence, word, letter, picture, and all matter used in the production of this work are not dangerous unless misused. You are responsible for your own actions, thoughts, imaginings, fantasies, mental health, friends, relatives, beliefs, and enemies (real or imagined).

If you refuse to take responsibility for your own actions, you are probably a psychopath and should not read this book.

Put this book down now and walk away slowly.

WE REALLY WE MEAN IT

Go back and read the warning. We know people avoid the warnings, but that is not an excuse that will hold up in court. The pages are numbered in an ever-increasing sequence so that you read every page. Don't think we won't check. We have people! Don't risk meeting one of our people in a dark alley. We are not making threats, but it goes without saying.

FINAL WARNING: THIS IS SUPPOSED TO BE FUNNY

If you believe any joke, picture, diagram, web link, opinion, comment, scholarly reference, quote, or degradation to be upsetting or blasphemous, you are mistaken. This book is a work of humor that contains religious, scientific, and marketing references to make the humor even funnier.

If humor about your religious beliefs offends you, we don't need your money or your pity. Put this book down. Now!

If you are really mad because of the contents of this book, please buy a few hundred copies and burn them. The fire will be spectacular, and the TV stations will happily cover any book burnings on the evening news. Special note: we chose the book's paper for its flammability and flame color.

Note: The eBook version does not burn very well unless loaded on a Kindle, Nook, Sony Reader, or iPad.

Deleting of electronic copies of this book is considered the same as book burning. Deletion is, however, not a very symbolic act of censorship unless you buy thousands of copies (we'll give you a volume discount).

Final Warning:

IF YOU CONTINUE TO READ THIS BOOK, YOU MAY GO DIRECTLY TO HELL.

The author takes no responsibility for damage to health, property or its loss due to puns, belly laughs, psychosomatic illness, catalepsy, or conniption fits. Reading this book will certainly invoke the wrath of the gods — your god or the one that is really in charge.

Do not use this book as a weapon. The police will track you down from the DNA, fingerprints, and fecal matter from reading this book in the porcelain library.

Read this book at your own risk. You have been warned!

NO REFUNDS!

Blasphemy

This book is considered blasphemy by almost every religion in the world. By reading this book, you may ruin all chances for eternal life in Heaven, reincarnation, or refunds on tithing to your church. You may already be guaranteed eternal damnation, but that's not our fault, and this book surely won't help.

A Notice to Girls

Please read this book. Just because we used 'Boys' in the title doesn't mean we are excluding you from the fun. Titles like *Unisex of Armageddon*, *He/She/Other of Armageddon*, or *Equal Opportunity Armageddon*, just don't make it to the Best Seller List.

A Notice to the Anal

The 'Boys' in Boys Books, is plural, not possessive. Don't call or write us to correct the title to be Boy's. All typos and grammar errors are for humor purposes and not the result of poor editing.

Pre and Post-Apocalyptic Contents

This page unintentionally left blank.
Please continue to the next page.
Please do not try to make the secret writing visible by exposing this page to 2% milk.

Apocalyptic Introduction

This book is a guide to the end of the world. Face facts, the end is near. Nature has gone mad. Mad scientists have gone wild. Mad terrorists are doing their mad god's will. Vengeful gods are punishing their creations, and the good old-fashioned biblical apocalypse from big "G," God, is getting ready to smite the sinners at any moment.

Yes, the world is ending, but you have questions. How the world will end? Why it will end? How will you prepare, profit, and survive? We have solutions to all your apocalyptic problems (also known as apocalyptic opportunities).

This isn't a negative book. This is the most positive book you will find about the end of the world. Sure we have to scare the socks off you, but that's to get you ready to live through the end.

The end of the world is opportunity knocking. Make lemonade from those apocalyptic lemons! If we can't make lemonade, cold hard cash is even better.

How do you make the end of the world a reason to celebrate? How will you survive the apocalypse in comfort and luxury? Why not become a successful entrepreneur at the end of the world?

Doomsayers are often wrong. How will you deal with such disappointment? What if this is all a joke? How do you survive a world that isn't going to end next Tuesday?

This book is full of information you need. How do you explain the end of humanity to your friends, church, fellow workers, family, and little children? How will it end? How can you survive a little longer or go end your life on Earth with flare, style, and have time for a witty last word?

You have questions; we have answers! Barring answers, we will let you know how to properly panic when the need arrises.

Why This Book?

We get asked, why did we write this book? The answers are rather mundane: for fame, to pay for our dog's food, to get chicks (little yellow chicks because we want to own a chicken farm, like our grandfather), and to survive the end of the world in our own bunker from the proceeds of this book.

Education is also important to us here at Boys Books. We are at heart teachers, especially to all boys under the age of 83. We love to teach. We have lessons on the prophets of doom, extreme religions, cults, science, survival, and marketing. With a wide array of subjects, we also get this book put on shelves in every section of the bookstore. Say hello when you see us smuggling this book from the humor section to the marketing isle.

We also believe people should laugh at the end of the world. Laughing at the apocalypse seems to be the ultimate goal of all humor: The last laugh.

This Book was Channeled from the Spirit World ...

We only typed the book. We're channeling a spirit that may or may not be the actual writer. We may just be insane and hearing voices. It's hard to tell the difference, and we usually take our medication.

You might have noticed that we said we. That's right, everybody in the Boys Books office is channeling. Not everyone at once, we take turns because channeling in five-channel surround sound is annoying.

We heartily recommend channeling as a method to write books. We have written other books and it's much easier to write books this way. No need to think. Just listen to the voices in your head.

Sadly, the spirit we're saddled with is as bad a speller as we are. Same goes for his grammar. The spelling and grammar issues are a sort of a disappointment. Obviously, we're not channeling somebody important or an alien from another dimension with a decent education.

We could have gotten a bigger advance on the book if it were in ancient Mayan or Sumerian, from a famous potentate or trusted advisor of the time. If we had been channeling Houdini, Joe Bob, or James Randi, we'd be a number one book in the apocalyptic science section of the best seller list–for a couple of days at least.

You Might Want to Know

> *James Randi is still alive at the time of this writing. As a channeled spirit he comes in quite clearly unless we call him on our AT&T networked iPhone.*

To channel some Joe Shmoe is just our luck. We'd prefer Mark Twain or Kurt Vonnegut. We'd even settle for Nero's food taster. The guy we are channeling is at least a hoot.

We don't always tune into the same guy. Sometimes it's a long dead ESPN 3 sportscaster or the sort of dead people you only see on bad cable community access. Imagine listening for hours about someone's Hummel figurines for hours.

We are not crazy. Voices don't tell us to kill the mailman, and we don't think it is CIA agents in the next room talking about us. It's just plain boring stuff picked up from the cosmic ether.

Every first Wednesday of the month we hear some city's chamber of commerce meeting. Sadly, the sound and video are so poor we can't figure out what city. All we know is that the voices go on and on about parking enforcement.

The clearest signal is from the real author of this book. Not as good as tuning in Walt Disney or Peter the Great, but much better than cable news.

Our spirited coauthor is not prominent on the front cover, or even the back cover. Our marketing department wouldn't let us credit him directly. Just imagine: "As channeled to us by a poor dead shmoe." The legal department didn't want us to publish his name either. Should the voice in our heads come back from the dead as a zombie or be reincarnated, we'd need to pay royalties.

There were a few issues. Channeling isn't a bed of roses, unless you are counting the thorns. This spirit has Tourette's syndrome. Remember Tourette's? That's the disease that causes you to twitch uncontrollably and cuss like a sailor's parrot.

Our channelled Joe Schmoe is good at the following poetic prose: profanity, cussing, taking God's name in vain, taking our name in vain, insults, sexual innuendoes, disgusting proclivities, and outright pornographic descriptions that would kill even a doubting nun. Our mother defines it simply as "a potty mouth."

Great feats of editing and rewriting were required to publish the book you're reading. This book was nearly 600 filthy pages before editing. Not that we have a problem with cussing and pornography, but Mom is still scootering about. She's okay with her kids being possessed, channeling spirits, or even with the prospect of us going to Hell, as long as it is a Christian-approved Hell. Profanity, though, turns her hair gray, and hair dye is expensive.

You can order the uncensored version for the price of a new car. We still have a box of the filthy unedited text. We expect only one person to want the naughty version, so that's why the price is so high, and we need a new car. Mom, if you are reading this paragraph, we are just kidding about the naughty version. Not kidding about the car. Send money, please.

Other Reasons for the Book

Some people are not going to believe that the world has ended until they are six feet under the rubble and meet Saint Peter. Others may need to feel the heat of Hell before they understand that life has consequences. A few people are a bit more observant, but you need some clues that the end is near.

We want to educate the masses about the end of the world. Educating the masses means more money. Even teachers need to drive exotic sports cars and have a house on the beach.

Can you spot the signs of an alien invasion? Do you know how to make a tin foil hat (copper mesh works better) to prevent alien overlords from controlling your mind?

We saw a gap in this type of information. Sure, there are many books on the end of the world. Are they humorous? Are they nondenominational? Yes, but this book is still better.

Take that to the bank, if your bank still exists, as the financial crisis is another sign of the end-times.

If you want a leg up on the end of the world, then that's why we wrote this book. This book is for you. We also need your money.

Some other important reasons why we wrote this book:

- ✓ Dispels myths that are silly.
- ✓ Reinforces myths that are good.
- ✓ Reads between the lines of myths to find the mything myths between the myths.
- ✓ Invents new myths, just to not myth-out on a good joke or pun.
- ✓ Teaches the best way to prepare and survive or just accept end-of-the-world myths.
- ✓ In general, this book is either hit or myth.
- ✓ This book has puns that could end the world all on their own and is thus a self-fulfilling prophecy.

Experiments

No book for boys is worth the cover price without experiments. That also means the inevitable statement written by our lawyers. Our lawyer says that warnings will keep us out of jail. Bright orange prison jumpers are not very flattering. We don't want to write the Boys Book of Prison Escapes that badly.

Please read the following warning and heed its advice. Then send us the contents of your piggy bank so we are able to pay our lawyer and put his kids through college.

> ***WARNING:*** *Ask your parents for permission to perform the experiments!*

We don't really care if you get parental supervision. We just need the warning to give your parents the illusion that we are responsible publishers. Parents never read past the warnings. Your parents have also now assumed we are responsible adults. Adults? Maybe… Certainly, a lawsuit short of being a responsible. The authors are not responsible for anything – we are quite irresponsible.

If you are a member of the *MythBusters*, do not attempt to perform any of these experiments. Yes, we know you are experts, but we also know this stuff is too dangerous for even MythBusters to handle. Also, we have never seen any MythBusters ask for their parents for permission to do a dangerous experiment – that's so uncool!

The experiments are not meant to be dangerous. That means we haven't made sure the experiments are safe; we just think they are reasonably safe if you use the help of a professional stunt man. You should therefore believe that every experiment will cause death, dismemberment, a criminal record, and a lengthy stay in a mental institution.

Each experiment has questions. This is to show your teacher and parents that you've learned from these experiments. If your parents and teachers aren't interested in your answers, please tell your mental health therapist your answers.

Wikipedia and Other Web Links

Much of the content of this book, when not completely born of fantasies from a sleep-deprived imagination, is based on research from the web. Most links are from Wikipedia, and others were found through Google searches.

When possible, the links to interesting information have been placed in the footnotes. Use these links with caution, as some are unsavory or have been changed by agents with nefarious purposes to discredit the information in this book.

Please report dead links to Boys Books Publishing® to aid in creating the subsequent editions of this book. Unlike the dead, we cannot bury our dead web links or raise them from the grave.

Learn This Word!

We like new words and phrases! We teach you at least one fun vocabulary word or phrase in every chapter so that mom and dad think this book is educational. Kids should expand their vocabulary! Words are cool, and we at the Boys Books offices love to learn new words. Here is your first word:

Learn This Word

> ***Warning**: Our first word is really important, 'warning.' We have used it a lot so far. A warning tells you that we think something is dangerous, that you might die, become crippled, go to prison, or be grounded by your parents. Warning is also a weak word. We gave you a warning, but you'll do whatever this book says anyway. You are now properly responsible for your actions, so go ahead. We have shifted the legal responsibility from us to you, so only you will suffer the consequences. We warned you! There is bad stuff in here and you can get hurt. You are old enough to read and old enough to know better.*

About the Author

This book was created by the team at Boys Books Publishing. That said, our leader and head writer is Daniel Brookshier. Because Daniel makes the big bucks and pays our salaries here at the office, we need to kowtow to our leader with a bit of praise. We have hopes that we might curry enough favor to get the fabled Christmas bonus. That said, onward with the inflation of Daniel's ego:

Daniel Brookshier was raised Baptist, fed by a Jewish family at least once a week as a teenager, married into and divorced Catholic, is a proud caretaker of a Buddha image, is agnostic in at least fourteen religions, atheist in five others, and a member in good standing in four cults. Daniel is currently a slack Sub Genius minister (http://www.subgenius.com).

Born with an ingrown funny bone, Daniel is a punographer of letters, has a punishing wit and dreams of writing the great American novel (tentatively titled Crime and **Pun**ishment).

Daniel's humor is legendary. Daniel won a pun contest at a regional Mensa convention by punning about nothing but chickens (well, there was one duck, but all puns were fowl). As the judge said, "I know punography when I see it."

Though living now in Texas, Daniel is planning a move to a well-stocked, abandoned missile silo in the Midwest to await the end of the world in 2012 (or whenever the world decides the time is right to snuff itself) and because it's cool to say you live in a missile silo.

Daniel has written several books that only a few smart people will ever read. Because smarter people love to laugh, Daniel wrote this book. This book is also a cunning scheme for Daniel to get interviewed by NPR, *The Daily Show*, and *The Colbert Report*.

You Might Want to Know

Sometimes we want to inform you of a fact or give a little advice. We call this, ***You Might Want to Know****. In this case, there is something you might want to know about Daniel's "winning" of the pun contest. He won by default. There were at least 15 other contestants, and Daniel was the first competitor. After Daniel's punishing performance, the competitors all forfeited, having no hope of beating such a skilled punster. Daniel's parting chicken puns were to taunt his competitors, calling them "chicken" and being afraid to compete because they might "lay an egg" or "fowl up."*

Eschatology

Did you know this book is a type of science? It's called eschatology,[1] which literally means "a study of the end." How cool! There is only one slight problem: the world could end before you get a proper job in eschatology.

Writing a book, like this is one, of the best ways for eschatology to win you real cash prizes. High paying eschatology jobs are scarce. An eschatology degree will get you a job as a cashier at Wal-Mart. You need to write a book or start a cult to make the big money.

We were too busy to start a cult, so you get to read this book. We didn't start a cult because need to file as a nonprofit with the IRS. Nobody wants to be the leader of the cult. That makes us non-prophet which makes the paperwork so complex we can't afford the legal fees.

There are a few professional eschatologists, but not many that write books. Some only write, "The End is Nigh" on signs and run around Hyde Park in London.

Why do nonprofit cults have prophets?

Dr. Brookshier, Eschatologist

The Dr. title is short for "Driver." We drive. If you do, we suggest putting that on your business card. Nobody is a legitimate doctor here at Boys Books. As eschatologists who drive, we write, "Dr. Brookshier, Eschatologist" on our business cards.

Why become an eschatologist? 'Eschatologist' is hard to pronounce! You get more respect when folks can't pronounce your profession. Better yet, folks are afraid to admit they don't know what eschatologist does. Sure they will ask, but not until late in the party, after much drinking and merriment. Luckily alcohol makes them forget your profession and they just re-invite that interesting doctor fellow.

---

[1] http://en.wikipedia.org/wiki/Eschatology

Eschatology is fun. You can't beat scaring the pants off folks with tales of the world ending. That's why they keep inviting you to parties. Not for the doom and gloom, but the suspense of how to survive it all.

As an eschatology practitioner, you don't need to be accurate, just creative. Most of the doomsayers were hopped up on drugs, addled by fasting in the desert, or just crazy. Imagine how easy it is to write interesting and scholarly works from the ravings of lunatics. It's even better if you treat the doomsayers as competent and infallible soothsayers.

Technology is a boon for the modern eschatologist. Google and Wikipedia do most of the heavy lifting. The news is also filled with signs of the Apocalypse. Republicans are always giving a new reason why the Democrats are triggering the Apocalypse, all delivered daily on cable news. Throw in a few 'fraidie cat scientists and you'll never run out of eschatology material.

A professor of Eschatology seems like an odd thing to find at a university. Happily, there are quite a few, especially at religious schools. These universities believe an eschatology professor is money well spent because of their many positive qualities, despite their negative profession.

An eschatologist is like a canary in a coal mine. When your eschatologist calls in sick, you should check the color of the sky. Double-check the bulges on the butts of the students, those are devil tails about to sprout. It's time to cash in that vacation time you were saving and get out of town before the brimstone starts falling from the sky.

At theological seminaries or those fancy private colleges run by TV preachers, eschatology is a valued degree specialty. Religious institutions are obligated to constantly recalculate the end as predictions fail to deliver. They insist on the best and brightest eschatologists come up with new dates and seek new signs. A religion without a properly predicted end of the world is like applesauce without Tabasco — not so hot.

Although we are eschatologists, we don't try too hard to predict the end. The odds of picking the right date are low. Doomsayers are all failures; eventually. So far, there is no such thing as a successful doomsayer. We don't see any reason to join a club of losers.

We prefer to work on the "signs" of the end and the panic between the signs. One of thousands of things could add up any second and cause the end of the world. The key is preparing — even if the signs are pointing the other way. We're an eschatologist specializing in the end or not end. We don't pick sides. We just want to scare you with everything, including what happens when the end does not happen.

Eschatologist Economy

There is an unimaginable amount of money in eschatology. Be a consultant to a TV preacher. Work at a religious university. Start a cult. Why not write a book on the end of the world?

We just did a search on Amazon for "eschatology." There are hundreds of books, tapes, and videos! You might well say that there are no eschatology books for boys … Well, yes, there is one now, but you get the idea. Yes, there are already thousands of doom-based books on the market, but many fertile niches remain for the creative eschatologist. Write about the end of the world for magicians, jugglers, or even *Girls Book of Armageddon* (send us 20% of the profits for each idea you use or any spare inheritance you can't spend fast enough after your parents find out what you are doing and have a simultaneous heart attack).

Don't worry about competition from other eschatologists or the ire of skeptics. Competition is good for eschatology and so are critics. Most predictions fail anyway, so feel free to cover any doomsayers past present and future.

Competition also means debunking your competitor's theories. You can make a very comfortable living debunking your critics as they would debunk upon you. It's not even necessary to promote your own counter theories! Just saying the competition is crazy, illogical, religious, or gets checks from big drug companies or the Church of Bogus is good enough.

Our best example of a debunker making a comfortable living is Phil Plait, writer of *Death From The Skies!* Phil is always debunking theories of a pseudoscientific or religious nature. Of course, as an Astronomer, he has his own idea about how space can and will kill us in the fullness of time. He isn't a full-blown eschatology expert, just an astronomer. Phil's genius is to debunk all manner of pseudoscience and doomsaying while promoting his own scientific doomsaying.

Astronomy is relatively boring and does not sell many books, unless you do a little death and destruction. In our book, right here, that's doomsaying that Phil's hawking.

Phil is not a fibber. The cosmos unfolds over millions of years. The chances of the Earth being destroyed by rather nasty unfolding of cosmic events could take millennia. Someday, millions of years from now, just before we are all cooked by cosmic rays or a stray black hole, someone is going to say, "Phil was right!"

Eschatologist for Hire

Did we mention that we do eschatology consulting? We charge very reasonable rates for our services. If you are reading this, then give us a call.

Why hire an eschatologist? Look at how useful the information in this book is. We cover life, death, salvation, damnation, and, especially, making money before and after the end-times. With all that useful knowledge running through our heads, why not get your own eschatologist for your home?

This is like a self-help book, and we are your personal self-help gurus. This book is well worth the cover price, but why not pay us a small fortune for quality one-on-one help? Think of us as an end-times success coach. Tempted to hire us yet? Don't wait too long, for obvious reasons. Note: We also do parties, weddings, and bat mitzvahs.

Experiment: Apocalyptic Monopoly

For our first experiment, we want to get you in the mood for the end of the world. Go to the closet and get your Monopoly game. Lay out the houses and hotels on each of the spaces. Now, creatively destroy every other space. Use your imagination and don't use the same method twice. Do not pass Go. Do not collect two-hundred dollars.

Here are a few suggestions:

- ✓ Rocks, thrown very hard.
- ✓ Fireworks
- ✓ Chili (meat, no beans)
- ✓ Hammer
- ✓ Bottle of water

Write down each of your methods. Post your pictures on Facebook for other students to compare.

Questions

- ✓ Did your sister tattle on you?
- ✓ How were the nearby Monopoly spaces affected by the ones you did destroy?
- ✓ Did you use 'The Voice of God' when you started destroying? If so, what did you say?
- ✓ How many in your family seem pleased that Monopoly will not be played on Thanksgiving?

Our Obsession With the End

Our fascination with the end of the world is fanatical and never-ending. Google "Armageddon" or "apocalypse" and you will see just how in love we are with the end.

This passion isn't coming just from religions, but also politicians, the media, and scientists. There are thousands of ways humankind will cease to exist, from the wrath of gods, to nature, to wars, to technology, to the pundits, elected officials, and their new or repealed laws.

Why do we seem to care so much about the end of the world? Why do we have religions praying for the world to end, or busily working on their get-out-of-hell-free cards to ensure salvation in the end-times? Why do ecologists talk more about the destruction of the Earth than about inventing solutions to reverse the problem? Why do scientists seem to get great pleasure from telling us about disasters we can't prevent? Why do scientists study things that will kill us if someone drops a test tube? Shouldn't scientists be inventing un-droppable test tubes? Nobody is working hard on anti-doom technology! It's all naysayers and problem finders.

Pink Monkeys

Mankind's obsession with the apocalypse started when our brains evolved a skill that animals don't have much of, imagination. We can imagine anything. Let's play with our imagination for a minute.

Imagine a pink monkey with gun.

Got that monkey imagined? Good! Now imagine the pink monkey hates smokers and likes to shoot anyone lighting up a cigarette. Once that idea is in your head, it is hard to get rid of. From now on, from time to time, when you see someone smoking, you will think of that pink monkey shooting the smoker. If you are a smoker, you will start getting nervous, imagining that monkey gunning for you (you are too young to smoke anyway).

Our ability to imagine something as silly and scary as a gun toting pink monkey, means we will certainly imagine avenging angels, killer asteroids, and Mayan calendars ending the world.

Imagine a vengeful pink monkey ready to destroy all of humanity for lighting up a cancer stick. See, easy.

As a new member of the Pink Monkey Church and BBQ, you now understand how powerful imagination can be. One minute you are reading a book, the next you're building monkey traps and thinking about how to destroy the cigarette industry with recombinant DNA that makes tobacco taste like Brussels Sprouts.

Imagination is Magic

Whatever we imagine seems real. It sounds like a flaw of the human mind, but it saves time that could be the difference between life and death. If someone tells you there is a tiger, it is better to start running than to prove the existence of the tiger with science.

Many of our ancestors survived because of imagination. Those that imagined a tiger, ran and survived. Anyone that took their time taking samples of tiger poo to send it off to a laboratory to validate the tiger hypothesis, became tiger food, and eventually tiger poo.

Our ability to imagine isn't all cupcakes and ice cream. We can't yell 'fire' in a theater because people would get trampled in the panic. You can't 'cry wolf' in a burning theater either because people will die in the fire trying to save an imaginary wolf from the flames.

Look what happens when someone on Fox News calls the president a Muslim? No truth required to get people running for the exits. Our paranoia is one hundred percent powered by pure and natural imagination.

Some say faith is plain old human imagination, not hard facts. It's a problem when people have faith because it is not based on reality. "Not so fast," we say here at Boys Books (mostly when people are running with scissors, not away from tigers). How is faith a problem?

Faith without evidence saves time. Sounds like a good thing, right? Just assume what a doomsayer says is real, you will be saved! Have faith in the end of the world before its too late! It's like when you hear a tiger, that's the time to run. You don't have the time to juggle test tubes to scientifically prove it is tiger poop. Take a leap of faith that a pile of poo and a tiger roar is enough evidence to run.

Imagination and this faith are problematic. Our brains have all sorts of emotions and motivations. Things get mixed up. We start imagining tigers in the darkness of the closet or lurking under the bed. When we start to get a little emotional and too creative, that's when doomsayers and their followers get into big trouble. Let's look at the things that make us imagine the end of the world:

Revenge

We are petty–not petty your kitty–we mean low down dirty bastard petty. Look closely at doomsayers and you will see a little turn of a smile, not because they are going to Heaven soon, but that everyone else will suffer horrible deaths. Simply, the end isn't really about being saved, but the sweet smell of revenge.

Think about a person that you really hate. The school bully. Yes, that guy. Okay, that's enough. There's too much angst in your young brain and we only need a little for our thought experiment. Hard to have a thought experiment simultaneously you're busy plotting revenge.

Now, imagine getting your revenge. Ignore the warm feeling you are having right now, just concentrate on the specific type of revenge you'll rain down on your mortal enemy.

Revenge isn't friendly or therapeutic. Don't be embarrassed, we understand, that guy is a twit. Revenge fantasies go from throwing moldy cheese at them to some serious maiming. We blame our revenge fantasies on video games. Not the violence part, but that we can't put our enemy's face on the monsters so that we get a little joy in our lives.

Learn This Word

> ***Metaphor**: A metaphor is another way of saying something another way. Metaphors help you understand something complicated by explaining a complicated idea it in a simpler way. Al Gore uses the metaphor of boiling a frog slowly. The frog understands hot and cold, but doesn't notice that it is getting really hot. The metaphor is false, but persists. Frogs are not that stupid. However, people secretly hate frogs so the metaphor works. Please, Jamie and Adam, test this Myth with a Mythturn, a cartoonish cannibal cooking pot and a Kermit Muppet. Ask for your mom's for permission first!*

Revenge is usually associated with prison or worse. Torture and death are illegal, even when there is a bully getting what they deserve. Unfortunately, the metaphor is lost in the reality. Bullies are usually chowing down on unjust dessert. We are left starved, unable to taste delicious vengeance.

Most methods of revenge have legal consequences. Your parents will ground you for at least a month. Imagine no video games for a month! Get caught at school for throwing stinky, moldy cheese at your enemies will get you detention where there are more bullies to torment you! If you are in a traditional religion, there is a trip to some kind of hell in your future. If you believe in reincarnation, a karmic nightmare is assured. Simply, you are not allowed to have personal revenge.

We are stuck with waiting on revenge from another source. We need someone else to do the dirty work. Why not avenging angels, gods, or just a convenient act of nature? We'd even settle for a terrorist, if they target the bullies in our lives.

We have great revenge fantasies for even minor annoyances. An eye for an eye is not really in our vocabulary. It's more a bucket of blood for a paper cut. When that guy cuts in line at the Starbucks, we don't just jump back in front of them, instead we glare at them and imagine some creative justice, like an eye-crossing wedgie. We don't all turn the other cheek. Even if we did turn the other cheek, deep inside, we'd prefer a small incident with the earth opening up and sucking them to Hell.

Somebody is going to deserve whatever nastiness that the end is going to supply, including a ticket to a never-ending damnation and eternal torment. Even better if their deaths are slow and torturous.

Ending the world is great revenge. Our enemies are destroyed in a very spectacular way and a bonus because the world's ability to create new bullies is neutered. No new people, so no more bad people. Ultimate revenge! See, everyone wins!

Learn This Word

> ***Xenophobe:*** *A xenophobe is someone who hates other people not like him or herself. Many xenophobes like only people of the same race, country, religion, and politics as their own. Xenophobia helps us choose friends. Knowing who your friends are is important when you are writing the invitation list for a bomb shelter.*

The world is full of **xenophobes**, hypocrites, and selfish bastards. Sure, there are a couple of saints, but most of us have someone to hate. You don't need a specific bully, just potential bullies that are not your intellectual clones.

We don't have to be directly wronged. Some think we are evil when we don't share our money, or good fortune. Simply, the have-nots want revenge on the haves. Even better though, the haves wan't preemptive revenge on the have-nots who are out to get theirs. Then there are the poor who think they will be rich someday and want revenge on the other poor that someday will hate them for being rich. Oh yes, lot's of revenge is in the air.

We believe that anyone who has wronged us, treated us impolitely, or given us a wedgie, should be subjected to a bit of divine retribution. We are just unforgiving **SOB**s with long memories.

Learn This Word

> ***SOB:*** *SOB stands for Sober Outstanding Boys. You might have heard that SOB stands for something related to children born to unwed mothers, but that is just a common misunderstanding.*

Why do we need the world to end, just to punish our enemies? Why isn't H. E. Double Hockey Sticks good enough for sinners and those who we find are ugly or just plain annoying? Why have an apocalypse when there's a perfectly good Hell? Simple, we want to see our nemesis destroyed in person or, if you are very lucky, on your Tivo, over and over. We also want those bullies punished here on Earth, just in case Hell isn't as bad as people say.

Bad people hardly ever get punished on Earth. We just have to have faith that Hell exists or an afterlife of eternal punishment of your choice. We crave revenge on a cataclysmic scale. We want the justice done right here on Earth, with no way to escape, not in a place we don't expect to visit. Hell isn't a reality TV show where we get to watch our enemies tortured (though it would get better ratings than *Survivor*).

Why punch someone in the nose when you can punch them with a space rock as big as your mother's home town? That's the other bit of good news, we don't need to get involved. We even have an alibi on the day in question. An act of God lets you avoid those embarrassing questions from the police.

Scientists want revenge too. Scientists are quite happy for us all to die of a killer comet, because that will serve us right for not buying more copies of their books on killer comets.

Revenge by way of apocalypse is final. More logical than the Christian Heaven and Hell to sort out sinners after they die. We get a satisfying revenge right here on Earth. We get to watch it on TV too!

Karma and reincarnation pale in comparison with a god smiting civilization. Ending the world stops all the bad stuff from happening. Nothing will ever go wrong again. End the world and evil will never again have a chance.

If you end the world, there's no more bad people. Kind of cool, eh? No more polluters! No more Democrats or Republicans! No more people with contrary opinions! No more schoolteachers and their dirty, dirty books! The door to Hell is locked, and we have thrown away the key.

Let's review. An apocalypse will kill everyone that is bad. The bad people will die horrible torturous deaths. All us good people go to Heaven with a warm smile on our faces, knowing our enemies are in a much warmer inferno of Hell. No more babies, no adolescent rebellion, no politics, no competing religions, and no other opinions. Nobody to call you names or point out your faults. Just you and your single minded clones in Heaven and everyone else in Hell.

Even if you are an atheist, this sounds sweet, doesn't it? Do you see why end-of-the-world fantasies are so popular?

Worry

We worry about the ends of our lives. We worry a lot! That's why the end of the world is important. We want it to all finally come to a clear and distinct end because all that worrying about the end of the world would be wasted! We hate to waste, so we need the world to end. Think of it as the ultimate in recycling.

Why worry? Worry is a huge part of our ability to protect ourselves. Worry helps us prepare for dangerous things. We are told that the world will end, and we believe it might be true. The brain has a tendency to believe things as a defense mechanism, We imagine there might be tigers and the fight or flight response kicks in. Time to grab a pointy stick, adult diapers and running shoes. With apocalypse, we just add canned peaches and start digging a hole to live in.

"Worry"–that's right, double air quotes worry–is the only true constant of end-of-the-world fanatics. We don't want the world to end, but we need to worry about it happening. We worry about worrying about the world being kicked out from under us. Religious battles, nutty professors, killer comets, the Sun going to become a super nova, or calendars that expire in 2012, we worry about it all. All that worry has to go somewhere.

A big part of the "worry" is to feel good about buying end-of-the-world books like this one. We find it hard to come up a better reason to worry. Tell your friends!

Why End the World Now?

Why now? This is a very interesting question. If this is all about wickedness, isn't there enough evil to end the world right now? If a god is going to solve the problem of evil, why is he/she/it taking his/her/its time? Many good people are being inconvenienced by evil right now.

This book is obviously blasphemy — why wait until it's in the third edition and fifth printing to strike us down? We think it is a damn good time for a final reckoning. It's high time for a battle between good book publishers and the evil book publishers.

Why dates like 2012? Round it all out and do it in the year 2,000 or even 2010? 2013 would be perfectly unlucky, especially on a certain Friday. If you were a god, wouldn't you want a nice round number with a divine significance? Celestial alignments can give a little more zing to the day that all live is erased, don't you think?

This sort of begs the question, why all at once? Why can't you just take out the wicked one by one? The blessed wake up one day and the nasty bastard next door who frighten the kids every Halloween is gone and a "For Sale" sign is on the lawn.

In the Book of Revelation, we also have a big fight against good and evil. This is true of several other religions, so not just a fad. It's like these gods are looking for a bit of entertainment. Strike the wicked down already. There is no need for knocking a wet cat upside the head of a demon. Just send a bolt down from the heavens.

A big war of Joe Good Guy versus Ultimate Evil seems a bit odd too. We're already having wars here and there. Why destroy the world all at once? Is this about efficiency?

We assume one of your neighbors is a bastard. Why not enlist the services of a vengeful god? Pray hard enough and that evil neighbor is killed by avenging angels which stops him from letting his dog poop on your porch.

How about sending your neighbor to war in a country? We need our neighbor to be far enough away so that we are not bothered by the sound of his screams as he is eaten by a demonic harpy.

This brings us back to Armageddon. Armageddon is not an event, but a rather big hill in Israel. Armageddon is where we are going to send our evil neighbors to fight the last war between good and evil.

Revelation implies Armageddon is the final battlefield. Somehow all the bad guys will show up in this historical tourist destination and shoot it out. Do they get teleported? Are they issued bus tickets? Why can't your boss be zapped into a war zone today?

Gods, being all knowing, why can't they prevent evil? Why not nip the nasty evil person in the bud? If you are against abortion, wait until they reach the age of five. That's not too late or too soon. By the age of five, you can guess they will be genocidal killers. They can't hold a gun properly until they are at least eight, so you have time to be certain. Remember, we don't condone killing. Just saying gods could be doing some godly brain surgery or divine group therapy.

We are not all knowing, but we knew a long time ago that Saddam Hussein was not going to be a saint. The first time he kicked his grandma in the shins for not giving him a lollypop, a god could have done something right then. A small asteroid aimed at Saddam's head could have corrected the mistake and prevented two wars.

Ending the World Isn't Brain Surgery

Why can't these gods study a little brain surgery? For decades, we have known a proper frontal lobotomy will convert a nasty criminal into a bag boy at the local market. Lobotomy converts a willful criminal to a useful pink-monkey-slave that can still tie his shoes and not drool too much at the family picnic. Faith is easier if you don't have that bothersome free will. We don't condone lobotomy, but if a god does it, lobotomy is okay, right? No messy ice picks, just the wiggling fickle finger of fate up a bad guy's nose.

You might have seen on the History Channel that Mesoamerican civilization performed brain surgery. Could that have been Mayans avoiding thoughts of 2012?

The brain surgery the Mayans practiced was probably just comic relief. Imagine the Mayan version of Moe, Curly, and Larry creating the same type of holes in their skulls.

Fruit Flies

Imagine you are a fruit fly. You started as an egg with five hundred brothers and sisters. You zipped through puberty to adulthood looking for a soulmate. This is just your first week of life. You are going to die in less than two months, so you are in a hurry.

Now imagine some biologist invents a pesticide to kill you and your entire race. You are all going to die a whole week before you go senile or see your great grandchildren. No natural death, buzzing, in your sleep! This is the fruit fly apocalypse.

An apocalypse for humans is the same as the fruit fly. We are puny bits of matter compared to powerful gods and the infinity of the universe. A biologist who specializes in killing insects is no less a god to the fruit fly or, if you prefer, a world-ending fender bender with an asteroid the size of Hoboken, New Jersey.

Humans have much bigger brains than fruit flies, so we imagine and worry about the end. We eat less rotted fruit and don't get much joy from flying up people's noses, but we are alike in how we would feel about the end of the world. We don't want the world to end before we die of old age. The universe is also not going to give a rat's sphincter when humanity is gone, just as we would not miss gnat-kind when they are gone.

Keeping It Real

Plain old death is just not interesting. Old age, disease, and accidents are not exciting. We want a grand death. We want to go out fighting demons or outwitting aliens trying to eat us for lunch. Death at the end of the world has its own immortality, if only for as long as it takes for you to gasp "cool" before the world is ripped apart.

Fighting aliens who want to eat our brains for the tangy aftertaste is much more exciting than death by heart attack from all-you-can-eat, deep-fried shrimp. Fighting evil or being called up to Heaven in the rapture or being Left Behind is far better than hiring Dr. Kevorkian to end a moderately annoying and boring life where you watched every episode of *Dancing With the Stars*.

Why die eating a lethal amount of fat in a double-decker, all-beef-patty hamburgers with that oh-so-special sauce? Why not be the chewy bits in an alien's soup bowl? Giving an alien a heart attack with your fast food laden flesh is significantly more fun.

Thinking about the end gives us a purpose. Fear drives us and we fight or simply to prepare to fight. Why not be prepared? Know your Armageddon and prepare accordingly. It's our motto. Not as catchy, but a lot scarier than the Boy Scouts, "Be prepared."Plain old death is just not interesting. Old age, disease, and accidents are not exciting. We want a grand death. We want to go out fighting demons or outwitting aliens trying to eat us for lunch. Death at the end of the world has its own immortality, if only for as long as it takes for you to gasp "cool" before the world is ripped apart.

Fighting aliens who want to eat our brains for the tangy aftertaste is more exciting than death by heart attack from all-you-can-eat, deep-fried shrimp. Fighting evil or being called up to Heaven in the rapture, or being Left Behind is far better than hiring Dr. Kevorkian to end a moderately annoying and boring life where you watched every episode of *Dancing With the Stars*.

Why die eating a lethal amount of fat in a double-decker, all-beef-patty hamburgers with that oh-so-special sauce? Why not be the chewy bits in an alien's soup bowl? Giving an alien a heart attack with your fast food laden flesh is significantly more fun.

Thinking about the end gives us a purpose. Fear drives us and we fight or simply to prepare to fight. Why not be prepared? Know your Armageddon and prepare accordingly. It's our motto. Not as catchy, but a lot scarier than the Boy Scouts, "Be prepared."

I'm Going to Die Anyway...

You might walk in front of a bus tomorrow. Especially one of those quiet electric buses — freaking dangerous! Crushed by the crosstown number four bus is a poor way to die.

We are all going to die. If you're Russian, eat yogurt, and drink vodka, you might live to be about 115 years old. If you eat fast food, you'll be lucky to live to the ripe age of 45, if you are lucky. You will die either way. That's not the point, is it? We want a cataclysmic event because we are bored silly with normal death. Life's a bummer. Death by catastrophe is exciting.

You want to die in an interesting way. Electric buses, heart attacks, cancer and old age are all boring ways to die. They just don't have the oomph of super volcanoes or a plague of locust.

We want a fighting chance in those last moments too. Survival takes planning and that requires worrying. If we can't worry about defeating mind-controlling robots, we will just worry about useless things, like what toilet paper works best on the naughty places. We'd rather think about ensuring eternal salvation, defeating demons, and surviving killer comets — wouldn't you?

Day to day death is hard to fight. «Dependent Clause Sentence Fragment.» Mainly because defeating a normal death is plain boring. Exercise, eat fruit, and look both ways when crossing a road, to stay fit and in good health. Those might keep you alive a little longer, but they are all boring.

A long, healthy, and productive life isn't as exciting or rewarding as having a chance to survive the last war between good and evil. We want adventure and purpose. We want to cheat death. We want to have an ace up our sleeve when demons, zombies, or the Antichrist come knocking on our door.

We want adventure, so why don't we get some adventure in our lives now? You would think that most of us would be out at sea practicing the pirate life. We are lazy, and there are just too many reasonably good television programs to watch. Pirating is cool, but it's hard to get cable on the high seas.

Apocalyptic possibilities let us put off any hard work until we can't put it off any longer. Better yet, all your favorite shows will be canceled and you will finally have some free time to kill.

Apocalypse and Life After Death

Those that believe in supernatural beings definitely see a life after death. Why? Heck, you gotta be with the big guys in the afterlife, right? There are three types of tickets into the heavens of most religions:

1. You will go to Heaven, or Hell based on your choices in life and how good a person you are.
2. You only get to Heaven if you are a fanatic.
3. Your god really is forgiving, and everyone goes to heaven.

Option number three is the best, but it hard to imagine a god is that forgiving. Imagine a god that does not care that you sinned or even worshipping them incorrectly (or not at all). Imagine that Hell/Purgatory or other nasty karmic destinations don't exist because that would be too nasty and impolite for a benevolent god to create. No jealousy from worshiping false idols, dirty dancing, or eating bacon. When your god meets you in the afterlife he/she/it will just chuckle and usher you into the glorious afterlife.

Our first two options are likelier. The first two require dedication and consequences for being a fallible member of humanity. You fight mortal sin, prepare for the end-times, be as good as nuns, priests, or benevolent witch doctors, goddesses, etc. Quite simply, we are either saints or spend all day and night confessing our sins and begging for absolution.

We live in the real world where sin is a part of the job description. It's damned (oops, minor curse word, be right back after the penance) hard to get past the pearly gates without a black mark on your record.

With the first two options, you are screwed. Sure, you might get to Heaven, but you either lived like a saint (boring), or lived a full and rewarding life (exciting, with an unpleasantness for eternity). Both are a bit rough and not at all fun.

Experiment: Enemies List

One way to feel good about impending doom is to create a list evil people that will die when the world is ground into hamburger. If you know their name, jot it down or just the time and place of their violation. Include organizations, political parties, and others that you disagree with.

Questions

- ✓ How many on your list are people you don't know personally?
- ✓ How many people on the list are older than you?
- ✓ How many boss you around?
- ✓ Would your life be better if all these people were gone tomorrow?

Gods Hate Us

Of all the ways the world will end, gods are usually the number one reason. If a god creates the world, they have the right to end it, right? Why would a god want to destroy the world it created? Let's start with the simple answer: Gods hate us.

Gods, for the most part, are jealous, anal, picky, insecure, vengeful, and creatively violent. Gods talk about being righteous, loving, and even forgiving, but this is a ruse. Gods do whatever they want, including being jealous, anal, picky, insecure, vengeful, and creatively violent. The rest of the time they are blowing smoke by telling their followers how righteous, loving, and even forgiving they are.

Why is there a Hell or Purgatory? How come there are so many rules? What's up with suffering and death? You'd think any god worth worshiping would have fixed this stuff. Instead, the gods punish us if we make the slightest mistakes. When minor disaster and threats of eternal damnation fail to set us strait, gods just wipe us off the face of the planet Earth.

Gods are supposed to be the good guys, protecting their followers, and generally making life pleasant for the faithful. That's the benefit of being a follower. Despite all the marketing from their prophets, gods rarely help us. The average god commits a few random acts of kindness and a heaping portion of random acts of horror. Devout follower or heathen, the mix is about the same with only a couple of followers getting their god's attention for a few moments in a lifetime.

Loving gods seem to have character flaws that cause death, destruction, disease, and the evils of traffic in Los Angeles. Sure there is love, but followed by terror. Gods also want huge sacrifices in exchange for eternal life. We even have to work hard for a good spot in the reincarnation queue.

The demands of the gods are impossible to meet. At some point, you are going to break a rule that puts you on the naughty list. As we fail to follow the rules, our sins add up. One human at a time we add another reason for a god to destroy the world to coverup the mistake of inventing humans.

We are seen as a pest to be exterminated all at once by a creator that is ashamed of its creation.

Glenda the Wicked Witch

Let's look at someone you might think is good but is in reality a very nasty person with a hidden agenda. Glinda, The Good Witch of *The Wizard of Oz*, is somewhat like a god or minor deity. Sure, she is good, but did she lift a finger to stop that house from falling on her fellow witch? Sure, she was from the East side of town and tortured the Munchkins, but she probably called her mother on weekends.

Glinda was so callous that she gives Dorothy her sister's shoes. How about all that nastiness with the flying monkeys? Did she lift her wand to help? Simply, Glinda TGW was not so good under all that glitter.

Gods are like Glinda. They look sweet on the surface. Turn your back and suddenly an Act of God is killing little babies, or monkeys are flying out of your nether regions.

Heavenly Rules

A Christian apocalypse results in only a few followers getting a ticket to eternal life. Why have rules to keep people out of Heaven? Simple, Christian Heaven is not as big as you might have heard. Makes sense now that you know, right?

Heaven could get crowded if anyone could get in. Heaven has to be exclusive to be worth putting in the effort. Nobody would be a good Christian if Heaven were just an apartment complex with good parking. We need gold, opulence, wings, and the airs of a snooty golf club to keep the riffraff and hoi polloi in Hell where they belong. If you didn't have to be selfless, like Mother Teresa to get into Heaven, nobody would be Mother Teresa. Not even Mother Teresa.

Only the devout who are currently caught up on their absolution and their sin debts are allowed to pass into Heaven. The rest of you (us) is working for the Antichrist when the world ends.

Did you know that you should be summarily executed for a carnal sin? There are carnal sins that cannot be washed away (baptism can't remove all the stains of man). Carnal sins are those unforgivable sins that are like wine stains on the soul. Of course, if you are Christian, Jesus is the laundry detergent that will clean a soul so that it sparkles and has the scent of a spring afternoon.

Here is a short list:

- ✓ Don't mess with the clown's props.
- ✓ Make fun of the freaks, but laugh *with* them, not *at* them.
- ✓ Never ever cheat the owner.
- ✓ Don't date non-circus folk unless they juggle or have a valued deformity.

Oops, sorry, those were carnival sins.... Here we go:

- ✓ Taking God's name in vain
- ✓ Chewing bubblegum in church
- ✓ Denying the Holy Spirit
- ✓ Smacking your lips after drinking the sacramental grape juice
- ✓ Fidgeting in church
- ✓ Sleeping around
- ✓ Drinking, even if you abstain on Sunday morning
- ✓ Complaining about going to church
- ✓ Not singing the hymns (humming or moving your lips isn't good enough)

These are just the sins we remember. We grew up Baptist, and they were very strict. More Baptists are going to Hades because of all these extra rules.

You Might Want to Know

You might have heard that Baptists classify dancing as a sin. All we know is that there was no outright dancing to be seen in a Baptist church. This isn't because dancing is a sin; the typical Baptist hymn just isn't much of a toe tapper.

Mortal sins, carnal sins, carnival sins, and Las Vegas are all going to send you to Hell. If you die before the world ends, you lose. If you are still living, you also lose because you aren't a saint.

If we find a church that doesn't make it sinful to fidget during the sermon, we'll probably sign up. We'd hate to go to that hot place just because the sermon was boring.

Then There is Gaia

Gaia[2] is the anthropomorphizing of the Earth into a big biological organism. Just in case you don't know what "anthropomorphizes" means, well, it is just putting something we don't understand in a dress and lipstick so it becomes easier to pretend we understand it.

So, Gaia is a cute woman, dressed in green and earth tones. She experiences pleasure and pain and throws a great party. Just make sure you put your used beer bottles in the recycle bin!

Gaia has motivations to survive and, like any animal, will defend herself against predators, disease, or parasites. We think of nature as a woman. She has wrath, anger, love, and some very tough love too. If she is crossed, she is going to even the score and will definitely get the last word.

You Might Want to Know

There is no Father Nature or Mr Gaia. There is no way we'd anthropomorphize nature as a man. Men can't even be bothered to put the toilet seat down. If Gaia was a man, volcanoes would erupt when you pulled Gaia's finger.

Gaia is currently sick. She is running a temperature. Things are not going well with Gaia. Her blood is polluted with human

---

2 http://en.wikipedia.org/wiki/Gaia_hypothesis

waste, her plants and animals are going extinct, and many areas are infested with human parasites.

Like a dog with fleas, Gaia will roll in the mud to kill all the nasty humans that are biting away at her flesh. Different to think of humans as parasites, eh?

Mother Nature, or her Gaia nom de plume, is dangerous! Add what man does to corrupt sweet missy Nature and you get real problems. Mother Nature could end the world at any time for her own reasons too.

Quite simply, we don't need a vengeful god to cause the apocalypse. All we need to do is poison our environment and, in return, our environment will poison us.

The problem with nature ending the world is that it's likely to be plain impossible to stop. Sure we might cut back on incandescent bulbs, but then we use low power fluorescent bulbs. Sadly, fluorescent bulbs are full of mercury. See the point?

You can't have your cake and eat it too. You can't make gasoline from corn without raising the price of Fritos. You can't have electric cars without rare poisonous metals. You can't be green and give up deodorant without smelling like bear poop. There is always a consequence that is worse than the cure.

If we assume anything about Gaia is true, we are in trouble. We can't live without harming nature. Eventually, nature will balance the scales by removing humanity. We are toast.

You Might Want to Know

Why do so many people loose their houses to floods, hurricanes, forest fires, and earthquakes? Is it a god trying to kill us? No, we're just not smart enough to avoid building houses on flood-planes, hurricanes, forest fires, and earthquakes. We are simply stupid. Blaming a god makes us feel smarter.

The Innocents

If you pray to the right god are you safe? Is there an escape clause? How about the divine gift of protection from your god (a Santa Claus)? Sorry, nobody is safe. Unfortunately, gods are sloppy. The innocents are doomed as if they had big red targets on their behinds.

There's always collateral damage whenever a god is dishing out vengeance. For example, hurricane Katrina which destroyed most of New Orleans, was said by many preachers to have been punishment of this wicked city and lovely tourist destination. Sure, a few bad guys got wet, but hundreds of thousands of churchgoing folks also got hurt, died, lost property, and were generally inconvenienced. Millions of dollars of damage and many innocent lives lost from punishing a few sinners. That's just one act of God, and not the first.

You Might Want to Know

> *We used the "capital G" God as the source of New Orleans' misfortunes because Falwell and others put the blame on the Christian God for this disaster. Many Christian sects agree, God hates New Orleans. God hates party towns, as the story of Sodom and Gomorrah shows.*

God-based disasters are messy. Rarely does a god destroy only the wicked; innocents are caught in the crossfire. Look at Bible stories to see how sloppy the Old Testament God is. When God flooded the Earth in Noah, innocent little babies were drowned. Skunks, Tasmanian devils, poisonous snakes, hyenas, and house cats got seats on Noah's Ark rather than make room for just one more innocent baby.

Innocents were killed at Sodom and Gomorrah, Jericho, and a dozen others. Throw in the Crusades, the Inquisition. Wherever gods are removing the wicked, innocents are sacrificed for the greater good. We have a long history of gods and their religions that have done the same thing.

Innocents are everywhere. Believers are classified as innocents too, so don't think your are safe. Cute babies too. They are all so cute and lovable, but that doesn't seem to matter. The gods hate sinners more than innocent babies.

Yes, there are a few devoted followers that escape destruction. Look at Noah's family as an example. Nepotism is best kept in the family.

In The Book of Revelation, there is no reprieve for innocents. Nowhere in the Bible does it say the destruction of evil will start 'after' the innocents are sent to Heaven.

Sorry, little babies.

Jealous Gods and Criminalized Prayer

Prayer is bringing the world closer to the apocalypse. Even the most merciful gods are just waiting for us to make a mistake, and we believe prayer is like a speed trap on a country road. The problem is that prayer is too easy to deliver to the wrong god.

The Old Testament God is the worst offender. Most of the killing in the Old Testament is directed at the followers of other gods. God has a zero tolerance policy when it comes to the competition. If too many people pray to a competing god, the big 'G' God will decide we aren't worth the trouble and pull the plug.

Why would the one true God be worried about the competition? You would think that if there were only one god, he wouldn't be jealous of our imagined gods. The only possible answer is that there are other gods or that the Christian God has faith that other gods exist. Even if our god doesn't exist, when we pray to them the Christian God is going to be jealous. In other words, having faith is bad, specifically when it is faith in a competing supernatural being.

We also have to contend with gods we are not even worshiping. According to the Bhagavad-Gita, part of the scriptures of Hinduism, the god Krishna claims[3] that it doesn't matter which god human beings worship; it's Krishna who answers their prayer. You are in deep doggy poo because the Jewish/Christian/Muslim God and many others require you have to pray directly to them. With Krishna intercepting your prayers, you can't get a direct connection and are sinning by default.

---

3 http://www.secularhumanism.org/library/fi/avalos_17_3.html

With the ever helpful Krishna answering the prayer hotline, you can't pray or you are breaking the rules of your jealous god. You could avoid prayer, but it's impossible not to pray. Just bang a finger with a hammer, stub your toe on a dog toy, or just get a wicked hangover and you'll be praying to your god for deliverance at the porcelain alter. Krishna answers even minor prayers, so you will go directly to Hell even if you pray for rain or a good night's sleep. Sorry.

A Religious Hijacking

You might assume that some Eastern religious gods have nothing to do with you. Well, we have a Western religion that is doing similar things: the Mormons. Mormons are the first religion to use multi-level marketing, and you are in big trouble.

Mormons baptize the dead. You heard us right, zombie Mormons! Mormons love genealogy because your family tree is where they fin their converts. The only rule it seems is that a family member needs to convert their relatives. If a Mormon figures out who your relatives are, they can baptize them as a Mormon.

FamilySearch.org is "A service provided by The Church of Jesus Christ of Latter-day Saints" A.KA. Mormons or their abbreviated nom de plume, LDS. Of course, they don't advertise on their sites that knowing who you are related to is their secret plan for mass conversion. Look up your relatives and boom, your relatives are wearing Mormon underwear and forced to listen to all boy choir music. Cool, your great, great, great, uncle was a French pirate, but now he's Mormon pirate, which is not cool at all.

Converts are important to a religion that started in 1830. Posthumous baptism is an innovative marketing gimmick. Baptizing the dead converts at a very low cost. For every new convert, Mormons convert generations of dead relatives with little mess or fuss and no resistance. Generations of the dead are converted without all the messiness of getting doors slammed in your face. Nobody can say no. It's like increasing the sales of Coke by watering the tombs of ancient Egyptians (obviously a pyramid scheme).

The true tragedy is for those already dead and in Heaven. Victims of Mormon conversion will find themselves in Heaven one moment and cast into Hell the next for incorrectly believing the wrong religion. All it takes is a well-meaning Mormon to goof up a good thing. One moment you are sipping tea with Saint Peter, and the next you are in Hell drinking stale coffee sludge with Hitler (converted

to Mormonism on September 4, 1993, in the Jordan River Temple, Utah).

Don't believe in Mormonism? Not even dead Atheists are safe! There you are, happily in Atheistic limbo, and bam, you're in Mormon Heaven. Welcome to Atheist Hell–it's full of Mormons!

In the end, which is coming, it doesn't matter what your religion is when the apocalypse comes. Somebody it going to convert you to their religion against your will. There you are, halfway to Heaven or reincarnation as a yackadoodle on the planet of Noodle-5 and then you are cast into hell of a god you've never heard of. Go ahead, pray to whom you want, but we think it is a waste of time.

Our lawyer wants us to clarify that we are not endorsing any course of action or religion. This is for entertainment purposes only!

You Might Want to Know

> *Religions use torture, mind control, hypnotism, magic (as in fakery, not the real stuff with tigers and sawing women in half), marriage (withholding of nuptials until conversion), taxes (Muslims do this), and did we mention torture? Birth is a productive conversion tool. Going forth and multiplying combines mind control and torture into parenting.*

On Suicide: Don't!

The publishers are a bit afraid of lawsuits, so we need to talk seriously about suicide. No matter how dire, painful, or unbearable your situation, suicide is a bad idea. Same goes for mercy killings unless it's your mother-in-law and she is possessed by a demon or about to become a zombie.

Don't get uppity and end things too soon. It's the end; why avoid the experience? Same goes for loved ones. Just because you don't want to see the end-times is no reason for you to take the experience from others? Nobody shoots nobody, okay?

You Might Want to Know

Mothers-in-law are difficult to distinguish from common evil monsters. Our now ex-(thank God)-mother-in-law was a great example. Even when a camera was set to do the double flash to eliminate redeye, her pupils still glowed a demonic-evil red in pictures (a sign of her demonic possession). If evil zombies were roaming the neighborhood and she rang the doorbell, we'd shoot first and look for bite marks later.

Think about the opportunities for interesting experiences during an apocalypse. If you are going to Hell or Heaven, you need something to talk about when you get there. We are sure Antichrist is going to be a hoot and quite an interesting person anyway. Telling people you knew the Antichrist is a great ice breaker. Nothing like a good story to make your time in eternity pass quickly.

Things could get better at any moment. What if a scientist figures out how to save the Earth in the last second? Wouldn't you feel stupid? What if the world is saved at the last second by disproving the existence of God? Keep soldiering on until you are dead, just to be sure. Even if a hellhound is eating your foot, all is not lost (Scruffy-of-hell could get full).

Hope is eternal, even if your brain is under complete control by your alien overlords. At least you get fed regularly and don't need to think about stuff anymore. Life as a meat sack is easy. When you can't form a thought that isn't placed there by your overlords, there's literally nothing you to worry about.

The end of the world is an event. You should enjoy it. Pull up a lawn chair and a beer and watch the world come to its final and glorious end.

Experiment: Prayer Test

The best ways to prove a god exists is through prayer. Our lawyer also said that here is a good place to warn you again.

> ***Warning:*** *This may be the most dangerous experiment in this book. Remember, some gods are jealous and don't allow for worshiping of other gods. With great danger, comes great learning.*

Warnings done. Let's start the experiment. Here's what to do:

- ✓ Get all the names of all the gods and minor deities throughout the history of humanity.
- ✓ Pray to each god and ask them to turn a glass of water into wine.
- ✓ When the water changes to wine, record which god answered your prayer.

Questions

- ✓ If you are old enough to drink wine, was it good?
- ✓ Was there an earthquake or other disaster during the experiment? If so, could you link it to a god that was mad at you for praying to the other gods?
- ✓ If no god changed the water to wine, does this prove that gods don't exist or just that gods don't believe in you?

Experiment: Create a Religion

Time to create your own religion. You should describe your faith in detail and the appropriate apocalypse that ends the world. When you are done, convert the masses!

Here are a couple of examples of religions we have started:

Church of Gravity–You don't need to understand gravity. You are not going to float away if you loose your faith in gravity. Gravity will always punish the antigravity heretics. Anyone testing the existence of gravity from more that a three story building will become a martyr. The motto of the Church of Gravity: Our faith is massive. Apocalypse: Space tourism allows heathens to escape gravity's wrath. Ultimate salvation: Lead underwear.

Last Church of New Calvinists–No rules or carnal sins. God will not punish us or end the world in an apocalypse if we don't believe in the First New Calvinists' god because he/she/it is busy reading a good book to care about your problems. Ultimate salvation: A stuffed tiger named Hobbs.

Questions

- ✓ Did you join your own religion?
- ✓ Were you successful converting your therapy group to your new religion?
- ✓ How long did it take to find this book after your parents hid it?

Explaining the End of the World to Children

Hey kids, this part is for your parents. Go fly a kite or teach your dog how to attack demon spawn.

The end of the world has many tough and heinous challenges. The hardest of these is explaining to kids why the world is ending.

If you are an Atheist and the end is a natural event easily described with science, this is easy. Monkey poo happens as do killer asteroids. Sit down with your kids with a couple of science books and you are done. A little explanation by Mommy and Daddy and the family can concentrate on fighting the zombies or eating the last of the creamed corn.

If you are an Atheist and the end is somewhat biblical or supernatural, you are going to have issues. You are going to look stupid, feel stupid, and probably say stupid things. Calm down, borrow a holy book and learn the correct religion really fast. You may have only a few minutes to convert before you are recruited into the Antichrist's army or eaten by a minion of Hell.

If you are a god-fearing fanatic and your god is ending the world (colored horses, demons, etc.), life is easy. Just hand your son a weapon and run screaming into the streets to kill anything not wearing your sect's cross.

If you are a god-fearing fanatic and something science-like ends the world, life is just as easy. Just hand your son a weapon and run screaming into the streets to kill anything not wearing your sect's cross. Science hadn't stopped you before, why let it get in the way now?

If you are somewhere between an Atheist and a fanatic, you have some explaining to do if the spawn of the devil knocks on your door. Kids need to know why a god would let them be eaten by minions of evil. Before being served up in a butter and brandy reduction sauce, you need to explain to kids why aliens aren't Christian.

Children will ask many questions. Why the cartoons were canceled because of 24 hour reporting about the world-destroying comet? Why can't we have dessert? Why can't we have another birthday party? Kids ask the darnedest things when zombies start roaming the Earth.

Children always ask, "Why is the sky blue?" Imagine when they ask, "Why is the sky on fire?" or "Will the aliens eat our heads or our feet first?"

There are many questions you should answer, and some you'll have to be honest about and say that you just don't know. Parenting is still parenting. Get Dr. Spock's book because it is still relevant right up to the last moment on Earth.That's Spock the child psychologist, not the Spock of Trek.

How do you balance going to school with fighting the final battle? Is a three-year old intended for God's or for the Devil's army? What about the actual date when you pull your kids out of school for the final battle?

Here's a little hint for the Christians and the Islamic believers. The Bible and Koran are clear that there are signs, but no mortal man will know the day. If the end didn't happen yesterday, get out of bed, eat your Corn Flakes, and get on the school bus.

Be strict with kids on skipping school until you know for sure it is the ending days of life on Earth. This is now like a snow day! Until the school yard is full of zombies, there is no reason for the kids to skip their homework until the school is a burning crater.

Educational Toys for Apocalyptic Events

Speaking of the end of the world and kids, there are many toys available to teach children about the wrath of God. Education should be fun, so toys are always welcome in the Eschatology 101 classroom.

Here at Boys Books, we love toys. While we were working on the Boys Book of Armageddon, we got nostalgic for the good old apocalypses of the Old Testament and started a Google search. We were not disappointed!

With a little searching, we found all sorts of cool things. There's even a plague of frogs! Our favorite, though, has to be the Ten Plagues Finger Puppets.

This wondrously educational toy is fun for the whole family–you don't even need to be Jewish! Jewish, Christian, and Muslims will have great fun with this toy. Even an agnostic child will get a thrill by pointing a plagued finger at a hated Egyptian overseer just to see what it would be like to believe in something.

Ten Plagues Finger Puppets

The finger puppets are made with polyester. We would prefer wool or cotton, though obviously not Egyptian cotton as that would be weird. We'd like a few threads to be Rabbi-approved blue dye. Apparently rediscovering a particular blue dye is a sign of the return of the Jewish savior. Imagine, a toy in your toy box brings on the end times...

Each puppet is lovingly stitched (on a machine in China) with the name of the plague in question. This is very helpful, as darkness is easy to understand (shown at 8 o'clock), but hail (6 o'clock) looks more like a plague of clowns, and the death of the firstborn child (9:30) is easily mistaken for the second born child.

Another cool feature is the cardboard holder for the puppets. This lets us hang our collection on the bagel tree for the holidays or on the front door in place of a wreath. We recommend hanging puppets on your front door. Mormons don't dare ring the doorbell.

The Ten Plagues teach the nature of Judeo-Christian branded apocalypse. It seems that God never eliminates the evil of man completely. God's follow-through is less than spectacular. Ten plagues would have been enough to wipe out the Egyptians, but no, God kills only a few to prove a point.

In the end, the Egyptians decided to free the Jews. Despite all the plagues, Egyptians change their minds and chase the Jews to the Red Sea. Of course, the sea is parted and the chase continues until the army gets a bit wet when the sea is eventually de-parted (love that part).

If God had simply killed all the Egyptians, He wouldn't need to keep supplying miracles and saving the behinds of the Jews. If you have a chosen people, why not avoid the confusion and kill everyone else and take away man's ability to exercise free will?

Things have gotten worse, at least they are for the Jewish people. Because God didn't kill the Egyptians, Egypt is now chocked full of Muslims. Maybe God wanted it that way? Are Muslims the real chosen people? Was God ejecting the Jews from what was to be the chosen people's oil soaked empire?

Noah's flood, Sodom and Gomorrah, and the Ten Plagues (plus Red Sea drownings of pursuing soldiers) never quite rid the world of heathens. Whenever the end does come, it's going to be a snoozer and far from perfect. The wicked will always be back for more.

Luckily, we have toys that celebrate a religion's hatred and intolerance for those not in their faith! Think of how cool it would be for all these plagues to befall your enemies? Isn't that cool! Our only wish is that the finger puppets also came with a little Egyptian doll to torture. Instead, we'll need to settle for giving the plagues to our sister.

You might think that Noah's Ark would be a good end-of-the-world teaching toy. Sadly, the Ark as it is usually sold is not very educational. Cute animals in a usually cute little boat will teach more about sailing and animal husbandry, not the wrath of gods.

Improve a toy Ark's educational value by buying a couple hundred Ken and Barbie dolls. Simply float the Ark in your pool with hundreds of dolls floating like the victims of Noah's flood. With Barbie's car and house in the murky depths of the flooded pool, you are teaching the folly of materialism too.

We couldn't find any Sodom and Gomorra toys. If you are desperate, try a five-pound bag of rock salt to represent Lot's wife. Not as fun, but you can always point to the pile of salt when your kids are on the verge of debauchery.

Boys Books Publishing will soon sell a commercial version of the bag of salt. We'll call it the "Lot's Wife Action Figure." It will come with an Old Testament-era, designer handbag, and matching sandals.

Speaking for a moment about a strange coincidence, why is there Noah's Ark *and* the Ark of the Covenant? Either you put animals in it, or you put the Ten Commandments in it and use it to fight enemies of God … see our problem? Could there have been a typo and instead there should be 'arc' like part of a circle? God is a geometry genius. Sorry for the detour. On with the story.

If you are looking for a good Ark of the Covenant, buy the deluxe Indiana Jones Lego action figure on Amazon. Sadly it doesn't melt Nazis like the real thing. Sorry.

Experiment: No school!

Okay, parents, your turn. In this experiment, tell your children that the world will be ending soon. Even if you are an atheist, get the family on their knees and pray for forgiveness. Back this up by taking your children out of school and going on vacation to a cave in the mountains. For fun, play spot the heathen (of course they all are, so it's an easy game for all ages). Don't forget to buy guns and ammo on your way. Stay in the cave for at least a month.

Questions

- ✓ Did your children cry much?
- ✓ When you told the school why you were taking your kids out, how long before you were reported to Child Protective Services?
- ✓ Did your neighbors start panicking when you started frantically loading the car with supplies and screaming kids?
- ✓ When the batteries on their games ran out, were the kids ready to battle evil?
- ✓ If you're atheist, did it seem less or more real to your kids?

Who's Who? Prophets of Doom

There is a true rogues' gallery of those predicting the end of the world. It's important to know your sources and what they are pitching as possible ways the world will end.

A mind-numbingly large number of people are saying the world will be destroyed, or otherwise made inconvenient for civilized living. This doomsaying is as old as mankind. From the moment we were created by supernatural beings, birthed by aliens, or if you can believe it, spawned by friends of Jane Goodall, we have been predicting when we would all die.

It's educational to look at a few of the famous purveyors of doom (small doom, not the big Doom which is a video game that simulates a doom-like world). We should understand their motivations, super powers, and their histories. You can't tell the doomsayers apart without a scorecard.

The History Channel

One of the most vocal of the doomsayer media is the History Channel. They are really pushing the end of the world. Especially during sweeps week. If it is Shark Week at the Discovery Channel, it's the end-of-the-world week at the History Channel.

For a history-oriented channel, pushing the end of the world is sort of odd. That's the future, right? We don't get this at all. They should be called the Future Channel.

How does the History Channel sign up advertisers for their apocalyptic programs? Who would spend money for a prime-time slot between *Squirrel Rabies Armageddon* and *Decoding Zombie Death Cults*? How does a dishwasher detergent company equate spots on fine stemware with spot-spotting demon hordes? Is gingivitis a concern when the oceans turn to blood? Should your clothes be snugly soft when asteroids are falling? All these questions lead to only one more question, does the History channel possess mind control technology?

The History Channel never admits to doing the actual doomsaying. Instead, they use a gallery of modern and ancient doomsayers like Nostradamus, cult leaders, Mayans, scientists and new-age book authors. Old-fashioned doomsaying in the guise of historical documentary. For variety they also push the natural stuff, like comets or asteroids, and even cosmic rays, adding their own spin by mixing real science with Bible-based Armageddon, sprinkled with quotes from a long list of doomsayers.

Add all the doom the History Channel plays and there's more tales of Earth's destruction than even an extra crazy TV preacher. To top that off they even give the evangelical preachers air time to spout their tales of doom for sinners.

Unlike other doomsayers, the History Channel does not have a traveling revival show with miracles and free Bibles. The channel doesn't have a congregation, just employees and Nielsen ratings. We really can't figure out why they'd push the doom stuff so hard.

The History Channel's actions seem like the minds of the employees are controlled by aliens. Their own show on alien mind control makes it seem a likely possibility.

Special message to History Channel employees: Please try putting on a foil hat. If you suddenly find your show schedule to be oddly stacked with nonsense, give us a call — ***and whatever you do, don't take off the foil hat!***

The History Channel is not the only pusher of doom on TV. The Discovery Channel and the Christian Broadcast Network (CBN) have their fair share. The National Geographic Channel has most of a day dedicated to the end of the world. The History Channel just seems to take some sort of joy from televising predictions of doom. The channel also has a wider range of end-of-the-world predictions and is not limited to the Christian faith. They are an equal-opportunity, non-denominational doom channel.

Want to get on TV? Just get the ATF to knock on your door just once and you get a show on the History Channel. If you are a cult leader looking to get the word out, the History Channel is your best friend on basic cable.

The Biography Channel has much higher standards. You need either an Oscar, or to kill a dozen of your followers before you get a show.

You Might Want to Know

The Bureau of Alcohol, Tobacco and Firearms are the number one agency for investigating doomsayers. The reason is simple: cults that believe in the end of the world like guns too. Oddly, you don't need tobacco or alcohol to get the attention of the ATF, just the guns.

Nostradamus

Nostradamus, next to John of Patmos, is the world's most famous doomsayer. Nostradamus would be a normal nut job, but he had French Royalty connections. If you have the ear of a potentate, you get into the history books and Wikipedia.[4]

Nostradamus is not his real name. His given name is Michel de Nostredam. Sounds like a movie about a hunchback haunting Saint Michael's. 'Nostradamus' sounds scarier, so it stuck.

[4] http://en.wikipedia.org/wiki/Nostradamus

Nostradamus: Original portrait by his son Cesar. We do not know the names of the cherubs in the corners.

Nostradamus wrote his predictions in poetry, so everything must be interpreted. In other words, he did not write anything we would call obvious. The best you could do is say, "Oh, that makes sense now" after it has already happened.

Nostradamus wrote in quatrains.[5] A quatrain is a fancy way of saying that he wrote rhyming poetry. Isn't that romantic? A Valentine's Day with death and destruction. Imagine getting a dozen roses and having the Earth crack open and swallow your lover.

---

[5] http://en.wikipedia.org/wiki/Quatrain

There are problems with poetry as a medium for predicting the future. Poetry is not literal. Poetry is symbolism and metaphor with a few flowery words thrown in. Poetry makes it impossible to pin down the exact meaning of phrases, and then it gets worse by using random words to make it rhyme properly.

You can twist the interpretation of poetry to say almost anything. For example, we proved that quatrain eight predicted that our dog Roo (as in kangaroo) would poop on our laptop keyboard. Don't ask, long story. The fact is, Nostradamus predicted the event.

Let's look at the eighth quatrain, and you will see what we mean:

How many times will you be taken, solar city,
changing the barbarian and vain laws:
Your evil approaches: You will be more tributary,
the great Adria will re-cover your veins.

First, you will note that nothing rhymes in the English translation. Here is the original French version:

Combien de fois prinse cité solaire
Seras changeant ses loix barbares et vaines:
Ton mal s'approche. Plus seras tributaire,
Le grand Hadrie recourira des veines.

Obviously, we are talking dog poo and laptops. Obvious to us, but it may not be obvious to you. We need to do a little more work to expose the true meaning by making the English version rhyme.

If we follow the rules of the quatrain, we need to put back the rhyming bit at the end of the line. Here's the English translation in its proper rhyming form:

How many times will you be taken, solar poo,
changing the barbarian and vain scrapple:
Your evil approaches: You will be more Roo,
the great Adria will re-cover your Apple.

Obviously, this proves that Nostradamus predicted a long time ago that our dog, Roo, would poo on our Apple's keyboard. It's all a matter of getting things to rhyme appropriately to get the right prediction that is obvious in hindsight. There is even a rhyming ending, "with doo" that ends the poem. Another sign that old Nostro, as he was known by his friends, was thinking about our dog Roo. Read it again and you will see what we mean.

Learn This Word

> ***Scrapple:*** *Seasoned mixture of ground meat (such as pork) and cornmeal set in a mold and served sliced and fried. This always gives our little dog a mild case of projectile incontinence.*

If It Don't Rhyme, Don't Do the Crime!

Nostradamus spawned legion of doomsayer poetry nuts. Because the Nostradamus poetry is a code, thousands are out there every day interpreting the poetry, looking for clues to the end of the world.

The people interpreting Nostradamus quatrains are *not* the same sort of uppity English majors you met in school. These poetry nuts usually live in trailer parks, hunt deer with a pickup and a six pack of light beer. Their psychologists would say they were delusional paranoid schizophrenics if their paranoia let them set foot in a psychologist's office.

You Might Want to Know

> *Nostradamus made most of his fortune interpreting his own poetry. He had a booming business selling Cliff Notes to desperate students during poetry week.*

Speaking of poetry, we suspect that Nostradamus was mentally damaged by a poetry teacher. We suspect the dark poetry started when Nostro got a D-minus on a poetry interpretation exam. The best way to get back at a teacher is to write dark rhymes to scare the willies out them. Teachers want to live vicariously through teenage angst, but not this much! Poetry of death, destruction and a few Antichrists will mentally damage the unsuspecting poetry teacher. The sweet taste of revenge.

When you are good at something, you dig in and make it your life. Poetry keep coming, despite the obvious practical joke played on the poetry digerati. Of course, ol' Nostradamus probably sent signed copies of his poetry to his teacher, just to rub it in.

Nostradamus was a "green" doomsayer, because his predictions are easily recycled. The first bombing of the World Trade Center - February 26, 1993 - was said to have been foretold by the same quatrains as the World Trade Center destruction of September 11, 2001. The quatrain has been recycled many times. Any time a big city has a bit of a nasty incident, like a building destroyed or a crime spree, we pull out the Nostradamus quatrains. It's just that easy!

Why are so many fascinated by Nostradamus? Nostradamus was a Christian. If his poetry predictions are proved right, then the Bible is right. Got to back up your fellow brethren, especially if you mix a bit of fear.

Nostradamus was no slouch in the apocalypse department. He has three different Antichrists and all the trappings for world-ending disaster. Nostradamus' third Antichrist looks a little like Osama Bin Laden. If you are a Christian Republican (there's another kind?), Osama Bin Laden, a Muslim and terrorist was very cool. Well, cool until he was killed by a Navy Seal team. Now everyone is an Antichrist short of Armageddon. There's a joke there about trained seals, a traveling circus, and the terrorist's daughter, but let's ask instead: If Osama was killed in Abbottabad, who's in Costelloabad? Third base!

Despite embellishing the Bible, Nostradamus is still the darling of the Christian devout. All it takes is a little love of your fellows and a History Channel special, and you forget all the flaws. "Nostradamus a little mixed up on the number of Antichrists, but it's the thought that counts."

The Bible's predictions of the end are not exactly clear. Embellishment and wild interpretation are part of the game. Throw in cryptic poetry and you have Christian gold!

You Might Want to Know

As far as we know, the only Atheist Republican is Carl Rove. It was Carl's anti-Christian super powers that created the Republican strategy to elect Bush junior with the extra votes from the Christian Right. Bush of course contributed to proving Nostradamus was right by reading[6] "The Pet Goat" on 9/11. The goat is of course the guise of the devil and thus Bushy was pushing devil worship to little kids while New York burned. It's all over except for the three Antichrists!

Bruce Bueno de Mesquita, PhD

We never would have thought it, but there's a doomsayer named Bruce. Bruce is a mathematician and political scientist, or rather a historian with a spreadsheet that tells the future.

Bruce Bueno de Mesquita, PhD, otherwise known as "The Good Mosquito," is a mathematical fortune teller. He uses game theory to make his predictions.

We'd explain game theory, but this is a book about the end of the world and we're in a hurry.

You might wonder how we know about Bruce. If you guessed that we met him at Disneyland, you would be partially right. Disney advertises on the History Channel and thus sponsored a show that applauded Bruce with his predictions as the new and modern Nostradamus. We watched with great interest the show and the Disney commercials. Yes, it's a Mickey Mouse connection, but it's all we have.

As a doomsayer, Bruce lacks the color of avenging angels, probing aliens, or even super volcanoes. Bruce just predicts nasty stuff, like terrorists, wars, economic collapse, George Bush (the latter), and other ways the world can end by mankind's hand.

The History Channel is sneaky. Because Nostradamus predicted the end of the world, and Bruce predicts future

---

[6] http://en.wikipedia.org/wiki/The_Pet_Goat

events, it is logical that Bruce is the next Nostradamus. Bruce has never publicly written a prediction of the end. The only reason we list Bruce as a doomsayer is that the History Channel says he's a doomsayer.

Bruce isn't big on doom, but he does have a few trappings of the doomsayer. Nostradamus was a mystic who used poems, and Bruce uses math, so neither could be understood by people who watch Oprah. This meets the requirement for doomsayers to be cryptic and mysterious.

Linking Nostradamus to Bruce saved the History Channel a ton of money. Archival footage from their dozen Nostradamus documentaries was used extensively. The two-hour special was created for one-fifth the cost of most documentaries because they never interview Bruce and everyone else they talked to was there already for an aliens apocalypse documentary.

Bruce never really says anything on the record about his Nostradamus super powers, nor did the History Channel interview close friends and family. We love the History Channel. It's history if you can interview someone who knows that someone told them that somebody did something.

Unlike some doomsayers, Bruce does not seem to take mind-altering drugs. He is also not part of a doom cult. He even has gainful employment as a professor, and does odd jobs for the CIA.

The only fishy smell, of course, is that Bruce works for the CIA. You can't confirm his equations, and you can't be sure it's all true, because all that work was for the CIA. Sorry, all top secret stuff....

The History Channel assures us that Bruce is as good as Nostradamus, so you don't need to bother with any inconvenient evidence. Evidence is for sissies and people who watch the Discovery Channel. Only real men watch the History Channel.

For most of the two hour History Channel special, Bruce sits on a park bench, either drawing on a napkin or typing into his computer. He does not seem too worried about the end of the world. We've heard that Bruce already has a place reserved in a CIA fallout shelter.

Bruce doesn't seem to be paid well. He used a couple of restaurants worth of paper napkins to make notes. Somebody should buy him a proper notebook. He also does not seem to have an office because he's always doing his work on a park bench. Apparently the CIA doesn't pay too well. No wonder he's doomsaying on the History Channel, he needs the cash.

Bruce isn't all doom and gloom. He believes the future can be changed. He's like a cool drink of lemonade on a hot day and the opposite of the 'nothing but lemons' Nostradamus. Of course, it will be a hot day because of nuclear war, and will require billions of gallons of lemonade to cool down.

There's little of the doctor's info on the web. Most of the doomsaying is by way of the single History Channel program that heralds Bruce Bueno de Mesquita, PhD, as the next Nostradamus. There are a few books by Bruce, but nothing with an end-of-the-world theme. The only real predictions put forward in the History Channel documentary are from Nostradamus, not directly by the Good Mosquito.

As we mentioned, Bruce has published a few papers and a couple of books. Supposedly his equations are available to anyone. If you want to be your own doomsayer, you too could predict the end of the world if you had the data to feed the equations. The data for the equations, the predicted apocalypse, and the important advice to avoid it are probably locked up in the basement of the CIA. Great!

Good news: math and science can predict the end and even avoid it. Bad news: the information is classified and too important for you to see.

Edgar Cayce

Edgar Cayce is one of our favorite hawkers of doom and mysticism. Cayce had it all from x-ray eyes to predicting horse races for his clients. He talked of the past full of the good people living in Atlantis and, naturally, of the end of the world.

Cayce predicted volumes of nasty stuff, including World War II. The big predictions include flooding (global warming), earthquakes, and the dead rising from the grave (possibly a reference to the Democrats in 2008).

Cayce's most quoted Earth shattering prediction is that the axis of the Earth will shift. That means new weather patterns and earthquakes big enough to move mountains. Even America will be split in two. Cayce does not end the world nicely.

Earth's axis shifting will be followed by the Second Coming of Christ. Christians can't fault Edgar because, well, you can't fault any Christian that predicts the Second Coming. Even if Cayce uses his God-given talents to play the ponies, he's still a member of the Christian club.

Cayce's visions of destruction and Second Coming were all to happen between 1958 and 1998. At the time of this writing, Edgar's end is already long overdue. Worse, the beginning of the end is more than 50 years late.

The good news is that Cayce made his fortune doomsaying, then died a relatively wealthy man. He died before his poor doomsaying skills could affect his standard of living. This is a lesson for all doomsayers. Either predict the end and leave town like a thief in the night, or be a little vague and be long dead before folks smell fraud.

Harold Camping: Serial Doomsayer

Despite 2,000 years of predicting the end of the world, Christians keep on dishing out new dates. Harold Camping has tried to end the world three times. Once in 1994 and twice in 2011. He can't seem to get it right, but that's okay because he's a Christian, right?

Harold Camping is racing against the Mayans to be the first to end the world. According to Camping, the Mayans were wrong about the end of the world and they are late to the party because the world would end in 2011, not 2012. Not that he disputes the Mayan calendar, Harold just won't make the appointment since he'll be busy in Heaven.

Learn This Word

> ***Rapture**: Rapture is when the good Christians get to go to Heaven and everyone (alive and dead) get judged for a trip to Hell or a vacation in Heaven. You may have noted that we said, 'alive and dead' which seems odd as*

> *most Christians believe that the moment they die, they ride the escalator to Peter's gate. Not according to Revelation. We get to rot in our graves until just before the world ends.*

Part of Harold's technique is to interpret the Bible's "Heavenly meaning." Unlike the Bible literalists, Harold believes the Bible is full of parables and it should be 'spiritually interpreted' to find meaning. This is a wonderful technique as it allows any part of the Bible to say what you want it to say.

You Might Want to Know

> *Google is currently working on technology that will make driverless cars a reality. Many at Google are Atheists. Atheists will be saved by their robot vehicles from accidents caused by the Christians praying so hard they drive like they've been raptured. In Save a life: Don't pray and drive!*

Harold interprets the numbers and relationships as a numbers which are then interpreted as spiritual words which then add up to numbers that predict the end of the world. The key is to interpret such numbers spiritually. We assume that an Atheist mathematician would fail miserably to predict the Rapture date because the accounting would be Godless.

Harold Camping is also a master of debate. In debate[7], we attempt to convince others of our stance on a particular subject. There are many tools that debtors use like logic, emotional appeal, facts, and insults. Harold uses logic, although it is special form of logic called logical fallacy. Logical fallacy is very powerful because it is immune to facts.

Harold also seems to be invoking another tool of logical inquiry called Occam's razor.[8] The technique cuts unnecessary assumptions and finds the better of two similar theories by eliminating arguments that are too complex or contain too many assumptions.

---

[7] http://en.wikipedia.org/wiki/Debate#Comedy_debate

[8] http://en.wikipedia.org/wiki/Occam's_razor

Here is Harold's razor: What's more obvious, the Book of Revelation or a silly Mayan calendar? The sillier Mayan calendar is "cut" and we are left only with what is probably true. Sort of like debating which is a better fictional character, Mickey Mouse or Luke Skywalker. Of course Skywalker would win because he has a cool lightsaber.

Applying Occam's razor to the apocalypse isn't difficult, especially when you use the Occam's razor with two blades. One lifts the humans off the world a bit, the other cuts them properly at their souls. You get a cleaner and smoother world that way. Then the whole thing gets a slap of aftershave.

You Might Want to Know

Occam's razor is a method used to select among two possible truths by choosing the explanation with the fewest assumptions. Christians are really good at this because they have only one assumption for most things: "God did it," or if something is bad: "The Devil did it." Of course, God created the Devil, so whatever the Devil does is also reasonably explained with the assumption: "God did it." This is why Christians believe in Creationism (also known as Intelligent Design) because evolution requires too many assumptions provable by science. So much easier to assume God did it.

Harold "Clean-shaven" Camping is also a fan of Sherlock Holmes. Remember the quote: "When you have eliminated all which is impossible, then whatever remains, however improbable, must be the truth." This is a favorite strategy of religious debaters. Even though the Book of Revelation is improbable, it must be true if you assume God wrote the Bible. Of course the Mayans ending the world certainly can't be true because Mayans aren't Christians. Sure, Sherlock is turning in his fictional grave right now, but it makes a weird sort of sense ... right?

Campings dates were, May 21, 2011 which is the beginning of the end and October 21, 2011 which is the full blown end. "The beginning of the end," is just the rapture. The actual moment that God turns off the lights was to be six months later, October 21, 2011. God simply empties the world of good Christians like.

Neither date seemed to be any good, but Harold is used to failure. This is his second and third attempt predicting the Apocalypse. Back on September 6, 1994, he had folks hanging out in a Veterans Center, Bibles open to Heaven and waiting for Christ's return. Come midnight, Harold went back to his Bible to recalculate a new date.

Harold was a maverick doomsayer. Harold's dates didn't fall on a solstice, no alignment of planets, not a prime, pun, palindrome, or mystic number. Just numbers that add up to a date. Damned inconvenient if the numbers happened to be a date in the past, say September 6 of 1994, like Harold's first pick for the return of Christ. Imagine if he had stuck with 1994. What good would that do? You need a time machine to keep checking too see if Christ is back yet.

You might think that a failed doomsayer wouldn't be popular. The opposite is true for Harold Camping. Harold went from dozens to millions of followers around the world. He'll have even more with his latest failures.

In our book, the one you are reading right now, Harold is not only a doomsayer but a successful cult leader too. AM radio is the best place for modern cult leaders to hang about. Harold has almost sixty AM radio stations in the United States and around the world. If AM radio station ownership indicates a cult leader's cult status, he is the top in his profession.

For Camping and his followers, the calendar ticked past May 21, 2011, just like any other day. There was no rapture or apocalyptic traffic jam, just a lot 'of praise the lord' followed by depressed crying. Harold failed to predict that the Rapture. That's okay, Harold later explained, the Rapture had been 'invisible.' In October, the destruction of the Earth turned out to be just as invisible. Hardly seems worth the effort to predict events that nobody can see.

Harold, though publicly he says he's retired from doomsaying, is busy recalculating again… Fourth time is the charm, right?

Since the world did not end, Harold, a spry 90 year old, will live to see the Mayans end the world in 2012.

Pat Robertson's 700 Club of Doom

Marion Gordon "I changed my name to Pat" Robertson started predicting in 1976 that the world would end by 1982. Marion even guaranteed the prediction during an episode of the 700 Club with this statement: "I guarantee you by the end of 1982 there is going to be a judgment on the world." Marion (Patricia to his friends) sadly failed to deliver on his guarantee and nobody saw one dime of their donations returned.

Marion's prediction was based on Bible math, like Camping's. Unlike Camping, Robertson has refused to recalculate a new end of the world and just says that it's "real soon."

In 2011, Robertson was recognized for his 1982 prediction with the Ig Nobel prize in mathematics for "teaching the world to be careful when making mathematical assumptions and calculations." He did not win the award alone and was forced to share his trophy with doomsayers who failed to predict the end before the 2011 prize ceremony. Here is the complete list of co-winners as documented by Ig Nobel committee, in the order of their apocalypse are, Dorothy Martin of the USA (1954), Pat Robertson of the USA (1982), Elizabeth Clare Prophet of the USA (1990), Lee Jang Rim of Korea (1992), Credonia Mwerinde of Uganda (1999), and Harold Camping of the USA (1994 and 2011).

Dorothy Martin, Homemaker, Doomsayer

We knew about Camping, but Dorothy Martin was a mystery to us, so we looked her up. Beyond Dorothy's standard doomsaying (relaying alien communications from the planet Clarion), the most remarkable thing was her representative, wait for it, Dr Charles Laughead.

Dorothy (Toto to her friends) holds a special place in social psychology as her predictions and their failure helped coin the term Cognitive Dissonance by University of Minnesota social psychologist, Leon Festinger in his paper, *When Prophecy Fails: A social and psychological study of a modern group that predicted the destruction of the world*.

Too Many Popes of Saint Malachy

Saint Malachy, the first Irish saint and coveter of the Blarney Stone, had a vision of the Apocalypse. In his prediction, written in 1139, he documented the end after the world after the 111th pope.[9]

Please, the last pope to leave the Vatican, turn off the lights.

We are on our last pope. Hard to say for certain because some people seem to be counting differently and assume the last pope was the last pope. Our world may have already ended, sorry.

There is also a 112th pope. The last pope isn't numbered, but it is made clear he is/was/will be in charge of the Vatican. So, we are on our last pope, but we might have one more.

Confusing....

Once we are on the last pope, things go downhill. The last pope to leave the Vatican in a pine box is the beginning of everything in the book of Revelation. We only wonder if in that pine box, will the pope wearing his pope hat? Probably costs extra to make a casket that long.

Saint Malachy was a doomsayer of very few words. Here is the end he predicts after naming the 111th pope:

> *"During the final persecution of the Holy Roman Church, the seat will be occupied by Peter the Roman, who will feed his sheep in many tribulations; and when these things are finished, the seven-hilled city will be destroyed, and the formidable Judge will judge his people. The End."*

This does not sound like Bible stuff to us here at Boys Books. Not enough blood and suffering by innocents. Sure there are sheep and judging, but it comes up short on apocalyptic visions of horror. The grand total of the apocalypse is two words, "The End." Saint Malachy is obviously rewriting Revelation for *Reader's Digest*.

---

9 http://en.wikipedia.org/wiki/Prophecy_of_the_Popes

As doomsayer predictions go, Saint Malachy's 111 popes lacks the uncertainty of generic doomsaying. Tribulations, persecutions of the Holy Roman Church, etc, are too simple and avoids the biblical symbolism we're used to in Christian doomsaying. The *"feed his sheep in many tribulations"* is like most prophesy, vague and mentions sheep. We are shrugging our shoulders and waiting for a scandal involving a priest and a sheep farm in New Zealand.

A secondary interpretation is simply that Saint Malachy was predicting the end of the Catholic Church. Imagine the yard sale when they move out of the Vatican! Our Uncle Jack would rise from the grave just to get a crack the Pope's golf clubs.

We would be sad to see the Catholic church go. No original church, no Revelation. Worse still, we don't have a Catholic Church to push doomsayers at us anymore. Good with the bad, we guess.

Saint Malachy isn't known as the patron saint of anything in particular. Not of travel, the lost, animals, zygotes or the poor. This lack of patronage might be the best evidence for his predictions being true. In other words, Saint Malachy is the patron saint of "The End."

Old Testament Daniel: Doomsayer

The idea that the world would end by God's hand goes way back. The Book of Daniel has some good end-of-the-world drama to scare little children. As an added bonus, the Book of Daniel is a decoder ring for Revelation.

Like all good prophesy, Daniel's vision of the end starts with our protagonist fasting and thus a little loopy. Well, not fasting, Daniel is on a veggie hunger strike. Daniel would not eat the king's meat (not a double entendre, the Bible is very clear about that sort of thing). The roughage from all the extra fiber caused Daniel to have very vivid nightmares of the end of the world.

Dreams are good stuff, as far as doomsaying goes. On the one hand, they don't need to make too much sense, because they are dreams. On the other hand, dreams are meant to be interpreted, so doomsayers can be very creative too.

Daniel gets referenced by most interpreters of Revelation as a sort of cheat sheet for some of the symbolism. This comparison between Daniel and the writings of John of Patmos is like tripping on LSD to understand your magic mushroom vision quest, or studying *SpongeBob SquarePants* by watching *Ren and Stimpy*.

You Might Want to Know

> *Our brother writes for the SpongeBob show. He is also famous for the phrase, "Yes, you can smoke a wet noodle!"*

Why would Daniel's dreams come up in analysis of the Book of Revelation? Simple: Bible scholars assume the imagery in the Old Testament was written by God specifically to help us understand the imagery in the New Testament. Like the clues in the earlier episodes of *Lost* without the flashbacks. It is akin to interpreting the relationship between Luke and Lea in Star Wars from the episode of Star Trek where Spock's brain is stolen.

Daniel was a pathetic doomsayer because he simply documents his dreams and moves on. Some of the visions did help Daniel make a power play in politics, so you might forgive Daniel of squandering his end-of-the-world visions. No reason to push the end of the world when you're already in charge.

In the Book of Daniel, we get a first-person account of the various steps that God takes to end the world. They are visions, granted, but they were Daniel's visions and written in the Bible, so they must be true. No angel is dictating the visions. It is like a direct link to God. No need for an angelic middleman for Daniel.

Daniel still gets interpretations from angels for some of the confusing stuff, so it may not be all that accurate. Angels are highly untrustworthy — remember Satan is an angel. Odd that angels are interpreting parts of the dream because Daniel is an expert at dream interpretation too. His resume includes the interpreting the dreams of King Nebuchadnezzar.

There's quite a bit of symbolism in Daniel's dreams. Our favorite[10] is the fourth beast in the Book of Daniel, 7:23:

> *Thus he said, The fourth beast shall be the fourth kingdom upon earth, which shall be diverse from all kingdoms, and shall devour the whole earth, and shall tread it down, and break it in pieces.*

Devoured and then walked on? When you think about it, that's rather nasty. The beast eats the Earth, digests for a while, poops it out, then tramples on the Earth poop. That's a really nasty apocalypse! Rather hard to get the stain out of the carpet too.

The glass isn't half full or half empty. The glass is destroyed by a beast when it devours the Earth, poops the remains out the beastie's sphincter, then tramples it to dust. Joy!

Back to corroboration between the Book of Daniel and the Book of Revelation. Like one of those find-the-word games without any rules. Try relating the previous quote from Daniel to any other word or phrase in Revelation. A square peg will fit into a round hole! Use a big enough hammer and some blind faith to ensure a proper fit.

To sum up Daniel, great for Sunday School, bad for doomsaying, good for doomsayers.

Isaac Newton

That's right, Isaac Newton was a doomsayer. The man that figured out gravity also dabbled in predicting the apocalypse. Isaac Newton calculated the precise date of the end of the world, the year 2060.The Earth will cease to follow Newton's Laws of orbital mechanics on that day as the Sun stands still in the sky and the stars rain down.

Newton calculated this number by analyzing the book of Daniel. Newton wrote his prediction on a scrap of paper that was never published. The scrap of paper was found in a shoe box of receipts for alchemy supplies in the back of Newton's closet.

---

10 http://www.Biblegateway.com/passage/?book_id=34&chapter=7&version=9

You Might Want to Know

> *Newton was a smart fellow with many intellectual hobbies. One of these hobbies was trying to turn lead into gold. Following Newton's lead-to-gold recipe, the History Channel and others have tried to turn that scrap of paper with the year 2060 prediction (the worthless lead) into gold.*

Newton wasn't much of a doomsayer. He didn't preach or run naked through the streets with 2060 painted on his unmentionables. Newton didn't use science or even calculus (which he invented) to predict the end. Just some Bible research and unfortunately the mathematical proof that the Earth is not the center of the universe. Sorry Catholic Church, Galileo was right. Luckily for the Church, the consolation[11] prize is the end of the world.

Isaac Newton is the patron saint of scientific doomsaying. Before Newton, all we had to predict the future were hallucinogenic drugs, mental illness, fasting, and inaccurate astrology. Now we have physics to calculate death and destruction on massive scales. Despite only dabbling in the math of apocalypse, Newton gave us the mathematical basis for a universe that will kill us.

With Newton's gravity we have the science to accurately imagine the world ripped asunder by wandering black holes, tilting of the Earth's axis, comets, and asteroids. Sure, it's harder to imagine the Sun standing still because of mass and inertia, but now the Sun will go nova and burn the Earth to a crisp.

Thank God for Newton!

The Little Apocalypse of Mark

The Gospel of Mark is really our first telling of doom in the Christian Bible.[12] There is an oft-quoted line:

> *There will be wars, and rumors of wars.*

---

[11] Here is another cool fact about Newton, he disliked the Catholic Church.

12 http://www.biblegateway.com/passage/?search=Mark+13&version=NIV

This is a sign of the Little Apocalypse. Of course the 'little' seems odd. How could one have a small end of the world? The trappings of Revelation are all there with talk of the Antichrist, killings, and revenge against the wicked Romans. After reading the Book of Mark, the Book of Revelation looks like copyright infringement.

The Gospel of Mark didn't go for the full death, destruction, famine, pestilence, like the Book of Revelation. There were no beasts singing about death, trumpets announcing death, seals broken to release death, or bowls full of the official breakfast cereal of the end of the world (with Satan shaped marshmallows). There isn't even a final battle of good versus evil. Just wanton destruction and a few good guys get a ticket to Heaven.

So what's up with this mini-me apocalypse?

The prophet of this Christian doom was Jesus. Mark is just a humble biographer and is quoting Jesus who is advising them on the coming apocalypse. Strangely, Jesus is talking about the coming of Christ. The tale is of the persecution of Jesus' followers and the destruction of everything before Christ comes.

Here is one of the juicy bits:

> *"At that time men will see the Son of Man coming in clouds with great power and glory."*

That's just one place where Jesus is doing the Queen of England thing and referring to himself as the Son of Man.

You Might Want to Know

> *Did you know that the prophesy by Jesus is used by the Muslims to predict the coming of Mohammed? Little known fact: Jesus is mentioned in the Koran thirty-one times!*

Imagine the question and answer session after Jesus gets done with his little tale of doom.

> ***Mark:*** *So, you say all these bad things are going to happen?*

> ***Jesus:*** *Yep.*
>
> ***Luke:*** *And then Christ comes?*
>
> ***Jesus:*** *You bet your sweet bippie!*
>
> ***Matthew:*** *But you are 'the' Christ, right?*
>
> ***Jesus:*** *Yep, Son-o-God with all the trimmings.*
>
> ***John:*** *Dude, how does that make you our savior? Seems like you plan on dying for all our sins, then evil people go ahead and have wars, and your dad is going to make a mess of the world just because the heathens didn't believe you were here on Earth the first time. Am I missing anything?*
>
> ***Jesus:*** *Nope, got it in one. Things gotta get worse before they get better. Heck, I get nailed to a cross just to make the point. Dad (the big G), says you all are just a bunch of morons who need to be slapped around before you have any idea He's in charge. Heinous, but true, dude. Next question?*

The Little Apocalypse is not exactly what we expect from good and kind Jesus. It has little forgiveness or parables of niceness. Here's our favorite part of the book of Mark:

> *When you see "the abomination that causes desolation" standing where it does not belong — let the reader understand — then let those who are in Judea flee to the mountains. Let no one on the roof of his house go down or enter the house to take anything out. Let no one in the field go back to get his cloak.*

We are warned that if you left your coat, and the Second Coming has started, don't go back and get it! On the coattails of doom? Not sure why you can't get off the roof, but a good guess is that he is implying the view of the carnage will be better.

Pregnant and nursing women will be really inconvenienced by the end of the world too:

> *How dreadful it will be in those days for*

pregnant women and nursing mothers!

You can't get off your roof, forget your coat, or be a mom, without something bad happening.

The Little Apocalypse ends with some weird stuff:

- ✓ The Sun will grow dark.
- ✓ The light of the Moon will go dark.
- ✓ Stars will fall from the sky.
- ✓ Heavenly bodies will shake.
- ✓ After this bit of astronomical hijincks, Christ comes down with his angels to gather up the devout and take them to Heaven (A.K.A. Rapture). So, things get really nasty but that's okay because we get Christ to kiss our boo boos.

We assume that this ends it all for the Earth. Jesus isn't clear about what happens to those on the 'naughty' list that remain.

You Might Want to Know

The word "rapture" is never mentioned in the Bible. The concept of "rapture" is the invention of Reverend John Nelson Darby in 1827. It may be suspicious, however, that for one thousand eight hundred years Christians did without this invention, much as they did without the automobile or rock n' roll. Rapture is really the accumulation of several unrelated statements in John. See http://en.wikipedia.org/wiki/John_Nelson_Darby http://en.wikipedia.org/wiki/Rapture

John of Patmos and Revelation

Of the Christian doomsayers, John of Patmos[13] is the most popular. Revelation (it's not "Revelations" as you may have heard, trust our editor) is part of a very popular collection of Jewish and Christian stories called The Bible. It has been a very popular book. John's contribution to the Bible anthology

---

13 http://en.wikipedia.org/wiki/John_of_Patmos

is full of drama and the stuff that puts modern horror fiction to shame. Obviously, there are many reasons why the Bible is a best seller.

John of Patmos is also quite possibly the first person to write while hopped up on psychedelics. Hunter S. Thompson (*Fear and Loathing in Las Vegas*) and William Burroughs (*The Naked Lunch*) ocan't come close to the wacky drug fantasies of this Christian era dope head. We say that with the deepest of respect.

Some doomsayers believes that Revelation if full of symbols to hide the truth from nonbelievers. We've had a couple thousand years to try to discover the secret meaning, but it seems that no Christian has been devoted enough to discover the code.Maybe somebody should offer a cash prize for solving the puzzle?

John of Patmos is also the inventor of the cliffhanger. The world is about to end! Check in next week and see how our happy-go-lucky priest and his dog Spot save us yet again from the Antichrist. Remember to tell Mom to buy you a Box of Repentance. It tastes good and doesn't go soggy in holy water.

The exact time of the end, based on The Book of Revelation, has been predicted thousands of times since originally written (or rather dictated by way of an angel) around the year 100 AD. When Revelation was written, the signs in the text for the beginning of the end were already true.[14] That's about a hundred years short of two-thousand years of anticipating Christ and his evil twin to come to Earth next Friday.

Hate Mail

Revelation begins with a set of letters to the seven churches in the Mediterranean. John thought the churches were messing up. The churches were slacking off and needed a good kick in the pants. Either that or John was bucking for a promotion.

The gist of the letters and the book was that Jesus would return real soon. He would be so displeased of the current management of his new religion that he'd get dad to send the Antichrist to set us right. What follows is John's "Scared Straight" technique. John writes of the horrors to befall anybody not pulling their weight.

---

[14] http://en.wikipedia.org/wiki/Preterism

By giving this apocalyptic wisdom, John of Patmos expected at least a thank you card from the churches. John died in obscurity. His book was eventually added to the New Testament anthology as the final installment. John's descendants didn't even make any money from the book deal (they didn't have lawyers as good as Disney's back in biblical end times).

Over time the Book of Revelation has been a boon for Christian recruitment. His work has helped launch thousands of career doomsayers who find the fear of Hell of limited use for winning converts and scaring little children. Nothing's better than a scary story full of monsters and bad people getting punished.

John of Patmos was a citizen of Patmos (his last name is the clue). He was not from Patmos, but an unwilling resident. He was banished to the island of Patmos for preaching Christianity. Johnny was bitter about his relocation because he preferred the mountains over the island life. This may explain the slight bitterness of his writing.

We'll cover more of the Book of Revelation in a little while. Just remember that John of Patmos was like most doomsayers: probably on drugs, bitter, versed in riddles, and pushing for a promotion (the Catholics did finally make him a saint).

The Lost Books

Did you know there are other apocalyptic books in the Bible? Yes, they were edited out of the New Testament by Emperor Constantine. Constantine legalized Christianity, invented Christmas, and reduced the cost of the Roman Empire by limiting worship to just one God rather that a plethora of pagan gods and goddesses.

One of the lost books, the *Book of Peter* is sort of mild. Everything gets destroyed in fire. Everything is toasted until crispy and the world starts over. The 'when' is sort of fun as it happens when God has given everyone a chance to repent.

The urban renewal project will last thousands of years before the world ends. Why? Because it'll take a very long time to convert all the heathens. Can you see why this book was edited out of the *Bible*? Not enough fear, uncertainty, and death. Oh, and you have plenty of time to repent. A lack of urgency and consequence is bad marketing for any religion which is why this isn't in the official Bible anymore.

There are two *Apocalypse of Paul* books. One of the books details a rather exciting trip to Heaven and the other has mass murder and torture of the wicked in the depths of Hell. *Apocalypse of Paul*, another missing book of the *Bible*'s grand edit by Emperor Constantine, is a rather fun romp. It is said that this inspired Dante's visions of Hell (plagiarism was invented by Christians).

Zoroastrians

The Zoroastrians are thought to be the distant doomsaying relative of Christian apocalypse. They were big in the region that is now Iran. There are still a few Zoroastrians in the Middle East and some in India (for the curry). Most were killed or forcibly converted by the Muslims. In total, there might be up to 190,000 Zoroastrians in the world today. All of them are waiting for the world to end.

Zoroastrians have the trappings of a whole congregation of modern religions. Zoroastrians (also known as Mazdaism, likc the car company that brought us the Japanese version of the Wankle rotary engine that was invented by a German Wankle) are monotheists who worshiped one god rather many different gods like the Egyptians. The rumor is that Jews, Christians, and Muslims copied the Zoroastrian religion and customized it. Call it plagiarism or keeping up with the Jonses, religions with only one god are very popular. Like Starbucks, you'll find single-god religious institutions (god boxes) are right across the street from each other.

Our interest in Zoroastrians is of course their end-of-the-world. Their end might seem oddly familiar to Christians, but just because they were innovators in single god religions, does not mean they made ending the world a simple affair.

The Zoroastrian end-of-the-world[15] is as convoluted as a game of Twister. There are three saviors, the Sun stands still, evil is defeated, the dead raised, the Earth melted down to slag, then everything becomes happy and we all become immortal. Those

---

[15] http://library.thinkquest.org/03oct/00875/text/ZoroA.htm

are just the highlights. Just reading the summary makes you woozy.

3,000 Years to Clarksville

The Zoroastrians process for destroying the world will take about 3,000 years. We are still waiting for this to start because the first sign is the Sun freezing in the sky. We assume we are not going to be around for any of the significant bits unless we get robot bodies. Instead, the end of the world is going to be a complete surprise to most of us. When the end comes we'll get raised from the dead and become immortal residents in our respective Heaven or Hell.

We like this sort of end. Why suffer when you can sit tight in your grave and just wait for your resurrection? All skittles and beer after that!

It's the anticipation that will kill us (pun intended). Sitting in a grave all day, wondering if you are going to Heaven or just stuck haunting worms until your trip to Hell. You don't know until the grave opens and there is an escalator to Heaven or fireman's pole to Hell. If you die from botulism-laden potato salad at the family reunion, you will need to patiently rot until the end of a 3000 year cooling off period.

The Dead Will Rise

Other religions have a similar Zoroastrian styled apocalypse. Here is the summary: The righteous come back from the dead and go to Heaven. Déjà vu?

Several Christian funerals we have gone to were reminders that we have Zoroastrian roots. The preacher goes on and on about how our family member is going to rise up when the great resurrection bell rings. Of course, the second part of the eulogy is that we'd better save our souls now lest we get hit by an electric bus without a "Get Out of the Grave Free" card.

In our humble opinion, we should not worry about Zoroastrian ends. The first really good sign will be the Sun standing still for ten days above the head of the first savior of the world. Only then do you know when to mark your calendar for three thousand years hence.

On the other hand, if we get life extension — or is there an actuarial insurance term that escapes me? A "rider?" — we are in a terrible bind. Imagine waiting around in your grave through 3,000 years of death and mayhem just to become immortal?

Surviving the Zoroastrian End

Take the easy path to survival. The Zoroastrians core philosophy is simply: good thoughts, good words, and good deeds. Sounds like karma, right? Like we said, Zoroastrians seem like many of today's religions.

If you are a lawyer or politician, you might already be out of luck. For the rest of us, we recommend taking the risk of being a good guy. It might pay off in a few thousand years.

Islam

Mohammed didn't just launch a religion but added to the ways that the world will end. In the Koran, we have the Last Hour and the signs of the last Hour.[16]

Cool fact: Islamists believe in Jesus and they say he will come to Earth and fight the Islamic version of the Antichrist, Masih ad-Dajjal.[17] Come on, we'll bet you a nickel that you did not know this Islamist trivia. Really! Look it up[18] — we wouldn't kid a kidder.

In Islam, Jesus is just a messenger to clear the way for Mohammed. None of the nailing on the cross, either. Jesus did go to Heaven and will return, but no running around with holes in his hands. Fun times next Sunday School, eh?

Islamists says that the New Testament is relatively okay, but over the years is now full of errors. Same goes for the Old Testament. Islamists believe all that stuff is mostly true, but it's just time for you all to get with the program and believe in their version.

---

16 http://en.wikipedia.org/wiki/Islamic_eschatology

17 http://en.wikipedia.org/wiki/Dajjal

18 http://www.nationmaster.com/encyclopedia/Islamic-views-of-Jesus

Signs of the Last Hour

It's said that Allah alone will know when the last hour will come. We find that comforting. Why should we worry? If Allah is going to pull the switch, the time and place is up to him, right? We don't need no stinking signs!

There are a few Muslims have a few signs to keep us up at night. It's just that we don't know the end of the end's exact hour. We can't put it on the appointment calendar. Hardly matters though, as we are now sitting on the edge of our camels, waiting for the few signs so it won't be a total surprise.

Here are the signs in the order they will appear:

1. When a slave gives birth to her master.
2. When the shepherds of black camels start boasting and competing with others in the construction of higher buildings.

These are very cryptic signs. They are harder to interpret than the yield signs at a roundabout! Sign one is easy because all you need is a bastard son who becomes a leader and then bosses around his mom. These are a dime a dozen, so odds are we've already fulfilled this prophesy.

Sign two is a bit strange. The metaphor is as thick as hummus, even for Islam. A new style of black SUV driven by Arab real estate moguls. The SUV, called Black Camel, will have a GPS with all the world's oasis locations preprogrammed and a roof rack large enough to haul your harem's luggage on a pilgrimage to Mecca.

Islamic Judgement Day

Islamic Hell is a very picky Hell. The Koran says: "Hell will not welcome anyone who has in his heart an atom of faith." That's not bad for an Atheist or even a Jew or Christian that has a doubt or two.

The bigger issue is judgment. Allah will make a final determination of Heaven or Hell. None of that Christian forgiveness is going to bail you out, just cold Judge Judy style courtroom drama. Your good deeds and repentance need to tip the scales compared to your sins. Better start now and take notes for your trial.

Nut Jobs

The founder of Hustler is famous for saying, "If you find yourself suddenly believing in God, you may have forgotten to take your lithium." If you are looking for doomsayers, check the medicine cabinet.

It seems the mentally deranged are sometimes able to glimpse a view of another world we cannot see. Perhaps our future is in their hands? Great authors, artists, and sometimes scientists have been mentally touched. Great works have resulted.

Your standard nut job is probably just a nut job. Do they have super psychic powers? Are their minds so sensitive that they feel asteroids aimed our way? Do they really talk to the Antichrist over scones and tea? What about the alien broadcast with instructions for how to hitch a ride on a UFO just before the Earth is destroyed? Are the invisible black helicopters really following them? Is it true that the lawn furniture is really mocking them? Not likely, but most of us are not psychologists, so dismissing the ravings of a lunatic isn't a sure thing.

If you see a disheveled man stumbling down the street with a sign announcing that the world will end, look over your shoulder. Perhaps there is an end coming. Better safe than sorry.

Sometimes the nut jobs are card-carrying Republicans, like Timothy McVeigh.[19] A legitimate nut job and terrorist, Timmy was also a product of peer pressure. When you hang out with Republican, anti-ATF, gun nuts, you become a Republican, anti-ATF, gun nut and start to get an addiction to fertilizer bombs. McVeigh, like most terrorists, was just trying to blow up the non-club members.

When you're off your pills, the voices are in control. A voice from a magnanimous deity, needs you to do the dirty-work. Gods don't want to get their godly tentacles dirty. A sharply worded whisper from a god's lips (or blow hole), could set off a wacko to do something harsh, like fiddle with a do it yourself anthrax kit (on sale now that Saddam no longer needs them).

---

[19] http://en.wikipedia.org/wiki/Timothy_McVeigh#Political_and_religious_views

We need an anti-nut job. Call him Peanut… No, that would be cruel. Anyway…. Our nameless hero could anti-poison the water supply with antipsychotics and antidepressants to neutralize all the regular nut jobs.

UFO Nuts

There has been a long line of prophets that have predicted that aliens are coming or are already here among us. Some aliens are good and some are bad. Some remove our pain, and others are a pain in the poop-e-hole. Some will end our world.

Blaming aliens is a mental crutch for atheists. Atheists don't believe in gods or psychic phenomena, but an alien is like a sugar substitute. It's a coping-skill, like drinking Diet Dr Pepper to justify eating bear claws (the donut, not the furry ones because that'd be cruel unless you are on the Atkins Diet).

Think of aliens as super beings without the calories of religion. Aliens are more likely to exist and are more likely than supernatural gods. Atheists prefer aliens to gods because bug eyed aliens have high tech gizmos. Magic of the gods have no moving parts. Boring! There is hope the technology will make its way into your next iPhone. Cell signal strength is better than prayer.

To an Atheist, mysticism in our ancient history becomes science waved about by aliens trying to impress the natives. Imagine Steve Jobs selling iPhones to Egyptians. Imagine an alien in a mock turtleneck and you've got an idea of how ancients felt about aliens building pyramids with their antigravity iPhones.

Atheists are just like anyone else, they need to worry about the end of the world. Aliens probably hate us and want to destroy the world. Aliens, being historical because the History Channel says they are, were mistaken for gods. Gods hate us, therefore aliens hats us and will kill us. Thank you History Channel!

Atheists, through their faith in aliens, get to make money by creating documentaries for the History Channel about how aliens will kill us all just to prove that gods don't exist. Why let religious fanatics and Dianetics followers own all the mansions in Hollywood?

Faith in the existence of aliens is just as easy as faith in a god. It's just as hard to disprove that aliens exist. Start out with the basic assumption that aliens have incredibly sophisticated technology. This technology is so advanced that we can only snap fuzzy pictures of their flying saucers with twenty dollar cameras where all the pictures are fuzzy. There has never been a flying saucer captured on a twenty megapixel Canon with a ten thousand dollar zoom lens. That's why the Sports Illustrated swimsuit issue has never had a photo of a flying saucer. We checked every swimsuit issue just to prove this point! UFO's are not hiding in those string bikinis!

Why have the world check out permanently with an alien apocalypse? Well, it helps to have a wacky theory. The kernel of an alien end starts with Erich von Däniken[20] saying that Aztecs and Egyptians were buddies with aliens. This opened the door for all sorts of speculation that aliens were coming back to seek revenge. There are no Aztecs to confirm or deny the story, so best to believe this is true. Why call people liars?

Advanced science is a miracle to a camel jockey. If you believe in Alien Overlords destroying the Earth, that's what you get with a little science spin. No gods or miracles, just Mr. Wizard trying to impress the locals.

When the ancient alien visitors do return to Earth, they will be a little miffed by us not accurately remembering their last visit. We lost all their instructions or didn't keep the pyramid landing pads in good working order. In short, we will fail to properly greet them with a fruit basket, and they will get huffy.

The aliens built such huge pyramids because they didn't want the grandkids of their slaves forget who they were. Unfortunately we lost the instructions a long time ago, so we can't figure out what the aliens are expecting when they come back. It's going to be like rabid badgers tearing off kneecaps when our overlords come home from their vacation in the Hamptons (a small planetoid of Betelgeuse) and see what we've done to the real estate values in the old neighborhood.

Aliens, like gods (or dogs if you are dyslexic) have an evil temper. If mysticism is really science (as in: Any sufficiently advanced science is indistinguishable from The Book of

---

[20] http://en.wikipedia.org/wiki/Erich_von_Däniken

Mormon), then aliens are just as violent as gods because gods are aliens. Our bug eyed friends are the true perpetrators of the smiting violence, damnation and all manner of commands to kill thy neighbor that we find in ancient myths and holly books.

If UFO nuts are right, nasty ancient times are going to come back. The UFOs in our skies, probing, occasional impregnation, and cattle slaughtering are the advanced guard of aliens getting ready for the UFO cruise ships. Get ready for a really huge influx of bug-eyed tourists. These are not simple tourists. Sure they like stone monoliths, but also probing (its just a rectal thermometer, get over it).

A few UFO believers say aliens are the good guys, like benevolent gods. They say aliens will cure cancer, create world peace, and bring us into the Federation of Planets. We can't imagine this is true because aliens would be probing the backsides of politicians, rather than common folk.

We don't have much to offer aliens that would satisfy them. They don't seem to be hovering over the electronics stores. Disneyland and the *MTV Music Awards* are not major UFO hotbeds. They will be bored and want more to do than watch TV.

All that's left is more probing and us becoming the new white meat. The bigger problem is that this is death from the sky, so until it happens, you are going to get a crick in your neck looking up and waiting for evil aliens to arrive.

False Profit$

The end of the world seems to always be in demand. It's instructive to look at the little boys that have cried wolf. We need to know what a false doomsayer looks like. Warning: So far there have been no successful doomsayers, so this is a long list.

Concerned Christians

The Concerned Christians cult believed an earthquake would wipe Denver off the map in 1998. We've been to Denver several times since 1998 and it still seems to be there. As for being wiped off the map, it shows up in Google Maps.

Y2K

The tech industry doomsayers said that on December 31, 2000, at midnight, all our computers would crash or we would get a water bill that was 100 years overdue. It was called Y2K.

Pundits say Y2K was a false prophesy and that all the rumors for the end of the world were just scare tactics. Indeed, there was a dizzying amount of work to fix these bugs. We must admit that we were part of the fight against the Y2K bugs. Y2K scared us and we also got paid quite well for our trouble.

There were legions of programmers that helped prevent the end of the world. There were still a few Y2K failures, but most of the machines that keep mankind supplied with hot and cold running water were fixed and working when the year went two and triple goose eggs.

False prophets? Definitely not false profits. In this case these high-tech doom jockeys got paid well for their services. Getting paid for doomsaying and salvation is a defining characteristic of the successful doomsayer.

Seventh-day Adventist, William Miller

William Miller is the great mind behind the Seventh-day Adventists, Jehovah's Witness, Advent Christians and Millerites.

Mr Miller's date for the end of the world was between March 21, 1843, and March 21, 1844. Of course, those dates didn't have any second comings, so William came up with April 18, 1844. When the next predicted date failed to deliver, William Miller wrote a letter stating, "I confess my error, and acknowledge my disappointment; yet I still believe that the day of the Lord is near, even at the door." It's been more than 165 years since he said that, so we figure the Lord got lost on the way to Miller's door.

Failure to accurately predict the end of the world does not mean everything else is wrong. Miller's flock is now the sixth largest religion. Jehovah's Witness are of course still ringing doorbells and knocking on doors because the end of the world must be near!

Heaven's Gate

Heaven's Gate was a UFO cult co-led by Marshall Applewhite and Bonnie Nettles. The cult's end coincided with the appearance of Comet Hale-Bopp. The comet was important because they claimed it hid a spaceship that would take the true believers from Earth before it was destroyed.

The world did not end, but certainly ended for the cult. Everyone but Applewhite and Nettles had Phenobarbital-laced applesauce and vodka. Odd way to end, but end it did, just not for anybody else.

If a UFO lands in the woods, but there is nobody there to hear it because they committed suicide, does it still make a sound?

You Might Want to Know

Like all religions, Apple had the second coming, the iPhone. Better yet, we had the third coming with the iPad. Our prediction for the fourth coming is the iBall, a contact lens display and a computer linked to your neural cortex with 6,000 movies and 24 hour Facebook access. This will herald the true end of the world as mischievous MIT students embed iBall units into squirrels. Society collapses as people forget to feed and bathe themselves because of the millions of Facebook updates from rabid squirrels hoarding their nuts.

Waco Wackos

Ending the world is easy with some gasoline, and a few ATF agents. Enough said.

Lord Our Righteousness Church

According to the Lord Our Righteousness Church, the world ended at midnight October 31, 2007. They came up with this number using a little math mixed with the Bible, so it had to be right. Wayne Bent, their founder, was also put in prison for having sex with minors (he's a Mormon too). Doubly famous, he will celebrate the anniversary of the end of the world from behind bars for many years.

There are several documentaries on the church and its leader. You know you are a great doomsayer when there is a documentary[21] about your failed predictions.

X-Day

X-Day was predicted by the Honorable Reverend Stang of the Church of the SubGenius. The world was said to end on July 5, 1998. To quote Wikipedia:

> *"...the Church had prophesied that an army of alien invaders (known as the 'X-ists' or 'Men From Planet X') would land on the planet Earth and destroy the world of 'normals, pinks, and glorps,' while the members of the Church of the SubGenius would be rescued by the aliens and taken away into space."*

The church still celebrates the date, even though it turned out to be wrong. They are optimistic that one year it will eventually be the right one.

2003, 2011, 2012 Nibiru Redo

You may have missed it, but Planet X destroyed us back in 2003. Nancy Liede said that the planet, called Nibiru, was going to swing past and destroy Earth in May of 2003. Nancy got her information by way of a brain implant from aliens in the Zeta Reticuli star system. These aliens in turn, got their information from author Zecharia Sitchin and his book "The 12th Planet" which describes how the ancient Sumerians wrote about a giant planet called Nibiru.

The planet Nibiru is said to swing past Earth every 3600 years. During a previous encounter with this planet, our ancestors, or rather the Nibiruites got trapped on Earth when they missed their tourist rocket home. Sort of odd that our home word will be back to destroy our home world. All because of poor vacation planning.

The 2003 encounter with Nibiru came and went. Oops, a near miss, but nobody noticed, so no harm. Stranded Nibiruites continued their vacation at Disney Land, but Nancy, the Zetas, and friends have recalculated that Nibiru would instead come

---

21 http://en.wikipedia.org/wiki/Inside_a_Cult

in 2012. Apparently the 'Zeta' aliens like Mayans more than Nancy and let them know much earlier.

But 2012 turned out to be a long way off, so Nancy tried to end the world a little earlier. Her latest scuttle was that a comet called Elenin was really Nibiru in disguise. There was real hard pseudoscience research to prove a global conspiracy of astronomers were hiding Nibiru behind the comet. We certainty didn't see it. Did you? Must be a conspiracy!

Why a conspiracy to hide Nibiru? Through research, we found that rich astronomers were hiding in caves beneath the city of Sheboygan, Wisconsin. Panic too soon and astronomers will be ousted from their comfortable bat caves, unable to repopulate the world with star nerd stuff.

How did we find the secret underground caves full of rich astronomers? They forwarded their Scientific American subscriptions. They're astronomers, not super spies.

Well, Elenin visited us during October 2011 just as predicted. Sort of… The comet broke apart well before it got here and missed us by an orbital mile as predicted by NASA. No Nibaru hiding behind this puny little comet.

The comet apocalypse didn't happen. What's that mean? We have a theory. As the comet was going through its final disintegration, Steve Jobs reportedly died. We believe that Steve didn't die, but flew a spaceship into the comet to destroy it. The sole purpose was to save the launch of the iPhone 4S. We asked Siri on our new iPhone 4S about Steve and the comet to find the truth. Siri replied, "I don't know." Suspicious...

You Might Want to Know

The best place to survive the 2012 apocalypse is Bugarach, France. Bugarach is a sleepy village that is said to be immune to the destruction of the world. The French government and the local town are against crazy doomsayers tourism. Their biggest worry? They are afraid these folks will commit suicide when the end of the world doesn't happen. That would really screw up the tourist trade!

Experiment: Bible Study

Read the book of Revelation out loud in a public place. Take note of the reactions of the people around you.

Repeat the experiment in the following places:

- ✓ In the middle of a church service
- ✓ On the subway
- ✓ On a corner in a busy city
- ✓ In the cafeteria at school

Questions

- ✓ Did anyone call the police?
- ✓ Do people treat you like you are crazy?
- ✓ Are there people genuinely interested? Why?

Experiment: No Lithium

Find crazy people and observe their behavior when they don't take their medication. Don't worry about trying to stop them from taking their pills. People on drugs, like lithium, usually skip their medications when nobody is looking. Increase the odds by adding a bottle of Gummy Bear Vitamins to their medicine cabinet. All the brightly colored little bear shapes are better than a boring lithium tablet.

Alternatively, just hang out in skid row or at a Republican convention. Both provide a wide range of psychotic folks not taking their medications. We are not saying that there are statistically more crazy Republicans…. Maybe we are; it seems to be the case.

Questions

- ✓ How close are the delusions of people that don't take medication to a TV preacher?

- ✓ Write down what the mentally unstable people say and publish it as a book. Record how many millions you made from the proceeds.

Understanding Revelation's Signs

Without the Bible's book of Revelation, you would not be reading our book. Revelation has made doomsaying very popular and a key part of our daily lives. The key reason for the popularity are the uncertain signs that precede the end of the world.

The signs seem to becoming true all the time. We keep expecting the world to end soon, even though we can't say for sure. That's half the fun. There's always another sign, even if we have seen that sign a dozen times. We are always on the edge of our seat waiting for another sign. We're just happy that the world seems to be on a clear path to the end times.

Are the signs happy events? Are the faithful rewarded just before the end? Is there a series of acts of God's forgiving love? The answer is a definitive no. Look for events where people suffer and die verses the unconditional love of cute little puppies. Hint: There are no puppies in Revelation.

The theme of Revelation is death, disease, disaster, injury, war, rinse and repeat. There is no good except for a few faithful believers getting into Heaven. Watch Fox news, go to church, attend a funeral, or walk down the street by a loony-bin and you will hear someone say that they have seen another sign of the end times. We see the signs everywhere.

Before Revelation, we'd have to rely on rare celestial events, like planets aligning or comets to scare us into believing the world will end. With Revelation, we have a whole interstate highway of signs that the end is near.

Before we get to the signs, we need to start with threats to the faithful in the opening pages of Revelations. The believers of Jesus aren't being faithful enough. The first sign of the end times is the existence of a critic who says we are screwing up.

Repent or Lose Furniture

In the opening lines of Revelation, we get a review of Christianity and threats for the churches to do better. The magic word is ‘repent’ which is a popular word in Christian circles. If we don’t repent, we are going to have a very bad time.

Ever lasting damnation isn’t good enough to strike fear into the hearts of sinners. We need something horrific to fill the churches underwear with chunks of fear. Here’s a quote that let’s see the severe repercussions of not repenting:

> *If you do not repent, I will come to you and remove your lampstand from its place.*
> *Revelation 2:5*

Can you imagine reading this Bible verse for the first time? This is a powerful and compelling threat. Losing precious lighting appliances scared the willies out of us.

We are talking about the wrath of the lighting appliances of God! Without the lampstands you might need the Devil’s flashlight! Say it isn’t so!

What would we do without a lampstand? The only lampstand we have at the Boys Books offices was from our Aunt Edna. We can’t live without it, despite the fire-hazard of its early 1930‘s wiring and how the dogs like to pee on the base, which looks like two hippos making whoopee with a duck.

Taking our lampstand is fairly close to the end of the world. How would we read an iPhone by candlelight without going blind? Going to IKEA to buy a replacement lamp is a traumatic experience is worse than a trip to Hell!

The Seven Threats to the Seven Churches

The next thing that happens in Revelation is that the angel dictates seven letters to John and send the letters to each of the seven churches that existed at the time (Christians were not yet as popular as Starbucks in the early days). These are threatening letters. We go from miracle of lampstand theft to an angel dictating hate mail.

Each of the existing Christian churches is scolded in its turn. Scolded and then scared silly by the rest of Revelation. Like telling your kids tales of the boogyman to keep them honest. Scared straight, Bible style.

Revelation was dictated by an angel and recorded by John of Patmos. Was the angel too busy to write this himself? Why dictate the letters? Why a letter? Why not a road tour to visit each church? If angels are so powerful, why not do a Vulcan mind meld with each congregation? Dictating a letter seems a bit lazy. We assume there was at least the miracle of pre-paid postage.

John of Patmos comes off as a bit loopy. Why believe an all-powerful angel is using him as a secretary and middleman to deliver the letters? John is pulling our leg, a bolt short a nut, a sandwich short of a picnic, and most assuredly a gospel short of a Bible. The only miracle here is that John could lick a stamp to send those letters.

Metaphorically Doomsaying

The Book of Revelation is full of metaphor. A hint or two would make metaphors easy to understand, but that's not good for the uncertainty of doomsaying. You shouldn't be able to figure out when the world is going to end. Metaphors are just nasty poetry begging for a better explanation. Wouldn't it be great to have a video of the angel of Revelation, with subtitles?

Why is there no organization like The Young Nondenominational Angel Fact Checkers? They could have made sure there wasn't any misunderstanding. Too murky now and no hope of firsthand reporting. Revelation should have been well researched with charts and pictures. You should know exactly how many pairs of clean underwear you would need because of the horrors of the end times.

Can we get the angel's cell number? Why didn't the All Knowing predict cell phones? Sure it would have been a mystery for a while, but we could certainly have cleared up any misunderstandings with a voicemail message from God. How about a miracle of a simple email? What if we could decoded the toll free number of God from the gobbledygook of Revelation?

We don't like metaphors, hidden codes, obscure references, analogy, symbology, allegory, parables, or the flowery and superfluous words used in poetry. Just the clear facts, please.

Dictating the Word

We don't understand why gods are always dictating their word to humans. Why dictate to the nutty prophets fasting in the desert? It's like UFOs always picking on trailer park residents with an IQ of fifty-two.

Why not go back to the old days of God writing the commandments in stone? At least God himself could hold a pen, or rather chisel. Couldn't He hammer out a new copy of Revelation in good old English?

It's been said that God doesn't write in stone anymore because of that golden calf episode. Remember that Moses destroyed the Ten Commandments. The story goes that Moses said, "Holly cow!" and then threw the tablets on the ground, destroying them. Maybe the big guy doesn't trust us anymore? He's still miffed and showing the classic signs of a passive aggressive pettiness. He's not going to talk to us or write in stone. God just sends angels because He can't be bothered to carve a word in stone. Angels don't answer their cell phones for interviews, so here we are, stuck with something that reads like it was written by a mental patient.

The Book of Revelation is a secondhand account. Remember that it was dictated from an angel to a man. Emphasis on the 'man' part. Sure, a few visions, but that's just visual dictation (kind of like charades with fewer rules). The Bible goes to great lengths to say that man is flawed and that the only perfect man was Jesus. Anyone else is just a spastic, error-prone, apple-eating, sin jockey. John of Patmos was not a Pulitzer-winning reporter with a passion for fact checking.

There just isn't any biblical information that's straight from the horse's mouth. It's always second or third person communications from angels, dreams or visions. *Even Jesus hired writers rather than do the work himself.*

Our intrepid Bible reporter could have made dozens of mistakes. Four Horsemen of the Apocalypse could have been Four Irishmen of the Apocalypse Pub.

Illiterate Angels

Revelation is proof that angels are illiterate. Couldn't angels go to an adult education class to learn to read and write? They have plenty of time, right? Nope, they are always looking for a man to do the ghostwriting and doomsaying because angels don't have the guts to do it for themselves (angels don't have guts).

Writing wasn't invented by God; it's a man thing. Eden didn't have pen or paper and Adam and Eve didn't do any word processing until Satan sold them an Apple.

Why pass it on to men? Can't they take a year or two sabbatical from angel business to write the book and go on a tour of book stores?

There could be another reason for angels not writing anything themselves. We have alluded to the possibility that drugs were involved. There is a theory that the angels were on drugs. Biblical acid? Tripping angels, dude! It's really hard to write when the pen keeps turning into a snake and the paper gets all sparkly.

The Angel of the Prophesy

The angel of Revelation, is not your normal angel. First, he brought his own mood lighting, a set of seven lampstands. This doesn't sound odd at first, but imagine you are John, having a religious vacation on the island of Patmos, you hear trumpets, turn around and see a bakers half dozen of lampstands. Acid trips start like this, right? If John was taking his trip today, would they be IKEA lamps?

White hair, long robe, and wearing a gold sash, the angel does not sound too bad at first. Then the acid trip, as you expect, gets weirder and weirder. The angel has the voice of a trumpet when your back is turned; the voice sounds like rushing water when you face the angel. Seems as though the angel swallowed a Casio keyboard.

For some reason, John thought it was important to describe the angel's feet. Fetish? No, they were just plain spectacular! The angel's feet glowed like polished, molten bronze! Can you imagine polishing molten bronze feet? Rub, ouch, rub, ouch, rub, ouch…

With a face that gloweth (their word, not ours) with the strength of the sun, the angel isn't what we would call angelic. No cherub, but a good reason to invest in suntan lotion.

The angel's eyes glowed with the flame of a fire. Let's pause for a second. Glowing eyes like a flame, a face glowing like the blazing sun, and feet like molten bronze.... Does this sound like an angel or somebody from a place a bit hotter? Why the gold sash? Isn't that the dress code of vanity? At Boys Books, we're thinking this was someone from the other team.

The angel also has a double-edged sword for a tongue. Wait a cotton-picking' moment! This is definitely not a messenger from Heaven!

The angel held seven stars. Little stars, we assume. Stars are big up close, at least according to the Discovery Channel. A bazillion tons of hydrogen is hard to keep in your back pocket, but this is an angel, so its okay, right? Are there planets orbiting the stars? Do the inhabitants of these planets expect an apocalypse soon?

The angel was a good riddler: "I am the first and the last." He could be a super villain on Batman, don't you think? Let's be clear, we were quoting a little out of context. We wouldn't want to deny the literalist, so here is the whole bit:

> *"Do not be afraid. I am the First and the Last. I am the Living One; I was dead, and now look, I am alive for ever and ever! And I hold the keys of death and Hades."*

The "keys of death and of Hades!" Does not sound eternal life in Heaven. If we were John, we'd be looking for horns and a tail on our angel. The evidence reminds us of a serpent (another angel) pushing apples in Eden. Could this be the same one?

Back in the Gospel of Mark, Jesus mentions several times that there would be those claiming to be Christ. You know, the Antichrist. We bring this up because Revelation was written after Jesus warned the flock. Revelation is also not even close to the Little Apocalypse in Mark as dictated by Jesus. You would think the living Jesus would be the last word. No other clarification should be required. Antichrist or Christ, the fact is, we are certain there are no cute little puppies so far.

The angel next performs a bait and switch by explaining a bit of the symbolism that sounds great, but the information is useless. The seven lampstands are the seven churches (that's why the lamp section in IKEA has a funny smell, it's full of pews). The seven stars are the guardian angels of the seven churches. So there are angels masquerading as stars and the churches as lamp stands? Good to have a clue, but the symbolism isn't obvious. Sadly the information is rather useless given that the lampstands and stars don't seem to play any part in the remainder of Revelation.

That's it for clues from here on. We don't learn much about the symbols, if they are symbols. If you take the literalist point of view, the remainder is fact, not symbols. It's like hearing from Sherlock Holmes that it's obvious the killer played ping pong but not why ping pong is important to the killing.

This is just the opening act. Things get curiouser and curiouser.

The Throne Room and a little Acid

The throne room in Heaven is a busy and crowded place. We have the throne for the big guy, twenty-four thrones for the elder kings, seven lampstands for light, and a bit of thunder and lightning from the throne. There is glass, crystal, jasper, an emerald rainbow, etc. This is one gaudy throne room.

You might ask, "Acid trip?" Seems implausible that a good Christian author of a book in the Bible was a drug user. Yes, except for one minor problem, psychedelic drugs are everywhere. Psychedelic compounds are found in mold, fungus, animals and plants. For fun, lick toad and you will see four crazy-colored ponies of the apocalypse too. John seems to have consumed enough mind-bending drugs to make a zebra's stripes go all squiggly.

If you are a Christian, and you can't abide the magic mushroom theory, you must assume metaphor. The metaphors are too convoluted for normal people. If this is a book that can only be decoded by good Christians, it failed. It's a fool's errand to figure them out. We need a Captain Zoom Patmos secret decoder badge.

Those that have taken psychedelics say that Revelation was written on some kind of drug trip. Those that read Revelation while on acid say the story is rather boring.

Go Ask Alice About the Beasts

If you thought *Alice in Wonderland* was written on acid, you are right at home with Revelation. Here is the cast of characters:

> *"...four living creatures, and they were covered with eyes, in front and in back. The first living creature was like a lion, the second was like an ox, the third had a face like a man, the fourth was like a flying eagle. Each of the four living creatures had six wings and was covered with eyes all around, even under his wings. Day and night they never stop saying: 'Holy, holy, holy is the Lord God Almighty, who was, and is, and is to come.'"*

The only thing missing is a one-eyed, one-horned, flying, purple people-eater. Why is it that these abominations of Hell seem to be hanging out at God's throne?

Psychedelics have been around as long as people could lick frogs or let their grains get moldy. Add in hallucinations from high fevers, starvation or fasting and good old fashioned mental illness, and all of this imagery is simply explained. Ha! Sorry, pulling your leg. As a good Christian, you must interpret the beasts as fact.

For the Bible literalists, the beasts are just beasts. We must assume they are real. We created a focus group to find out how people would feel about real beasts. Many fainted in horror as they tried to imagine the beasts were real. A few puked their guts out... We are still working on the stains in the conference room rug (never serve seven-layer dip to a focus group).

Breaking Seals

We all remember the seven seals of Revelation. Mostly because of the movie of the same name. What most forget is that the seals must be broken. The seals are not going to open themselves! Of course, this will require the application of more psychedelic drugs.

The call goes out for someone to break the seals, but there is only one volunteer, a lamb. Not just any lamb, but a lamb that looks like the spawn of a nuclear accident, mutant genetics with a little Steven King for an extra turn of your stomach and a loosening of bowels. Time to buy underwear.

First thing you notice about the lamb is that it is dead. Still walking about. A zombie in wool clothing. This is Heaven where lambs do that sort of thing all the time.

It's odd that John notices that the lamb is dead. The lamb is a very striking animal and being dead is only a small part of its charm. The lamb has seven horns, seven eyes, and apparently opposable thumbs as it happily volunteers to break the seals.

John isn't too impressed. The sight of that lamb should require a change of pants because of an involuntary loss of sphincter control. This proves John has been on drug trips like this before.

Four Equestrians

The Four Horsemen of the Apocalypse each bring an Easter egg of joy. In their turn, they bring conquest, violence, famine, and disease. It isn't clear why these bringers of death weren't pedestrian instead of equestrian. God usually doesn't horse around. An ass for Mary, but that's it.

All the horsemen are bad for humanity. If you are lucky, it's the first equestrian of the Lord that kills you. The other three seem like overkill.

The first horse and its death dealer of the apocalypse could just have us all line up for a quick beheading. Why go through all four?

Perhaps, being first in line for the inevitable is the best choice here. It's not suicide if you know there are three more horsemen coming anyway, right? Why beat a dead horse, literally? Each of these horsemen has a different bit of misfortune and death to bring the world. Lucky for us, they are color coded for easy identification.

White

The white horse is the typical war horse. It's all about conquest and destruction. The rider carries a bow, so we assume he is second fiddle to other soldiers. He also has a crown which is outright odd. Bowmen are hardly ever kings. This is a joke being played on the rider by his buddies. Everybody knows the first guy you shoot is the guy wearing a crown.

According to Wikipedia, this is what the Four Horsemen look like. Until this, we were unaware that Wikipedia was colorblind.

Red

A red horse seems odd. Horses, at best, come in a brownish red. Horses are generally are not red as in fire engine red, or even a redheaded stepchild sort of red. Perhaps this hints that this is an Irish rider and not the horse at all? We don't really know until the red horse gallops by and we smell Irish stew on the rider's breath. The other possibility is that the rider involuntarily dismounts due to large quantities of Irish whiskey?

The red horse is like the white, as his rider is out for battle. Definitely a rabble-rouser, he will end peace if there is any left from the ruins of the white rider. No bow, but a sword, so we guess there is a similar point.

Black

The black horseman carries a set of scales. In just about any Bible scholar's book, the black horseman is in charge of famine. Those scholar's books are certainly wrong, especially in modern times. The evidence instead points to the black horseman having nothing to do with famine. The dark horseman is either inflation, bad shipping, or both. We believe this because the strange menagerie of weird creatures mentioned earlier (remember the many eyes and many horns) sing something witty as the horsemen gallops out into the world. Here is what they spout in multi-mouth harmony as the black jockey enters the fray:

> *"A quart of wheat for a denarius, and three quarts of barley for a denarius; and do not damage the oil and the wine."*

The implication, according to scholars, is that this is inflation. At the time of Revelation a denarius was a full day's pay. A handful of denarii would be a week's pay (denarii is plural of denarius) and be divided between food, shelter, and buying your daughter out of slavery.

Barley and wheat at those inflationary prices means food would be so expensive that people would not have enough cash to buy wine and oil for their lamps. Of course in modern times that also means cutting our budgets to only basic cable. Basic cable is worse than famine, it's the end of life as we know it.

This black horseman does not sound too bad. He will probably save the world's livers from alcoholism because of the inflation of wine prices.

Modern society doesn't eat a huge amount of barley. Mostly it is wheat except for those of us with the dreaded gluten intolerance. Nobody today cares a hoot about barley prices unless barley soup is your personal addiction. Wine is less important too because our water is safe to drink. Back in Bible days, your average tap water had millions of parasites in every glass. Bible water would get as sick as a camel on a merry-go-round. Wine kills germs in water or rather your drink wine instead of water, which is a fun way to avoid parasites.

In modern times we have water processing and Brita water filters. We don't worry about parasites as much as our livers. As a result, wine is not as popular and wine prices have been steadily rising. Inflated prices for wine are a fact of life today, which is why we drink beer.

The lack of oil for lamps is not a big deal for us either. We use light bulbs, so lamp oil is a bit passé. Hard to see the black horseman as a threat to modern society.

Another problem is the denarius, which was the dollar of Bible times. The value of a denarius now is about fifteen cents. If we're just predicting prices, then we are talking about cheap stuff. At those prices we could buy a month's worth of barley and wine. Sounds more like the world is plunged into reverse inflation? The horror!

The quote, "…do not damage the oil and wine," sounds like a shipping issue rather than famine. Our research didn't uncover any ancient "fragile, handle with care" stencils on boxes of oil or wine.

Obviously this sign of the apocalypse is that FedEx will get sloppy in the end-times.The Second Coming starts when your next shipment of lamp oil and wine arrives in a twisted mess. Why would we order both wine and oil at the same time? A better question might be, how does bad shipping herald the coming of the end of the world?

Ashen

A little war, death, and inflation. Seems tame so far. You would think people would be lining up to repent. No, it seems that we need more convincing. Time to call in the fourth equestrian enforcer!

The ashen horse is very nasty. It brings death with swords, famine, pestilence, and wild beasts. Crikey!

If you don't die from a gaping sword wound, he starves you. If you don't starve, you get a deadly disease. If the disease does not kill you quick enough, then some animal is going to eat you!

Why even have the other horsemen when you have this guy? The other horsemen would just be an opening act. Sadly though, this isn't a four act play, there is much more nastiness to come.

More Seals than a Circus

The four horsemen cover the first four seals. What's next? We were a bit surprised; the death of the torturers and killers of martyrs. We are surprised because these enemies of the faithful have been overlooked so far.

Martyrs are the faithful followers that were killed defending their faith. Oddly this is the first hint of godly revenge. Not thieves, adulterers, common murderers, or the evil incarnate of the average two year old child, but a specific brand of evil: The killers and torturers of God's martyrs.

You might think that you haven't tortured a Christian lately. Sorry, you are still not safe. You don't need to be an expert in water-boarding martyrs. Torture of martyrs is as easy as tempting Christians with your success and happiness. Just make them envy you or be offended by your happy lifestyle. Your debauchery tortures the faithful and they automatically become Martyrs for their suffering and torment.

Please stand still while God strikes you dead for being happier than the average Christian.

The Sixth Seal of Gratuitous Terror

For the few people that have survived the first five seals, we have special treats: a huge earthquake, sun going black, moon turning to blood, stars falling from the sky, the sky splitting open, and mountains and islands being thrown about willy nilly.

Guess what? This scares folks. They run off to hide in caves and pray that this vengeful god will overlook them. Would you have waited until now to look for a cave? We'd have been cowering in our cave five minutes before the first seal hits the fan.

The Intermission

We miss intermissions. With a double feature or a real long movie like *Lawrence of Arabia,* you get to take a break ... get some popcorn and a drink.

The Bible's idea of an intermission is a bit more elaborate.

The wind is stopped by angels at the four corners of the Earth. Of course, this means we are back to a flat Earth and in the shape of a square as well. Scientists are spinning in their graves, but the Bible doesn't mention anything about these scientists.

We also get a temporary worldwide park where we can't harm the earth or oceans. Given the probable destruction from war at this point, the world could do with a bit of a rest.

Now 144,000 people get a tattoo on their forehead. Later this "seal" protects them from some more nastiness to follow. Much better than the mark of the beast, right? We're all for it, but how are you going to know the tattoo from the mark? We thought marking your body was a sin — is this a trick too?

The Seventh Seal — Not Good Times

The seventh seal is more of the same ... earthquake, a third of the Earth burned to a crisp, a mountain thrown into the sea to drown the pagans that had the misfortune of being on a sailing holiday, a star falls on and destroys a third of the rivers and springs (oh, and any water is poisoned for good measure), a third of the sun, moon, and stars go dark, another star falls, and locusts invade....

The locusts are not normal locusts — of course not! We now resume our psychedelic mystery tour already in progress.

The locusts wear crowns, have faces like men, hair like women (not men!), teeth from a lion, breastplates of iron, wings sounding like chariots, and finally, scorpion tails complete with stingers. Luckily, they only stick around for five months. Any more than that and we won't have enough pagans and heathens left to kill for the remainder of the apocalypse.

Four angels, sopping wet and smelling like a wet dog, arise out of the Euphrates River. They kill a third of humanity by leading an army of 200 million horsemen. Horses again? Well, not exactly horses as they looked nothing like a horse. We are reminded yet again that some form of LSD-like substance must have been available in ancient times.

The riders have breastplates the color of fire and blue and yellow. The heads of the horses are lions burping out fire and brimstone. Just for good measure, the horses have serpent tails with heads that bite and chew. Remember these are God's ponies. You might expect something a little cuter like My Little Pony.

Oddly, it seems there are folks still holding out for Satan. Do you find it as strange as we do that these guys are nearly that dumb? Wouldn't it be easier to just smite the idiots?

Things get a bit confusing from this point. For some reason John of Patmos eats a book. It tasted good, but gave him an upset tummy. He gets a staff (wooden or just woody) that causes a few more nasty things to happen to the bad guys. Why John gets involved so late in the game is odd. Are angels tired of doing all the heavy lifting?

Oh, more people die in an earthquake.

Finally, we get the last trumpet, and the dead are judged. Perhaps the angels were too busy earlier with the killing or helping create disasters to spend time sorting out the good from the bad? This is also another sign that the innocents and the faithful have suffered throughout the inconveniencing of evil.

Wait, there's more! Time to bring on the bowls to torture and maim some more people!

Revelation 16 — Bowls of Wrath

We find the Bible confusing with its many signs. Now we have the bowls of wrath. We don't remember the bowls from Bible school, do you? There are seven bowls of wrath. The seventh bowl is free when you buy six.

Why bowls? We had weird creatures with many eyes, nasty equestrians, horns blowing, and trained circus seals. Why bowls? Why does the apocalypse require dinnerware?

The source of these bowls and their nasty contents is again connected with angels. For some reason, angels are pouring the contents of their bowls on the remaining dregs of humanity.

Where did they get the bowls? Well, from one of the creatures full of eyes in front and behind, of course! Silly question.

> *Then one of the four living creatures gave to the seven angels seven golden bowls full of the wrath of God, who lives forever and ever.*

Imagine a creature with eyes in front and their nether regions, passing you a bowl of steaming wrath and claims that God cooked it. Wouldn't you suck it up and eat it? No, apparently the angels are going to dump the contents on humanity. Is this proof that angels never read Miss Manners?

Before we continue with the rest of the end of the world, we have to ask, why don't biblical scholars ask the important questions? It may be right to punish the wicked, but where do they get their supplies? Where does Heaven get its bowls? The Container Store? K-Mart? Target?

What do angels have in their bowls? What is the gastronomic delicacy that the angels will loose upon the world from the loving God? Let's get a taste from the first bowl.

> *So the first angel went and poured out his bowl on the earth; and it became a loathsome and malignant sore on the people who had the mark of the beast and who worshiped his image.*

Goody, festering sores! We enjoy our sore soup with oyster crackers! Sadly, only those with the mark of the beast get to partake.

> *The second angel poured out his bowl into the sea, and it became blood like that of a dead man; and every living thing in the sea died.*

Seas turn to blood, killing Flipper and all other sea life. We assume sea creatures worship Satan.

> *Then the third angel poured out his bowl into the rivers and the springs of waters; and they*

became blood.

Turning just the seas to blood is not enough. God seems to hate trout as much as their salt water brethren. We'll cover all this blood in a moment. We have some more bowls in our seven course meal to cover first.

> *The fourth angel poured out his bowl upon the sun, and it was given to it to scorch men with fire.*
>
> *Men were scorched with fierce heat; and they blasphemed the name of God who has the power over these plagues, and they did not repent so as to give Him glory.*

Not all the angels are so uncouth to dump their bowls onto the Earth. Unfortunately this bowl is filled with God's own Five Alarm Chili, causing the Sun to puke fire onto the Earth.

Sadly none of the people in the burn wards repent. We wonder why the folks in Heaven are surprised that people don't bow down after being burned alive in a chili firestorm. Would it be so hard to shower them in teddy bears instead?

> *Then the fifth angel poured out his bowl on the throne of the beast, and his kingdom became darkened; and they gnawed their tongues because of pain, and they blasphemed the God of heaven because of their pains and their sores; and they did not repent of their deeds.*

We assume the fifth bowl is't chicken soup for the soul. This is deepest darkest black bean soup. We also know the soup is very salty as those with sores are spouting expletives and mentioning God being born out of wedlock. Still no repentance.

> *The sixth angel poured out his bowl on the great river, the Euphrates; and its water was dried up, so that the way would be prepared for the kings from the east.*

Because of the sixth bowl, the Euphrates River dries up. Probably a good thing, considering the river was already filled with blood.

Now we get our first mention of Armageddon.

> *And I saw coming out of the mouth of the dragon and out of the mouth of the beast and out of the mouth of the false prophet, three unclean spirits like frogs;*
>
> *for they are spirits of demons, performing signs, which go out to the kings of the whole world, to gather them together for the war of the great day of God, the Almighty.*
>
> *("Behold, I am coming like a thief Blessed is the one who stays awake and keeps his clothes, so that he will not walk about naked and men will not see his shame.")*
>
> *And they gathered them together to the place which in Hebrew is called Har-Magedon.*

Let's summarize: Three frogs jump out of the mouths of a dragon, a beast, and a false profit, and begin a recruitment campaign for the battle at Armageddon (also known as Har-Magedon). Dumping bowls of wrath only seems to be making the wicked even more mad and ready for a fight.

Somehow, between the frog and Armageddon, we are given some very sage advice: If you keep your clothes on and don't sleep, you won't be walking around shamefully naked. Good advise if you are a naked sleepwalker. This may explain why Christians get insomnia.

One little side note. Remember the sixth bowl emptied the Euphrates River for the kings of the East to cross? That adds another army for Satan. Oops. Sort of the opposite of God parting the Red Sea. Long time to hold a grudge, but it makes sense if these angels aren't really the good angels.

One more bowl. This one is filled with a rather nasty pea soup.

> *Then the seventh angel poured out his bowl*

upon the air, and a loud voice came out of the temple from the throne, saying, "It is done."

And there were flashes of lightning and sounds and peals of thunder; and there was a great earthquake, such as there had not been since man came to be upon the earth, so great an earthquake was it, and so mighty.

The great city was split into three parts, and the cities of the nations fell Babylon the great was remembered before God, to give her the cup of the wine of His fierce wrath.

And every island fled away, and the mountains were not found.

And huge hailstones, about one hundred pounds each, came down from heaven upon men; and men blasphemed God because of the plague of the hail, because its plague was extremely severe.

Here is the summary: Lightning, rumblings, thunder and a severe earthquake, God remembers the queen of Babylon and gives her some bad wine, Jerusalem splits into three pieces, cities collapse, mountains are missing and show up on the side of milk cartons, islands flee (don't blame them, we would run too), hundred pound hailstones – the wicked complain only about the hail.

Somebody take the bowls away from the angels!

Do we have enough evidence that this is all from the point of view of Satan? No mercy, no love, just destruction. We can ear you saying, "If this is Satan pouring out bowls of hate, what about the bad guys getting hurt? Well, they are just collateral damage. If you are Satan, hurting your followers is perfectly okay.

Satan's followers like a little pain and suffering. They are probably happy that this doom is happening. God is getting some bad press and won't be reelected. Looks like Revelation is the first act of the Antichrist, not a warning of the coming of the Antichrist.

Welcome to the 'Satan Wrote Revelation' conspiracy. You're welcome!

Oceans Turning to Blood

One of our favorite parts of the Book of Revelation is the oceans turning to blood when the second bowl of wrath is spilled. How cool would it be to see that? Much better than David Copperfield making the Statue of Liberty disappear.

Seas of blood are not all bad. The Red Cross just needs to park a Blood Mobile at the beach and use buckets. Blood is nutritious, so the world could see the end of hunger, though it would be stuck eating blood pudding and blood sausage. Threats by vampires go to zero. There are other benefits to oceans of blood. Just think through the possibilities. Get creative!

There are downsides to seas of O-negative (we assume it's a common blood type for oceans). Fish die along with dolphins, whales, and cute little penguins. Real estate prices would drop for beach front views. A day at the beach is out of the question. Disney cruises will go bankrupt.

There is a nasty rumor that this blood is just symbolic and not really blood. Scientists call this red tide and is nothing more than algae. This is a scientific and thus atheist replacement for a really cool miracle. What's the fun in that?

Red algae, which is toxic, could have same effect as blood, killing all life and ruining Disney cruises. Scientifically minded Christians think that we are poisoning the seas and that a red tide will bloom.

Red tide will cause shellfish poisoning, especially if you eat sushi. There are worse things than upchucking your sea shells by the sea shore. If the scale of the tide covers most of the world's oceans, a red tide could qualify as an apocalypse by destroying the planet's ecosystem. Almost all life wold be affected. Well, all life except for the red algae.

Red tide has one flaw. It's boring. If a god is going to be dramatic, he isn't going to substitute the impressive miracle-making bloody ingredients just to conform to some biologist's wet dream. We'll take real blood over algae any day of the week.

Antichrist Enters Stage Left

You may have the misapprehension that Jesus would already be on Earth. Isn't it the savior's job to *save* us? You hear preachers all the time saying that Jesus may already be on Earth, or that the Antichrist is among us right now. Well, you and those otherwise flawless fanatics would be wrong. All this frightful nastiness has happened without either a Christ or even an Antichrist.

Most of the people on Earth are long dead before the corporate reps for good and evil arrive. The world isn't just a bit roughed up, it's a rotting hulk. How could there be anybody left to see Jesus come to Earth? Who's left for the Antichrist to corrupt?

Just Signs

Some say that all of this nastiness up to this point in Revelation are just 'signs' that the end-times are near. We smell monkey poo in this sort of explanation. When most of the world is dead, it is already a bit late to be 'warned,' don't you think?

You can't mistake most of the world being burnt to a crisp as a sign. Why 'signs' and not clear evidence? A few PowerPoint slides would clear things up. So far things look less like signs to be interpreted than just plain nasty facts. Either you have 666 on your forehead and get a bowl of wrath poured on your head or it isn't the end times. A bowl of hate falling from the sky is less a sign of the end times than a running commentary of the end times in progress. As a sign to repent, it's a bit late.

Armageddon, It's Just a Place

Ever hear the Bible thumpers talking about the "coming Armageddon?" The word Armageddon is a proper noun, not a verb. Armageddon is a mountain in Israel (original Hebrew is Har-Megiddo or Har-Magedon). In the Bible, Armageddon is where the final battle of good and evil is to be located. Armageddon is a GPS coordinate, not a time or an event. You find Armageddon by looking at a map. The only signs of Armageddon are the directions to Armageddon and its Christian tourist traps.

If you hear some yahoo preacher spouting about the "coming Armageddon," let them know it's a big mountain and isn't going to be "coming or going, as it's already here." Please buy your incompetent doomsayer a copy of this book with this section highlighted.

If you can't be an accurate doomsayer, why be a doomsayer at all? Armageddon is a place!

Har-Megiddo sounds like a rather pleasant destination.[22] We'd go as far as saying this pleasant hill overlooking a fertile valley could be an educational destination vacation. There are tours, many active archeological digs, a museum, and an educational walking tour.

Har-Megiddo is less a mountain than a rubbish heap. This rubbish heap was created by city after city being built on the rubbish heaps of the cities before them. Why were they built on each other? These cities were destroyed, usually by war. War, build, war, build, rinse and repeat for a millennium or two and you get a hill-sized rubbish heap with a good view.

By the time Revelation was written, Har-Megiddo was already quite a pile. The hill has about thirty cities that were destroyed and rebuilt on top of each other. That's just a few more than what John of Patmos knew about, so the hill was about the same as it is today minus all the dirt and broken pottery the archeologists have hauled away to museums.

The fact that Armageddon is a real place may or may not be good news. If all the fighting is going to be on some hill in Israel, we don't have to worry about putting plywood over the windows in suburbia.

No need to stockpile canned peas, or buy guns to fight the evil masses threatening to trample the rose bushes. Your bushes are nowhere near Armageddon. One location also means that the lucky few that remain on Earth will watch the battle on CNN.

If you do visit Har-Megiddo, you may see signs. Not signs of the end-times, but signs like,"Napoleon slept here." Napoleon, like other short-tempered little warmongers, fought wars here. In 1799 Napoleon said that Megiddo was a "fine place for a battle," or at least something like that … only in French.

---

22 http://tinyurl.com/c97p7w

Battlefield of Good and Evil

Let's be clear: the Book of Revelation is true! At least the battle at Armageddon. If John of Patmos was writing about a future battle of good and evil fought at Armageddon, he is indeed a soothsayer of unquestioned accuracy. Right on the money! At least two great battles were waged in 1799, 1918, and many earlier skirmishes since 100 AD when Revelation was written. Armageddon is a very popular destination to fight a war.

Napoleon fought and won there in 1799, and the British fought and won as well, in 1918 against the Turks. The Turks could be considered reasonably non-Christian and thus, by Christian standards, a tad evil. That means the most recent battle royal of good versus evil was fought in 1918.

We'd be a bit reluctant to vote Napoleon as being on the side of good, so the later battle with the British beating the Turks is the right battle — even though Napoleon did invent champagne and canned peas.

The point is that we can officially call the battle of Armageddon fought and won many times over. The last battle was unquestionably the last battle. All we need is a good resurrection of Aunt Petunia from her cozy grave to seal the deal. Since you haven't seen Aunt Petunia, what's going on? Where's our 100 years of peace and then eternal life?

Verifying Revelation

Are we missing a sign? Seems like the story of Revelation should have ended, but it keeps going. There's been more imagery of disaster than a Hollywood movie. The need for all this nastiness does not make too much sense. Why not just a simple smiting and then everybody good is relocated to Heaven or Hell?

The exact order is a bit murky too. We didn't even start numbering the paragraphs until King James came along. Suppose somebody dropped a copy of the Book of Revelation and it got out of order? Could have happened. God isn't everywhere all the time, just ask Poland.

If you died right now, you'll find yourself looking down from a good neighborhood in god's country (a gated community where Zeus is your neighbor). All your questions will be answered.

That terrible confusion you're having right now about this wacky Revelation will dissolve away in a godly flow of information.

We don't recommend that you die by suicide just to answer such important questions. Untimely accidental death is preferable. We aren't going to eat potato salad at a picnic just because we are curious. Nobody should come within a mile of any mayonnaise-based food products just to prove John of Patmos was a liar with his pants on fire.

We can't be sure that Revelation is, ah, well, gospel, without proving John really did have a conversation with the angel of Revelation. A time machine could solve the problem. Compared to faith, a time machine is much more fun!

If we had a time machine, we could go back to the afternoon of the 'great dictation' and ask the angel for clarifications and check those glorious molten bronze feet (and look for horns and a spiked tail).

The end of the world should be obvious to a casual observer. By 'casually observe' we mean 'lazy.' If the world cracks open, it might be the end of the world. When your couch falls into the depths of Hell, there might be an apocalypse. The future is easier to predict when it is the past. We call this history.

A good old fashioned time machine could sort this out. By traveling to the future, we could learn when the end of the world would really happen. Going into the past to hear the predictions of mad men and avenging angels isn't going to help as much as seeing the Earth destroyed in person.

Time travel can be dangerous, especially if you overshoot the date of the apocalypse. Imagine arriving in the future after the end times when nothing exists! Nothing! All the people are already in Heaven or Hell? Why would God keep the universe ticking? Time would end too, so you'd be stuck in a time machine with no time to run it.

We already have a poor man's time machine and are slowly traveling into the future, one day at a time. We'll eventually see if the world is going to end, but it could take a long time. It will take a long time to invent time travel too, so we just as well watch TV and eat popcorn while we wait. Pass the butter.

Shibboleth: Code Word of Apocalypse?

Do you know the code word? Study the Bible, kids! The secret word is "shibboleth." This word was used way back in the Old Testament in the Book of Judges[23] and was used to figure out who was on the side of God.

Good people can pronounce shibboleth. Evil people, it seems, cannot pronounce the word properly. The evil ones just cough up sibboleth (missing the first 'h').

Here is a little bit of how it played out in the Bible:

> *...whenever a survivor of Ephraim said, "Let me cross over," the men of Gilead asked him, "Are you an Ephraimite?" If he replied, "No," they said, "All right, say 'Shibboleth.'" He said, "Sibboleth." Because he could not pronounce the word correctly, they seized him and killed him at the fords of the Jordan. Forty-two thousand Ephraimites were killed at that time.*

Shibboleth works as a great evil detector. At least forty-two thousand people were killed for being evil Ephraimites. As we all know, Ephraimites are very evil because they are Ephraimites.

There is a slight problem with the technique. Though it may detect evil, it may also catch people with a bad lisp. Of the forty-two thousand dead, a few might have survived if they had gotten speech therapy.

You should get ready now and practice saying, "shibboleth." Never know when you are going to be tested. If you do have a lisp, put a fish on the back of your SUV.

The "shibboleth" technique [24] has been used over the years. For example in World War II, U.S. soldiers asked each suspected spy what they knew about baseball. Germans, being evil, knew

---

[23] http://www.biblegateway.com/passage/?search=Judges+12&version=NIV

[24] http://en.wikipedia.org/wiki/Shibboleth

nothing about baseball, so the American soldiers shot them. Germans, of course, asked our spies about German strudel.

At Boys Books, we use a similar test and have people say, "I was born on a pirate ship." If they fail to end it with a hearty pirate 'argh' or pretend there is a parrot on their shoulder, we know they aren't one of us.

Jesus Returns, Antichrist Disappoints

At this point in our story, the Antichrist is useless! Those who have been denying Jesus are probably not going to drop to their knees for an Antichrist. Nobody will be ready to switch sides after all this. Who would want to worship a bully?

While we're here, why bring back Jesus? Almost everyone is dead and the world is generally a nasty place to live. Civilization has been destroyed by disease, war, and disaster. What good is a savior when real estate prices are in the toilet?

Either you're smart enough to follow God or you are dumb as a rock, which happens to be dumber than most rocks. Rocks are dumb, but you need to be a super dumb rock to think the Devil is somehow on the winning side after all this. There are dead bodies as far as the eye can see.

Perhaps, because of all this death and destruction, people are starting to worship Satan? Who could worship anyone who breaks seals, blows horns, and dumps bowls that are so inherently evil? Most of the destruction and violence has been indiscriminate so far. Would you follow such a wrathful god or look for someone that would be a little nicer?

Let's summarize the remainder of Revelation with a few Cliff Notes:

- ✓ Whore of Babylon and her seven headed, ten horn beast shows up and gets destroyed.
- ✓ The lamb gets married.
- ✓ Christ comes and a dinner is served of human flesh of the wicked and their wicked horses.
- ✓ The beast and the Antichrist are killed, eaten by birds.
- ✓ Satan sent to Hell for a 1,000 years.

- ✓ Those few luckily enough to be beheaded by Satan's minions, get resurrected and live with Christ for a 1,000 years.
- ✓ After a 1,000 years, Satan returns, makes trouble, gets sent back to Hell for eternal torment for violating his parol.
- ✓ God comes to Earth, kisses boo boos.
- ✓ Jerusalem is rebuilt in gold and gaudiness. Yea piety! Oh, and night is banished so solar power is finally worth investing in. A good time is had by all as long as you are pure, chaste, and Republican.
- ✓ An angel dictates to Joe Bob of Patmos his marketing plan for selling Revelation part II. The end!

Let's stop here and put the Bible back on the shelf to collect dust. Th Bible is a silly book. Until we see few brightly colored horses coming our way, Harry Potter books are a much better read.

Christians and the Book of Revelation

Christians have a vested interest in the contents of the Book of Revelation being true. They can't be wrong, not even a little bit. It's the word of God, after all. If one thing is wrong, it all collapses like a house of cards.

Being Christian is hard work! Your job is to believe any wacky nonsense from your fellow Christians. This includes the entire Bible, and any wild thought related to the Bible. As long as it sounds like it might be from the Bible, Christians will believe anything. Most people don't read the Bible and that's why this works.

In the Book of Revelation, the end of the world is explained with symbolism and a lack of exact dates. You don't get better doom mongering than that. Every day you'll find something that looks like one of the signs. It's the ultimate in doom recycling as every day is your last day.

Christians are very creative people. Their ability to link modern day events to various parts of the Bible and the Book of Revelation is astonishing. Before you know it, those little marshmallow peeps will be the Antichrist, and eating waffles on Halloween will be a sign of the coming war between good and evil.

We remember an encounter with a door-to-door doomsayer who worked for one of the many Christian sects. He used a concordance, a sort of Bible super index, to show signs and relate them to our history so far. Quite fun and sort of like using a secret decoder ring from Captain Zoom. He's able to connect the dots between Old Testament, current history, and Revelation, to show that the Catholic Church was the secret identity of The Beast. Certainly a revelation of biblical proportions.

Apocalypse spotters are truly masters of their art!

A concordance is the ultimate reference guide for a diviner of signs of the apocalypse. It contains references of every word used in the Bible and where to find it. Look up the word "lamb" and you'll find many references in both New and Old Testaments. Some references to lambs are for cooking, some for herding, some for puking your guts out–remember the lamb in Revelation?

Spotting the Antichrist is a sport for Christian doomsayers. Armed with a concordance, the savvy doomsayer cross references words that appear in difference sections of the Bible. They are looking for clues to translate something in an absurd context like Revelation to the same word written in a clearly written section like Leviticus (that's were we are taught biblical hygiene and cooking techniques). Look up the same words on Google to locate the same words in news and you will find clues to doom everywhere. Think of it like train-spotting without the trains. Doom-seekers are attempting to link the present with the past of the Bible to the symbolic blither blather of Revelation.

The end of the world is also a recruiting gimmick. The 'End' could be true and right around the corner. Supposedly, only the 'true' believers will be saved. Not a believer now? Sorry, no ticket to salvation. It's a hook for conversion. Sermons, weddings, eulogies, all will have some talk about the end-times. Save your soul by converting now and avoid the rush. Ensure you are reserving your place in Heaven with a healthy donation to the church too.

If you hear the world will end, and that there is a free ride out of town to paradise, wouldn't you sign up for advanced tickets? Not saying you shouldn't. Just remember that the best recruitment for a religion is to scare you so bad that you need to get a fresh pair of underwear.

A great sign of choice for Revelation doomsayers is the Antichrist. Even though the Antichrist does not make his appearance until most of us are dead and gone, he still makes a great image to hang your fear mongering.

The rich symbolism of the Bible is used to make us see signs wherever we look. The best way to scare you is to dispense with imaginary demons and point to the President, the Pope, or your neighbor and say they are the Antichrist.

The easy targets for Antichrist are people whom you already hate. Politicians and their political parties are easy targets. The trailer-park vote bows easily to the hate-bait and fill the churches and the voting booths.

The Pope, for some reason, is also a target of doomsayers. Seems odd that the head of the Catholics would be seen as the Antichrist, but it is obvious for Christian sects that are not Catholic. We think the real reason is the Pope's pointy hat. That weird hat just makes some people mad as a hatter.

You Might Want to Know

The phrase "mad as a hatter" comes from the days when hat makers used Mercury in the process of making their headwear. The result was brain damage and madness. Coincidentally there were a several mad popes. Could it be the Mercury-laden pointy pope hats?

Surviving Biblical End-Times

Can you survive a Christian end? Let's rephrase that, would you want to? There is nothing good about anything written in Revelation or the 'little' Apocalypse of Mark. Sure, in the end their is a 'savior,' but nothing else is good. We have the capacity to survive, but why?

If you have tortured a martyr recently, you definitely won't make it out of the end-times alive. They really hate anyone that has inconvenienced a martyr. We don't plan torturing anybody, true believer or not, just in case.

Avoid worshiping anything material. Avoid all possessions. Owning anything could be seen as the sin of greed, avarice, gluttony, etc. Avoid materialism by renting everything. Living in a cave is not recommended unless the cave is rent controlled so that you aren't contributing to the sins of materialism of your landlord.

Don't deny that this Jesus fellow could have died for you. It could have happened. Why not? Things are bad if you can't believe in this just a little bit. It seems that this is really important for surviving apocalypse. We love science fiction and make believe. Why not put Jesus in the same realm as the Force from Star Wars? Go ahead, have a little fantasy, it might save your soul someday.

Why commit to Christianity until the third horseman or wait around for the fifth bowl before you get some Jesus? Seems unwise. Heed our advice and commit early to avoid the next disaster. Once things start getting too bad, just drop to your knees.

Then again, commitment doesn't save you from the end of the world. There doesn't seem to be a free pass, even for the faithful. Just wait it out and hope you get a free pass.

You Might Want to Know

> *Be warned that God does not accept converts who believe based on facts rather than faith. God would rather you believe in him for no good reason. God doesn't have the time to sprinkle facts of His existence for scientist to discover. God isn't going to stand around in a lab all day just so a scientist to shine a laser up his butt. He'd be a little silly to accept converts because they witnessed His wrath in person.*

What happens if Revelation isn't true? Mayan gods could kill us, what then? Your choice, faith or bad luck. Hard to recommend a perfect strategy. Use a dart board for your important decisions of faith. At least you can blame fate.

Experiment: Write Your Own Revelation

You don't need to take psychedelic drugs or fast yourself into hallucinations to write your own personal apocalypse. People write apocalyptic horror all the time. Just read the Congressional Record and search for the words apocalypse or Armageddon and you will find many fine examples.

Imagine something you don't like, then link its existence to the end of the world. Success is ensured! Imagine the creative torture and death whomever forces you to confront that one thing you hate. For example, should there continue to be the eating of oatmeal at breakfast, deformed rabid badgers will begin raining from the sky to punish the wicked oatmeal lobby. No more soggy Quaker Oatmeal and the evil ones are punished. Serves them right for supporting a breakfast product that is less than 80% sugar and has no prize inside.

Next, write down all the words that describe your nemesis and your creative revenge. Look up each of the words in an online Bible (avoid the paper cuts). Those that appear in your descriptions, Revelation, and any other part of the Bible are now quotable out of context to support your vision on doom.

If you really want to curl the toes of your readers, use a few simple tricks to add a sense of the bizarre. Try randomly adding words by throwing darts at Grandmother's encyclopedias. Whatever words you get, just sprinkle them through the text. As long as you have a legal sentence, use whatever words you want.

Questions

- ✓ What is the reaction from your parents?
- ✓ How long did you need to spend in therapy?

- ✓ If you were committed to a mental hospital, after they put you on meds, do you have an easier time believing what you wrote?

Experiment: Oil, Wine, and Barley

Order some lamp oil, wine, and barley. Use denarii (denarii is the plural of denarius, the coin of Revelation) as your money instead of dollars. Shop for denarii at your local coin collector for around four thousand dollars each. Do not use toy denarii coins which are about three dollars per hundred, as these would void the experiment.

Order all of this online and have it shipped to your house. We want to see if there is any shipping damage that might be a sign of the coming apocalypse.

Questions

- ✓ How much did you have to pay for each antique denarius coin?
- ✓ Were you able to exchange the denarii coins for lamp oil, wine, and barley or did they only except Visa or PayPal?
- ✓ Was the price of lamp oil, wine, and wheat expensive enough to qualify as a sign of the Second Coming?
- ✓ When you accepted the shipment, was the oil or wine damaged in shipping?
- ✓ Why would United Parcel Service abbreviate its name so that it would be pronounced 'oops?'

New Revelations

The Book of Revelation is a good read, full of horror and salvation. It makes a compelling end of the world. The only problem is that it only works for Christians. It was also based on a narration by an angel, and we know how reliable they are.

The Boys Books office is full of computers and researchers. Why not use them to discover an alternative to the original classic end of the world theories?

No expense was spared — except for psychedelics, which were already available from the *Boys Book of Carlos Castaneda* — to find the most probable ends.

You Might Want to Know

Sadly, the Boys Book of Carlos Castaneda will never be printed. To get into the mood, the staff tried to do a vision quest like Carlos in The Teachings of Don Juan: A Yaqui Way of Knowledge. We tried to save a little cash by not hiring an experienced Yaqui shaman to prepare the magic mushrooms, and opted instead for a guy that lived through the 60's at Berkley. We learned to never scrimp again! Only a few stained pages of the book galley survived the episode, and we are still trying to get the smell of sautéed lizard out of the break room.

The Last Foosball War

Foosball is a simple game. A little table with little people you spin and, with great skill, slap back and forth a ball with little men impaled on poles. The game's origins are murky, though evidence points to the inventor's fascination with Vlad the Impaler and European Football.

The last foosball war will be fought by Christ and the Antichrist on Mount Armageddon in a small pool hall. They will not play a game of pool. No, that's not Christ's style.

Christ also loses quite often at pool, because the Antichrist keeps making up "house rules."

The foosball game will be played fairly, with the winner taking the best out of six games, with a possible tiebreaker. Everyone will be drinking beer except Christ, who will be drinking water that turns to a California Bordeaux with a fruity hint of berries and a clean oaky finish.

Why foosball? Why not? Our faith teaches us that God likes games of skill. We see nothing in the Bible that contradicts this belief and such faith in divine assumption is rewarded with everlasting life in Heaven. Even an Atheist can get a day pass from Hell for Tuesday night dart league at Saint Peter's Bar.

Foosball is the equalizer. Very hard game to cheat at if you disallow miracles. The Antichrist will try to distract Christ by spitting nasty puns about Christ's mom and her pre-birth transportation. Christ will counter with polite taunting that Satan isn't the Antichrist's real dad, and that he was adopted by the Whore of Babylon — all true.

In the end it will all come down to hand-eye coordination between the forccs of good and evil.

Upping the Antichrist

There will be a poker tournament that will have the misfortune of being called "The Last Battle." Nobody will notice, but Christ and the Antichrist will enter the tournament.

Christ will get to the last round because He is good. The Antichrist will get to the last round because he cheats. Because Christ is at the final table, further cheating will be impossible.

There will be four other players at the table. They are all rodeo clowns that are passing through town. They are the Four Horsemen of the Apocalypse. They will all lose their money to the Antichrist.

The last hand has Christ with too few chips to cover the Antichrist's bet. The house will allow Christ to put mankind on the table to cover the bet. Christ has a possible royal flush, and the Antichrist may have a fourth ace in his hand.

You'll have to wait for the cards to be revealed. Think of the suspense! The game will be televised on ESPN5, so all but a few chosen will know.

Candid Camera or You've Been Punked by Christ

The end of the world is just a practical joke. The angel of Revelation was Christ in a white wig. You won't know how funny the joke is until you finally die.

Imagine meeting Saint Peter at the pearly gates of Heaven. Saint Peter gives you a glass of milk and then tells you the funniest joke you've ever heard.

In Heaven, they have a complete 3D video recording of your entire life. Everyone you know who is currently dead gets to laugh at you and the things you believed in.

You Might Want to Know

> *God invented 3D when he created Heaven and Earth. Smellavision was created when Adam and Eve eat of the tree of life and found they were both naked and were in desperate need of a bath.*

One of Christ's famous practical jokes is near-death experiences. Christ does his white light thing, or lets you talk to Grandma. All just to make it seem real. There are no bright lights in Heaven. The atmosphere is like a comfy bar lounge with little candle lamps on the tables. Christ sometimes lets a few people see something like Hell, but it's really just a movie set in a back lot of a porn studio in Burbank, California.

To complete the hilarity, in limbo there are only dribble cups with the only form of refreshment being milk. You are either spilling it down your shirt or laughing so hard that milk spurts out your nose.

Revelation is one of the longest setups for a joke in the history of mankind. Everyone is called down from Heaven in various costumes, from the four horsemen to slathering and putrid demons, just to make it all seem real. Nobody is really killed, just put into limbo until the final gag.

For the next million years, we watch movies of it all while eating popcorn and drinking milk from our dribble glasses. We get to giggle and laugh as each person on Earth gets individually punked, poops his pants, and dies from fright as his Aunt Edna, dressed in a rubber demon suit, bites their head off.

You Might Want to Know

> *Little-known fact: Christ looks like Allen Funt. This is because Christ is Allen Funt. Yes, another of Christ's hilarious jokes on us all is that his Second Coming already happened. Christ just wanted to do Candid Camera to hone his skills for the ultimate joke on humanity.*

Republican Apocalypse: Doom in the Air, or Just the Grape Juice?

Why are there so many Republican politicians and far right Christian preachers yelling that the end is near? Why don't you see Democrats or even moderate Republicans digging bomb shelters? How come it is just crazy Christians, not Methodists, who have so many reasons to believe in the end-times?

What in the blue nether regions of brass monkeys do these guys have for breakfast that makes them feel like the end will come before supper time?

From the economic Armageddon to the apocalypse of the Employee Rights Act, there have been enough imagined horrors to fill an Ark much bigger than Noah's puny umpty-umpt cubits by insignificant cubits. There are so many doomsayers that you would need an Ark so massively huge enough to bring them in as threesomes instead of just two by two.

What would true Republican apocalypse look like? We've already seen something close when Obama was elected president. Republicans were buying guns, stocking up on canned goods, and bottled water in anticipation the horrors of horrors; a Hawaiian-born Democrat. Would republicans be forced to wear grass skirts? The horror!

Obama hasn't really delivered a clear apocalypse for Republicans to rally behind. The healthcare bill hasn't killed grandma and the economy is recovering. Republicans need to turn up the heat! How about enforced libel laws? Republicans could pass hard laws including prison sentences for fear mongering or hate speech. That'll show those Democrats! How about pouring millions into the invention of a device that detects lies? It would be the end, surely. Of course, politics would be dead as a profession too. No lies, no politics. All we would be left with is honest people in charge. Yep, the true Republican apocalypse!

Bad Timing?

Geologists are smart people. Geologists are smart people. Yeah, said that twice. Trying to convince you it is true before we say that geologists have a few rocks in their head.

Carbon dating? We say that's silly straight away. Who would date Carbon — she isn't very cute, is she? What does having a date with Carbon have to do with the age of things?

Geologists think it took a very long time to create the Earth. There is no reason not to believe them. Even when you talk about creating it all in six days, those are God days, not people days. There is no way to know the real context.

Even when you are as literal as the Baptists or their Southern "Christian" cousins, the age of the Earth is all up in the air when God rests. After that much creation, you'd take a long nap too!

What if the actual timeline for apocalypse is not so cut and dried when mounted in a picture frame? It could take the next million years before we even get close to the fight between good and evil at Armageddon. Are you prepared to wait that long? We could all die from the Sun dying. Nobody wants that!

Whoops, Wrong God

The Devil turns out to be the real guy in charge. The Second Coming goes as planned, but when we are all called to Heaven, we find we are at the pearly gates of Hell for our final judgement.

Hell is a great place. Imagine healthy frolicking and the best food you have ever tasted. Debauchery and gluttony are Olympic sports in Hell. Interesting people from history are everywhere and there is never a dull moment.

Isn't it odd that we are born with original sin and it is so hard to get rid of? It's hard to be as perfect as Christ because the Devil is in your DNA. No soap is going to clean that deep.

The story of Adam and Eve was just poorly edited too. The hero is really the serpent. The serpent was just a humble fruit seller and God a heartless landlord who casts out his tenants to live homeless, naked, and ashamed. Seems right. Why would a perfect God create a conniving serpent, hungry humans with free will and a fruit tree in the same garden? It's all a smear campaign and human kind is due interest on their cleaning deposit.

You Might Want to Know

> *It is often believed that Adam and Eve were tossed out of the Garden of Eden because they ate from the tree of knowledge. God had made mankind too noisy because Adam and Eve were always talking or making a racket from the mischief caused by God's unfortunate mistake of making some parts interlocking. The apple business was just an excuse to evict the troublesome creation from the garden so God could nap in peace.*

Heaven will turn out to be a really nasty place. You sit around on clouds all day with little to do. The only company you have are a couple of popes, some priests, tons of nuns (none of the fun ones, in case you are wondering), and fanatical right wing Republican Christians who never bought an SUV. The true torture is that all these people like to talk your ear off about how good they were on Earth.

Sadly, once you are in Heaven you can't just shoot yourself.

As the great Saint Augustine[25] (patron saint of brewers, printers, theologians, and sore eyes) famously prayed to God

---

[25] http://en.wikipedia.org/wiki/Augustine_of_Hippo

after breaking up with his prepubescent eleven-year-old mistress:

da mihi castitatem et continentiam, sed noli modo

Loosely translated: God, grant me chastity and continence, but not yet.

Experiment: Start an End-of-the-World Rumor

There are an infinite number of monkeys typing at typewriters, all trying to create the great works of Shakespeare and episode VII of Star Wars. Steal some of those monkeys and write a new scenario for ending the world.

Your doom scenario (doomario) might kill all the bees, make people allergic to hamburgers, or destroy the Earth and/or universe with a deodorant that's so effective that it eliminates anything that stinks.

Questions

- ✓ How long is it between when people notice the end and when it happens? Note: Extra points if it's impossible to predict and seems like its going to happen any second.
- ✓ Is there a specific type of person that will die first?
- ✓ If a woodchuck could chuck wood, how much wood could a woodchuck chuck before the world up chucked?
- ✓ If it is a supernatural end, which supernatural deity destroys the world and why?

Deadly Scientists

Name a complex subject, scientists will end the world with it. If nature won't kill us, a scientist can whip up something that will do the job ten times better.

We can blame scientist for global warming, the atomic bomb, lip syncing, smog, the ozone hole, and traffic. It's just a matter of time before a scientist does something that unintentionally kills us all.

Who needs vengeful gods when we have scientists at 3M creating a new glue for Post-It-Notes that will dissolve the Earth's protective layer of dirt. One moment you are leaving a not on the fridge for your mom, the next minute you're dancing on lava.

Scientists are doomsayers too. Their unique spin is that no supernatural beings are involved. Oceans of blood become red tide, or the great flood is just global warming. This makes an unbelievable mystical event into a scientifically plausible event. Scientists scare the pants off both the religious and the atheists. Even Agnostics are afraid of scientific doomsayers, but will hold their final opinion on the subject until the world is officially ended by scientific mischief.

Here's a short list of ways that scientists have found that could end the world. Some are man-made, and others are just scientifically plausible. They are all frightening.

Genetically Engineered Corn

Native Americans domesticated corn. Originally corn was wild, hunted in packs, and eat small babies. After hundreds of years, corn is now fully domesticated and used in tacos and corn chips. Hardly the end of the world unless you count diabetes and obesity.

Scientists are always looking to improve on nature. For corn, they want to make it resistant to weed killer, up its sugar content for use in fuel, and perhaps as mindless slaves in the wheat fields of northern South Dakota.

Corn genetics will eliminate un-popped kernels of popcorn but the mutants genes will cause the corn to grow a brain and tell jokes (all corny). Bad corn genetics. Corn so bad that it can end the world as the world's corniest comedian.

What if a scientist decides to engineer corn to produce medicines? A plant-based pharmacy lowers the cost of making drugs because plants are our slaves and don't form unions. That's good, but what if the drug corn mixes with regular corn? Suddenly, we are all eating drugs that weren't prescribed.

Imagine sitting in a theater munching on popcorn crossbred to create the Viagra drug. Oh, the humanity! Civilization collapses (rises?) into debauchery as we develop an addiction to seven layer dip and internet porn. You will be amazed!

Antibacterial Soap and Antibiotics

Oh, the woe of preventing something deadly only to make that thing like superman. Let's start with antibiotics.

Antibiotics help cure the one thing we know that will kill us: germs. Antibiotics helped cure us of hundreds of diseases that that used to kill us. The only problem is that germs are learning to fight back.

We have been pumped full of antibiotics over the course of our lives. Anytime a doctor sees a little green snot, a needle is poking you in the butt or you are popping pills. Sure antibiotics kill billions of little germs every year, but a few survive. Those survivors are plotting revenge for their brethren and creating an army that will kill us all.

We keep inventing new antibiotics to kill the ones we can't kill with the old antibiotics. Billions of germs die, but a few hearty microscopic souls survive. These survivors will start pumping iron from the supplements we take, buying microscopic guns, and learning microbial kung fu. Before you know it, we all catch a nasty diseases by these super diseases. Someday we run out of new antibiotics and we collectively sneeze to death.

Antibacterial soap is just as bad. Try this experiment. Put dirty dishes in a sink. Fill it with sudsy antibacterial soap. Now leave for a week or two. We do this all the time because we are just plain lazy. One week later, when you look again, if you can get close enough, the kitchen sink is a putrid mess. It may even be moving (a slow crawl or a shambling walk if its had enough time to evolve). You know you are in trouble when it looks you in the eye and demands your wallet.

We suggest you only do this sink experiment when you can call in a nuclear air strike. The creatures that grow in a sink of dirty dishes and antibacterial soap are very scary. Even when there isn't a sentient creature, you still need something real strong to kill it. The gagging smell will linger too. You can kiss your cleaning deposit on your apartment goodbye. Millions of dollars are lost to sink monsters every year.

The next problem with antibiotics and antibacterials: What if one starts working too well? Imagine Grandma flushing a bottle of antibiotic pills down the toilet? What if too many restaurant employees start washing their hands after they used the potty? Zillions of penicillin pills and millions of gallons of antibacterial soap floods the world, killing the good germs.

We could all die because the wrong gut bacteria croaks. Nobody is able to digest food! We all die because we get sick from eating and pooping the same hamburger and fries over and over again.

Forget gut bacteria, what if all the yeast in the world dies. Without yeast we can't brew beer, wine, and other fun alcohols. Riots start as Coors Light disappears off the store shelves. Despondent trailer-park red necks start rioting because they sober up enough to realize how ugly their trucks are and how nasty country western music sounds.

This is another of those end-of-the-world scenarios that we find very likely. We have a cache of Coors Light just in case the riots get too close to our home.

Particle Colliders

A partial collider causes atoms to go round and round in a big circle until they get dizzy and start running into each other. The goal is to get them going so fast that they smash together and create subatomic primordial belly button fluff.

Particles get shot at each other with such high speeds they create black holes. The theory is that the faster they go, the higher the relative mass, the more mass, the more likely you'll create enough compacted mass with the gravity of a black hole.

The black hole then gets bigger as it pulls in everything in the local solar system.

Black holes suck. Black holes suck so hard that they beat any vacuum you have ever seen — even the cool Dyson vacuums. The entire Earth could be sucked into a black hole the size of a pea. "I don't want to pea on your parade," has a whole new meaning.

Some say this end of the world scenario is impossible. Their evidence is that the universe throws these particles at each other all the time. Sort of. Imagine all the combinations of particles these scientists will try. One could be the wrong mix. Scientists are pranksters, so this isn't too hard to imagine. Imagine bean dip and a Dorritio[26] colliding at the speed of light. Yummy, but perhaps unwise…

Scientists are not good at calculating risks. They calculate the 'odds' as low for black holes, but nothing is certain. We put this type of end-of-the-world scenario at the top of our list of most likely methods for us snuffing it. Odds are good, but bad.

Imagine scientists and Alec Baldwin discussing particle physics in a bar:

> ***Scientist 1***: *Hey, let's recreate the big bang!*
>
> ***Scientist 2***: *Cool!*
>
> ***Alec Baldwin***: *Don't you think that's dangerous?*
>
> ***Scientist 1***: *Nope.*

The next day, Pittsburgh gets sucked up into a black hole. The black hole grows and pulls in every bit of the Earth without losing suction (black holes, like Dysons, are bag-less).

Scientists say that man-made black holes will evaporate before they do any damage. Really? What if black holes are like ethylene glycol in your car's antifreeze? We spilled some in our car and that stuff never evaporates! It just gets stickier!

---

26 http://www.urbandictionary.com/define.php?term=Dorrito%20damage

There won't be much warning because these things are quick with all their relativistic bending of time. Black holes get stronger the more they suck, and it will really suck as the black hole grows and gets more to suck on.

If you're lucky, the hole will be big enough that you'll live on the event horizon (it is like a normal horizon, except it's sunset forever). This could be good news and bad news. Bad: You are being ripped apart by tidal forces. Good news: The event horizon slows time down, so you will live forever as you're atoms are slowly peeled off your body one by one. Nope, sorry. We were wrong. It's all bad news.

Nitrogen Trifluoride

Scientists love to create new chemicals. For some reason there is always something bad that scientists fail to predict.

Nitrogen trifluoride (NF_3) is used to make microchips and flat-screen TVs. Researchers[27] analyzed air samples and found that atmospheric NF_3 is growing by eleven percent per year. NF_3 lasts for 550 years and is 17,000 times better than CO_2 at causing global warming.

Our deaths will be caused by a 30 degree warming of the Earth as the demand for 3D HD TV sets rises when the Dallas Cowboys are finally Super Bowl favorites in 2027. Alternatively we all get super rich and want to have the same 160 foot long big screen TV that is in the new Cowboys Stadium. Cowboys and NF_3 will be the death of us.

What do you think about when you buy a new TV? There is price, true colors, response time, and features. Never have we walked into an electronics store and asked where the TVs were that are made without NF_3. We just stare at the prices until we have to pee real bad and then we flip a coin.

Of the predictions you will find in a scholarly list of end-times, this one is the most probable. The Texas Rangers baseball team will also pull off a miracle and make it to the World Series again (the Rangers being in the 2010 World Series twice in a row is currently being evaluated by the Catholic Church as a divine miracle). Imagine the number of people buying new flat-

---

[27] http://www.agu.org/pubs/crossref/2008/2008GL035913.shtml

screens for the game watching party! The double threat is that both teams make the playoffs in the same year. Global warming from NF_3 and food riots caused by a limited supply of Doritos. All the ingredients for the end of the world, Texas style.

Cell Phones

Cell phones operate on a frequency similar to your microwave. When using a cell phone, your brain is cooked in a similar way to a steak in your microwave. Like a bad pun, tough and tasteless.

Microwaves are not good for the brain. The world ends as we all get progressively stupid and chaos ensues. Poor people without cell phones end up croaking as cell phones of dead people flood the world, offering cheap phone calls and microwave popcorn.

There is an upside to cell phones. Their tiny waves are nearly deadly enough be used for zombie defense. A slow death, but a cell phone strapped to a zombie's head would be more humane than a garden spade to the neck. The world could still end when you get the cell phone bill for the seven day phone call the zombie had with your aunt Petunia (she can talk the ear off a corpse).

Global Warming

Let's blame global warming on scientists. It's good fun and only harms scientists. We're not blaming them for the cause, but the solution.

Scientists and Vegas bookies have calculated that global warming won't kill us for a couple hundred years. By then we'll invent interstellar drives and have nicknames like Kirk and Spock.

Sure there are floods and bad weather. Even famine and disasters. The net result is that beach property changes locations and we sell more raincoats.

Yes, doom and gloom doomsayers hedge their bets by voting for global warming. They are all barking up the wrong tree — especially because the tree just died. Not going to end the world fast enough for anyone to care.

Despite being true, global warming, or climate change as it is called when there is a blizzard in Phoenix, is an uninteresting and a very slow way for the world to end. When we try to fix global warming, that's when really do something stupid.

Back to blaming scientists. What happens when the scientists come up with a solution? At Boys Books we have a bet on which disaster we get when the solution to global warming backfires. Right now the two top contenders are that the sky catches fire or we are plunged into an ice age.

Hole in the Ozone

A hole in the ozone is a nifty way to die. You get a glowing tan and then quickly die of radiation poisoning. Think of it as a sunburn that goes all the way to the bone.

The ozone layer protects us from radiation. Sadly, they don't sell a sunscreen for that kind of radiation. Only ozone will protect us from the Sun's glowing personality.

Where did the hole come from? Scientists of course.

We have reduced some of the chemicals that cause ozone to disappear. You may have noticed that taxi drivers smell a lot worse these days, and this is a direct result of removing these chemicals from deodorants. The chemicals make it easy to spritz your underarms on the go. The banning of these chemicals has temporarily saved us from radiation, but body odor is the new threat.

Yes, we have banned the CFC's and other chemicals that were putting holes in the ozone, but then a scientist invents a new chemical that will destroy the ozone. You never know when the next can of Silly String you use has a new chemical that will wipe out mankind.

We could also get a solar storm strong enough to do similar damage to the protective ozone layer. The Sun blows a big burp of gas or even a nearby star goes supernova and we lose our protective shield. If its not one thing, its another.

Living deep underground will save you. Because of H. G. Wells, we all know that we will lose our humanity and start calling ourselves **Morloks.**[28] The good news is that some humans will survive on the surface, and we will use them as food.

Learn This Word

> ***Morlock:*** *Morlocks are not real, at least not yet. You need to travel to the future to meet one. A Morlock is a human that evolved to live underground. They don't look much like humans and seem sort of stupid. Morlocks are also ugly. A baby Morlock even looks ugly to a mother Morlock. The primary food for Morlocks is humans. Normal humans in the future will be rather stupid, but very tasty.*

Gray Goo

Gray goo,[29] or the attack of the nano machines, is the only other cause of death that is almost as tiny as a Bird Flu virus. Imagine an artificial microscopic creature that could munch down on molecules and transform them into something useful.

Little nano machines will escape from the labs and start eating anything and everything to stay alive. They would produce whatever they were to told produce. Doomsayers think the nanites (that's what they are called on Red Dwarf) will poop gray goo. We think that's wrong. Scientists don't want gray goo, they want their creations to literally poop diamonds.

Imagine tiny robots that could eat your garbage and poop diamonds. Who wouldn't be excited about some of that?

Nanites will do exactly what they were designed to do, just a lot more of it once they are free to roam the world outside a test tube. Given that garbage is something you don't want, and diamonds are what you do want, then diamonds in quantity will be the good news and the bad news. Imagine tons of diamonds.... Tons of diamonds are just as worthless as tons of garbage, only prettier.

---

28 http://en.wikipedia.org/wiki/Morlock

29 http://en.wikipedia.org/wiki/Grey_Goo

What if the diamond-pooping nanites escaped the lab? They would still have an appetite for garbage and in particular, carbon, which is the only required ingredient of diamonds.

One man's garbage is another man's treasure. For a nano machine that likes carbon, most of the world is pure treasure. That means almost every living thing is a cordon bleu dinner for a diamond-pooping nano machine.

Nanites need to create other nanites. No, there will be no naughty nano interfacing. There is no nanite robo sex — they build their children. They make their kids from what they don't use to poop diamonds. That's where things get really bad. If only one of these machines gets loose from the lab it will make billions of copies of itself that will also make their own copies who make other duplicate nanites that are making more nanites with all of them pooping diamonds as fast as they can. In the end all we have left are nanites and diamonds.

See the problem? Chain reactions from atomic bombs and chain letters are not as lethal as a chain reaction of nano machines that defecate diamonds.

Left-Handed Sugar

The wonders of science have created the ultimate sweetener: left-handed sugar. Same as sugar, but it zigs when it should zag. The result is that nothing, especially fat people, are capable of digesting this sugar.

Left handed sugar goes from popsicle to poopsicle without breaking down. All you need is and Eskimo and some wooden sticks and you have the world's next frozen confection. Global warming is nothing compared to The Great Sweetening.

Think of the side affects. The soft drink industry implodes as tap water becomes sweeter than root beer. A visit to the beach will make you feel diabetic. Washing your car will just make a sticky mess.

In the end, we'll just commit global suicide rather than live in a world as sweet as the Small World ride at Disneyland.

You Might Want to Know

Scientists have a fun loving side. Science isn't

all about test tubes and counting the bowel movements of laboratory mice (lavatory mice?). With all those brains rattling about, there is a great percentage of science dedicated to inventing, perfecting and testing practical jokes. Nothing is more fun than a good giggle around the lab's coffee pot.

Experiment: Designer Death

Use your school's biology lab to create a recombinant DNA that will make humans sterile.

Questions

- ✓ Did your teacher get quiet when you told him or her what you were doing?
- ✓ How many weeks of therapy did the court order?

Natural Ends

We shouldn't manufacture the apocalypse. We should choose paper over plastic and have an ecologically minded end of civilization. We don't want an artificially flavored end-times. You wouldn't want the sky to turn red, only to find out it was Red Dye #3.

Destroying the world in the name of religion is just as bad. Demons from Hell are not of this world and don't make good compost. We don't need the environmental damage from wars and rumors of wars. We need a natural end of the world with only natural and recyclable products like asteroids and super novas.

A natural apocalypse is comforting. You feel like you are close to nature, and probably are if you are sandwiched between the Earth and an asteroid the size of Portugal.

Speaking of asteroids, or rather writing unless you are listening to the audio book, let's start our natural disasters with the sky falling.

Asteroids/Comets

A rock from space ruined everything for the dinosaurs. We could be next. The Earth is hit by meteors every day. Comets cross our orbit on a regular basis. It is just a matter of time before a space rock as big as the dinosaur killer stops by for a little humanity smackdown.

If a space rock is headed for us, we won't know until it's too late. Only a few people are looking to the sky with their telescopes for these interstellar hit men. Knowing about the killer soon enough to send Bruce Willis won't happen–even if Bruce wanted to go again.

Learn This Word

> ***Cosmophobia**: A strong fear that, in the near future, the Earth will be destroyed by some cosmic event. This is also known as "the sky is falling" or being a "Chicken Little." There is*

another meaning: The realization or belief that you are an insignificant speck as compared to the vastness of the cosmos.

There are killer asteroids that are coming our way right now. If you have **cosmophobia**, you think about this every day. One asteroid is already planning to hit us in a 160 years. How many asteroids are out there with an earlier appointment? What about the ones we haven't spotted yet?

Comets look like an easy threat to avoid, right? Big tails and they glow for months before they get close, no missing that. Comets are unfortunately too big to move out of the way. You can't just put its turn signal on. It isn't possible to dodge out of the way of a planetoid. It's coming, and you are not going to change its mind.

Comets are just snowballs, right? How could that hurt us? Comets have a good bit of rock with that ice, so no snowy winter wonderland when it hits. If you have ever been hit in the face with a dirty snowball full of gravel, you know what we are talking about. It's going to sting!

You Might Want to Know

An iron meteorite hitting Pittsburgh will be the cruelest of ironies.

A big comet could dig a crater the size of North Dakota and create a super volcano. Unfortunately we can't fill the hole with South Dakota. Modest sized comets hitting in the ocean could boil the ocean or create tidal waves taller than a skyscraper. If a comet hits land or sea, we will get an ice age from the explosion and a bit of sky catching fire. It isn't going to be a good day for a family picnic.

Comets and asteroids often break apart before they hit. Instead of one big one, we get a swarm of smaller, but just as deadly pieces. Imagine hundreds of mountain-sized pieces hitting everywhere in the world. One of these rocks has your name on it.

Comet Shoemaker-Levy 9 broke into twenty-three pieces and slammed into Jupiter over the course of a week. Just one of the fragments caused a 500 meter per second shock wave with a radius half that of the Earth. That's just one piece! Jupiter looked as if it needed to call the Battered and Abused Hotline when it was all done.

Imagine the pieces of Shoemaker-Levy 9 hitting the Earth. The pieces would hit us so hard that we'll skip the stone age and go straight to pointy sticks. This is assuming there would be any sticks. With all that destructive power, we might have only toothpicks.

Asteroids are sneakier than comets. Asteroids don't glow or shout, "Here I am!" These things are stealthy as ninja cats. Asteroids are zooming around the solar system at great speed, but it is a very quiet zoom.

Asteroids are attracted to Earth like ants to a picnic. Things are worse now that we have hundreds of thousands of SUVs adding to the mass of the surface of the Earth. All that metal was safely buried, and now they are in our driveways attracting obese space rocks.

It's unlikely that an interstellar extinction-sized rock will be spotted. One these killers comes out of our blind spot and poof! One day we are here, the next we are worm food, provided that any worms survive.

Don't believe us? Want proof? Ask a dinosaur.

Armageddon-Scale Asteroid

One of the things you often see in the news is "Armageddon-scale" asteroids. Let's take a moment to look into this false reporting and the actual Armageddon scale.

There are many false reports of Armageddon-scale asteroids. This is just poor math used scare the poop out of people. One specific asteroid, about the size of New Zealand's Parliament building (lovingly called the Beehive), was said to be Armageddon-scale. This was complete disinformation or somebody used a rubber ruler. The folks that called it Armageddon-scale were including the inflated egos of the politicians in the parliament building?

At 60 meters, this New Zealand Parliament-scale asteroid is not a killer, just a mass murderer of inconvenience. It's not even close to Armageddon-scale and not apocalyptic-worthy.

A Kiwi-sized government building is rather big, but it could not end all life. If this parliament-oid hit far out in the ocean, it might not even ripple a wave on a beach. Largish cities would just have a day of horrible traffic and lose a few Starbucks. It wouldn't be a slow news day, but the next day would be really slow, as reporters interview disappointed end-of-the-worlders.

At 60 meters the asteroid is less than 1% on the Armageddon-scale. Megiddo is a smallish hill in the Middle East that is at least 500 by 1,000 by 40 meters (based on reckoning using Google maps). If such a hill came from outer space, and then hit us square in the nose, that would be a certified One on the Armageddon-scale of apocalyptic destruction.

What if the Armageddon-scale of the rock from space was the same size of, well, Armageddon? Bigger than a breadbox, but a reasonable size for destruction if it comes out of deep space. How much damage and will it ruin your dinner plans?

We need to an asteroid that has twenty-million cubic meters of rock, dirt, and "Napoleon Slept Here" signs — yeah, Napoleon slept at Megiddo. We need to add the signs to the total weight of the asteroid to be extra accurate.

If you have this rubble-pile-of-an asteroid, what kind of damage would it do? We found a convenient asteroid-damage calculator. Here's the web site address:

http://www.lpl.arizona.edu/impacteffects/

Unlike a standard calculator, Impact Effects Calculator is specialized for "death from space." It has only one job, to calculate the damage of stuff from space. The calculator even lets you place an observer any distance from the impact to see if they are burnt to a crisp by the fireball. You have the option of selecting a dirty snowball, a block of nickel or just a pile of rubble like Megiddo. Imagine being there just as the asteroid hits and knowing how dead you'll be!

Time to measure an Armageddon hit. We set the observer's distance at 300 miles from the impact. This is probably about as far as you can travel by car once you figure out the CNN news report is true. If you stay to see an interview with a doomsayer who says that God hates you and we are all going to die, you will only get about five miles, so just grab the kids and drive!

After things are setup, all we need to do is let the super computer do its job. We hit the calculate-the-death-from-space button and sit back for a a millisecond or two to wait for the results.

An Armageddon-scale asteroid is not very impressive. The crater is only forty-three miles wide. If you use metric, it's an impressive seventy kilometer crater (metric always makes things look impressive). Big hole, but not huge. About as big as Los Angeles and a few suburbs.

Sadly, our observer will likely die of third-degree burns and/or the 211 m/s (473 mph) air blast. At 473 mph you wouldn't lose your shirt in the wind, but you would lose your arms if they didn't burn to charcoal nubs from the heat first.

The shock wave will send your house into the air like Dorothy's house in The Wizard of Oz. Dorothy's tornado driven-house only fell on one wicked witch. An asteroid wind-driven house would take out dozens of witches and a squadron of flying monkeys.

Obviously, an Armageddon-scale asteroid isn't going to cause the Apocalypse. Despite being a certified "one" on the Armageddon-scale, that little pile of rock is only big enough to wipe out Walla Walla Washington, not the entire Earth.

Sadly, it will take a rock a bit bigger than Megiddo to take out all the non-Christian heathens of the specific church that is not properly genuflecting at the moment of impact.

Rubble doesn't sound like a very scary asteroid. But what a rubble pile looses in impact, it gains in its ability to hit more parts of the Earth. With a little divine intervention, each little chunk of stone could whack every heathen right on their noggins!

An asteroid 100 times the size of Armageddon would kill most of us, cause an Ice Age, and send any survivors back to the Stone Age. The bad news is that it wouldn't technically be a Christian Armageddon. This is fudging the Armageddon scale and Bible literalists don't like fudging. It has to be a literal

Armageddon. Any surviving literalist will be hunting with stone tools and praying for a little less Armageddon.

Cosmic Rays

When a star burps in our interstellar neighborhood, we are toast, literally — so burnt that we can't scrape off the charcoal bits. No bread left, just charcoal. Imagine a couple of slices of bread popping out of a supernova-powered toaster.

You might think, "I'll just be on the other side of the world when it happens." Your location won't matter, or how deep a hole you are hiding in. These beams of death could last for years. Even a quick burst could rip away atmosphere, deplete ozone, or kill enough stars in Hollywood that we will be forced to watch only YouTube cat-dancing videos for entertainment. The humanity!

You might also think a reasonably thick tinfoil hat will save you. Sorry, but this is going to sterilize the Earth. Foil hats are not strategically placed to prevent sterilization. You need is lead underwear.

If we did survive sterilization, we would no longer be human. Cosmic rays cause a high number of mutations. You would grow a cool tail or a third hand in the middle of your chest. For every cool mutation you get a bad mutation. So, cool tail but the brain power of slime mold.

Meandering Mini Black Holes

You always hear about black holes, but nobody has ever seen one. We'll skip the obvious reason. Our problem is with mini holes. Not only are they black and hard to see, the are also very tiny. Supposedly they are zipping around the universe and headed our way.[30]

There are a few signs that there's a mini black hole coming our way. If you start feeling heavier or your feet seem five miles from your head, suspect a black hole is about to rip our world to pieces.

---

30 http://news.nationalgeographic.com/news/2008/01/080110-black-holes_2.html

Mini black holes have the mass of a few planets stuffed into the space of a golf ball. The mass would change our orbit, making it either colder or hotter, and make people weigh a few tons more because of the new gravity. The Moon would crash into the Earth too.

No upside to mini black holes. Maybe just one. Stock in weight loss companies will rise as people try to shed a few thousand pounds of new weight.

A mini black hole does not need to hit the Earth. The hole has enough gravity to drag around all the trash it passes. The black hole could miss us, but all that trash could hit us and wipe us out. Just entering our solar system would tug the Oort cloud or the Asteroid belt and sends all sorts of space rubble whizzing around the solar system. Death by space garbage.

Methane Ice Meltdown

There are huge deposits of frozen methane in our oceans.[31] The methane ice comes from ancient dead things. Sort of like ancient farts buried at sea. The methane gas is compressed by the deep ocean pressures to form methane ice. Spiffy cool stuff. Looks like ice, burns like charcoal briquettes.

Methane is flammable as anyone who eats beans and has a cigarette lighter and a juvenile audience will attest. Methane is also a potent greenhouse gas. Vast quantities released all at once might raise the world temperature really fast. Of course, the cloud of gas could catch fire and burn all the oxygen in the atmosphere. Good to have choices.

What causes frozen methane to be released? Start with global warming. When the ocean warms up, that deep water methane ice will warm up enough to turn back to a gas. Tons of methane gas bubbles will start rising to the surface. As more methane hits the atmosphere, the oceans get warmer, which melts more methane. Eventually the world is hot, sticky, and smells like a cow's butt.

A release will be caused when an asteroid, even a small one , hits in the right place in Canada or Siberia. In the wooly north, where millions of tons of methane are locked up in the

---

[31] http://en.wikipedia.org/wiki/Methane_clathrate

permafrost, a well placed asteroid (a meteorite once it hits) will cause the same problem.

Methane ice deposits are a very cool solution to our fossil fuel problem (pun intended because methane is a cool fossil fuel fart). Engineers are already looking for a way to mine their stinky riches. As we all know, there is always a chance for an accident. One mistake creates a chain reaction that releases the gas of millions of years all at once. The methane causes the Earth to warm which causes more methane to release into the atmosphere. Eventually someone lights a match to hide the stench but that's what sets the atmosphere ablaze. Yes, apocalypse by lighting a billion fossil farts.

That Persnickety Sun

The Sun has its good days and its bad days. Things get cooler or they get hotter. We don't really have a good handle on what's possible. We could die a very sweaty boots on when it gets hotter or with our ice skates on if it gets cooler. It could happen quickly or in just a few days or decades. Suns are unpredictable, and we should be considering ourselves lucky so far.

The Sun could be very quiet too. This is a rather new threat that was just discovered. The solar wind keeps nasty radiation and high energy particles out of our solar system. With a quiet Sun we get radiation poisoning or we all become mutants with super powers. We like super powers, but we might have a super war among the super mutants. Super powers are not as fun when everyone has one.

When the Sun gets a bit angry, there is solar wind to worry about. Sort of a solar fart without the stink. Depending on if it's a small squeaker or a huge blow, we have other problems.

A Sun squeaker could knock out satellites and fry our electronics. Imagine the chaos as millions of teenagers trash the world because their video games and cell phones become useless. With no satellite TV to calm them, they start gangs that act out Angry Birds and destroy civilization.

Bee Mites

Bees are scarce these days. The cost of honey is rising and agriculture is in trouble because bees aren't pollinating. After blaming cell phones, bee mites or rather mites on bees are a leading candidate along with cell phones, and bad puns on valentines cards (bees go mad when they read 'will you bee mine').

The best theory is that bees are being killed by a puritan god's hatred for the naughty congress between bees and flowers. Pollination is an X-rated threesome between two plants and a bee. You should only rub your stamen against another's stigma in your own species. Naughty bees! We cast thee into Hell for your sins!

Scientists paint an apocalyptic world without bees. Without bees, they say there is an end of food. Without bees pollinating our flowers, we have only a short time to live.

We don't think there is much to worry about. Many foods are bee free.[32] For example, many grasses (rice and wheat) and legumes (peas and peanuts) don't require the indentured servitude of the honey bee.

Scientists say the world does come to a screeching halt when apples, watermelons, and the like disappear. All we would have left is peanut butter (hold the jelly) sandwiches. Without bees, we will not have those nasty vegetables crowding our plate. The world will be forced to choke down steak and potatoes for dinner. Even with a food shortage, we will still be able to survive on Soylent Green on whole wheat toast.[33]

Bird Flu

Bird Flu is scary. Think Hitchcock and "Tippi" Hedren scary. A Bird Flu starts with a duck farm outside Beijing where a duck destined to be Peking Duck catches the flu, doesn't call in sick as he should, and then sneezes in a farmer's face. The disease spreads to humans and we all die in our beds drinking NyQuil.[34]

---

32 http://en.wikipedia.org/wiki/Self-pollination and for the kids: http://www.mbgnet.net/bioplants/pollination.html

33 http://en.wikipedia.org/wiki/Soylent_Green

34 http://en.wikipedia.org/wiki/NyQuil Are you as amazed as we are that NyQuil has its own Wikipedia page?

Bird flu spreads quickly because of bird migration. Generic Swine Flu is spread slowly because pigs are rather lazy and don't travel business class.

Birds top the list of "evil signs." Horror movie writers use birds as their favorite plot device to deliver a message of death. With bird flu, the message of doom and disease is convenientlyat the same time! We love coincidences like that!

Why Bird Flu is so much worse than pig-based flu is not really explained by scientists. Pig Flu has been just fine for hundreds of years. As pigs are the closest to humans in many ways (cannibals say pig and human flesh taste the same and are just as delicious), pigs can transmit a flu that humans can catch too.

You Might Want to Know

> *It's important to understand that in Beijing, Peking Duck is called Beijing Duck. There is no difference between the two, except that one is a communist triumph of cuisine and the other is a monarchy's dish to rule the masses.*

Why not Horse Flu or Flea Flu? We think it all goes back to Hitchcock. He made birds scary. Who's made a movie on the horrors of fleas or horses? Birds are at the top of the horror list no matter how dangerous they really are when they have a bad case of the sniffles.

It's hard to spot a duck with a cold. Pigs, with their big snouts oozing green slime, are obviously sick. Bird flu can't be spotted because farmers don't see the signs. If you can't send your birds home for plenty of bed rest, fluids, and a few days watching soaps, the virus gets more infectious.

Could you cure a duck with Bird Flu? A cure and proper treatment would require a doctor. This is impossible because all duck doctors are quacks.

Bird farmers don't know how to cure Bird Flu. Imagine the horns of dilemma (assume the horns are bull) on a chicken farm. How does a farmer cure his chickens? The best medicine is a big bowl of *chicken* soup! Will the stress of nepotistic cannibalism cause the flu virus to mutate and become even deadlier?

Bird Flu is a low probability in our book (well, this book), but still possible. Our belief is that doorknobs the easiest way to transmit flu germs, so birds can't transmit the flu to humans. We have never seen a bird sneeze *and then open a door*. What are the odds? We've never heard a bird sneeze, have you?

Bird flu is definitely a fowl killer.

The H1N1 Pandemic

As we write this, thousands (well, it turned out only fifteen) are already dead in Mexico from a deadly strain of the H1N1 Flu.

Regular old flu kills hundreds of thousands every year. The H1N1 pandemic strain killed fewer people than normal flu in the US. It seems the more press a flu strain gets, the fewer people it kills. People start washing their hands and more buildings get self-opening doors without doorknobs. Farmers in China kill hundreds of thousand of pigs, fearing they would sneeze on them. Of course doctors loose money like crazy because people don't get sick and their cholesterol is free falling faster than the value of gold as fewer sick days means a thriving economy. The horror!

Pandemics are bad. H1N1 is bad too. Not because of a dangerous strain of sniffles. The real killer is a plot to poison everyone (except rich people), by forcing everyone to get a flu shot. The vaccine will kill most of the population a few weeks later… Wait … We hear black helicopters flying over the office. Spread the word, flu vaccines are a conspiracy to kill poor people.

Generic Flu

Swine flu pandemics kill thousands every year. Farmers live with their pigs and touch the same door knobs, transmitting disease. Pigs are very close to us genetically, so bugs that will kill a pig will kill people just as easily minus the smell of Christmas ham.

As evidence for a looming epidemic, we submit that nobody has invented pig-friendly Kleenex. Mud in the average pig pen is 80% pig snot! These unsanitary conditions at pig farms will mutate a flu into a disease that could kill billions. With all that pig snot, we die faster from a pig sniffle than a bacon heart attack.

Pandemics don't just happen. They require business travel. Complicate that with business hangovers. Lower immunity because you stayed out too late, drank like an alcoholic fish and French fries are at the top of the hangover food pyramid and you get an immune system ripe for a repeat of Typhoid Mary (or Ted). The clincher is that flu is easily transmitted by air travel. Imagine the layers of runny poopy squirts from Stomach flu embedded in a coach airplane seat (never, ever, sniff an airline seat).

Have you ever been on a plane and not be allowed to get off because someone was sick? We have. On a trip between Japan and Dallas, Texas, a couple of people started getting sick. By sick, we mean a faces that was pretty shade of jaundice yellow and disturbing noises from the toilets.

Moments after landing in Dallas, the plane was quickly quarantined. Paramedics in gloves and masks entered the plane and examined the plague carriers. Our first thought: How many would die?

Bad news, nobody died, that we know of – at least from a strange asian disease. Sixty-eight percent of the passengers now have shorter lives due to the chemicals used in the process of dying their frightened-white hair after the incident.

We loved the refreshing the medical advisory forms the airlines give out as you exite the airplane. Something about going to a doctor if you feel any of the three symptoms of death; stopping of breath, a room temperature fever, and a fondness for warm brains.

The incubation period of the worst diseases don't show until little sally spreads the disease to everyone at Disneyland. It's a Mickey Mouse way to start an epidemic. Well, maybe Goofy.

Most diseases don't seem deadly until you are showing signs of dying, like your skin turns a shade of purple-black while green pustules squirt yellow goo every 20 minutes like an Old Faithful at Yellowstone. Any symptom you might have before the onset of death is easily confused with an allergy to cats. Nobody thinks cat allergy can be spread, so they go to work, shop, and ride the mass transit to the theater so that everyone shares the coming black death.

Plagues are only deadly because we tough it out a few days at work with snot flying through the cubicles. This human denial that something is wrong, allows the flu to spread faster and we get a little more time in the office before we all die.

Germs are invisible, so we don't know we are spreading them. We crawl out of our death beds to spread phlegm to the four corners of the world.

With the long incubation, most defenses are too little and too late. You are sneezing before you know that the pandemic has arrives.

More people die if there is vaccine. Where are the biggest crowds of sick people? Standing in line to get a vaccine!

Bird-Pig-Ferret Flu

We can now create the flu of your choice. All you need is a little recombinant DNA and a high school biology lab. If you feel lucky, put a few sick animals in the same pet store and wait for a five-year-old snotty-faced kid to sneeze.

You may not know it, but most diseases are caused by people and animals rubbing up against each other. If it wasn't for animal husbandry and frequent flier mileage, we would hardy get the sniffles.

The next pandemic will start when a pet smuggler attempts to hide a bird, pot belly pig, and a ferret in his underwear. Bird-Pig-Ferret Flu will kill half the planet before we find that kibble is a cure. One-third more of humankind will die because they fail to add water to the kibble to make the delicious and life saving gravy.

Space Germs

The stars are raining space-born disease on us. We love this idea because we also loved the original *Andromeda Strain*. Helpful hint, don't watch the remakes or you will wish you had a space-born disease.

There is a theory that space germs are spread by sunspots, comets, and asteroids.[35] Perhaps even blown on the wind by a dying star? An astronomical wonder has sneezed and space is spreading germs. Sunspots are just germ-filled zits on an adolescent Sun.

How comc there is no space-based hygiene? You can't fight space germs by shooting soapy rockets into space! Would soap in space make space smell like flowers? Will it mask that awful smell from Uranus?

Antibacterial soaps always say they kill 99% of germs. Are the 1% that it can't kill, from Alpha Centauri Prime?

Gotta love death from space, even if it is space cooties.

The Hitchcock News

Alfred Hitchcock loved to scare people. If Hitchcock was alive today, he wouldn't be making movies, he'd be a network news anchor. The news is ten times scarier than any horror movie.

Learn This Word

> ***Fear Mongering:*** *Fear mongering became popular with McCarthyism and the hunt for the Communist Menace. Since then, politicians, news show hosts, and smart marketers have used fear, real, imagined, or crafted for the purpose to influence voters, consumers, and TV ratings. For example "Shark Week" on Discovery and the Armageddon shows on the History Channel during sweeps week.*

Fear mongering in the United States surfaced during the era of McCarthyism. Since then, politicians have used the technique to poison the minds of voters with the certainty that any political opponent is the Antichrist.

The master of fear mongering is the news. Fear mongering on the news always increases ratings. Fear mongering also moves products too. How many surgical masks and gallons of

---

35 Fred Hoyle and Chandra Wickramasinghe, "The dilemma of influenza" http://www.ias.ac.in/currsci/may102000/opinion.pdf

antibacterial soap were sold to the masses during the H1N1 scare? Combine the news and products that target the consumers worst fears and you'll make billions. Fear sells!

Look at the hype about Bird Flu. Top notch mongering! We suspect the tobacco companies are behind it. Why give up smoking if you are going to die young from Bird Flu? Follow the money!

How will this end the world? Simple, panic in the streets. We could have a five pound asteroid, a sniffle, or other meaningless event over-hyped by the news as the end of the world. The fear mongering will destroy our ability to think rationally, and we will run into the streets with an unstoppable panic. The world will end as the fear of the end becomes worse than anything we could imagine.

Experiment: Candid Astronomer

Learn how to use a telescope, a camera, and Photoshop. When you are well-skilled in astrophotography, start using Photoshop to add little dots to your photos that look like a killer asteroid. Make sure your celestial mechanics are accurate. Put the trajectory behind the moon so that it is a few days before the asteroid is expected to hit. After that, all you need to do is give the data to a few astronomers and wait for the fun to begin.

Questions:

- ✓ How long is it before the astronomer calls every observatory?
- ✓ Does the astronomer believe you because you sound like a scientist?
- ✓ For extra credit, make sure a fundamentalist knows about your fake asteroid. Does he behave differently than you would expect now that the world seems to really be ending?

- ✓ For extra-extra credit, find a real killer asteroid. Repeat the above questions.

Mayans and 2012

December 21, 2012, at 11:11 p.m. GMT is the Mayan's "Long Count" that will mark the end of a 5,126-year era. Think of it as a super-sized New Year's Eve. It will even be on a Friday so plan to sleep off your hangover over the weekend.

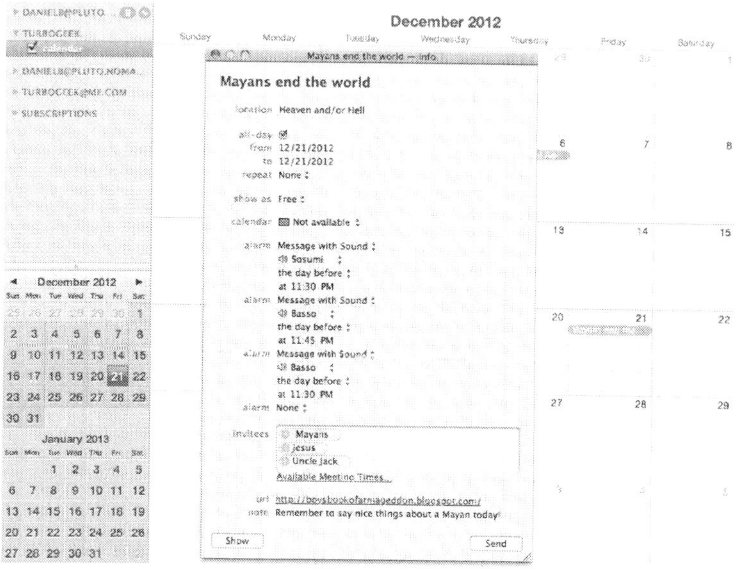

The December 21, 2012 on a modern calendar.

Calendars do not lie. Our calendar predicts all sorts of things like Easter on a Sunday to President's Day always on a Monday. The calendar is full of mystery. The Mayan calendar is much like our calendar, except it is round and made of stone.

The Mayan end seems a little anticlimactic. Seems silly to end the world just because the calendar runs out of Tuesdays, but end it does. Hard to argue with that.

The lion's share of Mayan calendar propaganda (a pride of propaganda) is from the History Channel. The 2012 date has existed since the Mayans created their calendar thousands of years ago. Popularity is swelling because the date is near.

The History Channel is very creative. The best ratings the History Channel has ever had was when they did the Mayan apocalypse during sweeps week, so they know what people want. It seems that all the 2012 specials were put together with stock footage from other programs. Throw in a few Erich von Däniken, a little Nostradamus, sprinkle some Armageddon, and you have aliens landing in 2012. Abracadabra, a myth is transformed! Aliens coming in 2012 to enslave humanity. Quatzecoatl isn't a feathered serpent god, but a wacky alien.

2012 is bandied about by the Christians too. Somehow they find the Mayan calendar a corroboration of the Book of Revelation. Christians justify this by saying that the Mayans were hyped up on magic mushrooms, and mistook Jesus for a feathered serpent.

Mayans loved to predict eclipses, equinoxes, and all sorts of things. If they could predict all those events, why wouldn't the Mayan calendar be a correct prediction of an end in 2012? It helps to have a track record for accurately predicting events on your doomsayer resume.

Scientists have so far been able to predict the same types of events. Scientists predict eclipses just as well as Mayans! Scientists have unfortunately failed, like doomsayers, to predicted the exact end of the world. Scientists have a great track record on the astronomy stuff, but scientists are not predicting the end of time. Mayans do both, so they must be much smarter than scientists.

Aliens may be a key part of the Mayan end. If the aliens helped the Mayans build pyramids, then it seems obvious aliens will return in 2012 to show their grandkids what they did when they were teenagers.

Aliens are coming back to punish the Spaniards for messing with their Mayan buddies. It's just taking a long time to pack the alien version of the station wagon. These are theories of course. All we know is that the Mayans have an appointment December 22, 2012 with somebody important.

You Might Want to Know

We're starting a Pyramid Late Payment fund. The aliens built the pyramids for Mayans and the end of Mayan calendar in 2012 when the final payment is due. We need a fund to pay the Pyramid debt or the aliens will get mad and reposes something important, like our souls. If nothing happens after 90 days, all profits go to the Brookshier personal wealth trust. We'll spend the money wisely on personal luxuries to help boost the economy by paying luxury taxes on fast cars, espresso machines, and yachts. We call this our pyramid scheme.

What if the calendar only ends for the Mayans? There are about five million Mayan descendants remaining. Suppose the Mayan gods came and just took Mayans? Who would notice?

The Mayans believed[36] they were built from clay, then destroyed, then made from wood, then destroyed, then from corn and, well, they are still here eating corn (essentially cannibalistic corn people). We don't know. Seems a little strange to be made from corn flower. If we are destroyed again, we hope the gods make us from carbon nanotubes or something cool.

You Might Want to Know

Mayans, Aztecs, and other New World civilizations share common myths and their calendars are similar. Mayans just happened to be one of the last major societies to rule the Americas. Doomsayers judicially pick random myths from history and use them to confirm the bad things that might occur when the Mayan calendar ends.

Why the Mayans didn't choose a round number like 5,000 years or stop at midnight is left to the anthropologists and true believers to explain. Time is messy. Gods (or aliens mistaken for gods) have better things to do with their eternity. Prayer is nice, but why would a super being listen to your ramblings at the the kitchen table - even if it is Thanksgiving? Better to book an appointment and perhaps that's what the Mayan calendar is for. All those hearts ripped out in sacrifice are collecting interest. Time to pay up.

---

36 http://en.wikipedia.org/wiki/Maya_mythology

We know Mayans suck at seeing the future. The Mayans certainly missed the Spaniards invading, raping, pillaging, giving them smallpox, crabs, killing, and forced religious conversion. Do you think they know what's happening in 2012?

Mayans loved their calendars. They were among the first to have cute little animal calendars with cute little animals like dogs and other imagery we use on calendars today. Mayans never graduated to The Far Side, Dilbert or word of the day calendars, they were still sophisticated. The Mayans also avoided buying calendars as gifts every year for Christmas by having a calendar that lasted 63 million years (alautun). Why have a calendar for something that far in the future? Imagine hating new calendars that badly.

What kind of end are the Mayan gods planning? The Aztecs have Montezuma's Revenge,[37] which is extremely bad, and that's just from drinking the water! What could be worse? A massive apocalyptic disaster, Montezuma's squirty poos, or just a way to sell end-of-the-world books?

Archeologists believe Mayans end their calendar as an excuse to throw a party and get blind drunk. We do the same thing for New Years. The Mayans must throw a wild party if the hangover lasts 63 million years.

There many questions and no satisfying answers to the Mayan calendar question. We will all need wait until December 2012 to find out. Luckily for us the publisher of this book doesn't offer refunds.

Mayanism

Mayanism[38] is a new age religion. By "new age," we mean made up by people on drugs or some sort of mental illness. A key theme is that Mayans knew aliens and that in 2012 they will return. When they return, they will bring world peace.

New Age people don't believe in Mayan gods. These mystics gave up believing in Christianity back at Berkley after an LSD trip. Without a god they need a fact-based entity. Why not

---

37 http://www.weturl.com/3748/

38 http://en.wikipedia.org/wiki/Mayanism

aliens? They also claim that angels and their brethren are just visitors from another dimension or visitors from the planet Crazy For You. The only thing we think they've got right for sure is that Myanisim sells books and videos shows.

2012 Doomsayers

We have already mentioned Erich von Däniken, so let's just add to the list of Mayan wackos and what they have added to the Mayan myth.

José Argüelles

José Argüelles is big on aliens and spaceships. He has a PhD in Art History and Aesthetics. We are sure that this is perfect training and makes him quite an expert on Mayans, the 2012 event, and aliens.

José is a repeat offender. His first foray into predicting the future was with the Harmonic Convergence. Remember August 1987? This was the alignment of the planets and the universe. This was also the day that burning incense became an in thing to do, even if you weren't trying to hide the scent of pot from your mom.

The year 1987 was known as The Great Enlightening. Primarily by the sellers of crystals, voodoo pharmaceuticals, and New Age books. The enlightenment was how much money you will make if you opened a New Age store and sold worthless crystals for a hundred times their value.

Milking enlightenment only goes so far. Once you've had your Harmonic Convergence, the bank account starts to get low and you need a new marketing strategy. You need a new set of books and spiffy things like calendars based on the Moon to break into new markets. Enter 2012.

Let's look into how José got to 2012. First, he took the I Ching (pronounced eeeee' Chiiiiing or simply ca'ching at New Age book sellers), laid out the sixty-four symbols and put them on a calendar. The symbols conveniently lined up with significant events in history after fiddling, Jose got things to line up in 2012, just far enough in the future for a book deal. Then, all the Mayan stuff started getting popular and Jose did a little more fiddling to match the end of the Mayan calendar.

You might think that this is very cool. The I Ching is just a few lines. Easy enough to just shift the lines around until yo get something to fit on your graph paper. The best comparison is throwing noodles at the wall to do your taxes.

After throwing noodles at a wall for a while, José happened to get things to line up in 2012. There is criticism for the actual date selected and its relationship to the Mayan calendar. José left out little things like leap years and other minor glitches and something to do with Mayan squirrels (yep, Mayans had cute animals on their calendars too). Like any other prediction, it is in the eye of the doomsayer to make the call, not the critics.

Unfortunately for Jose, the I Ching is Chinese and not in any way related to Mayan mythology. These two issues cancel out. Jose is able to ignore the problem and write best selling books about his theories.

Soothsayers, doomsayers, and New Age profiteers are masters of argument. Your criticism bounces off of me and sticks to you like glue. Arguing facts and logic doesn't make a dent in their credibility and only adds to their book sales. It's amazing that they don't become career politicians.

If you will excuse us, we need to make a few stock picks by checking the cardinal relationships to magnetic north of our dog's poo.

Terence McKenna

Terence McKenna is a math guy, but he was also a psychedelic drug user. Are you starting to see a pattern?

Terence's brush with the Mayan calendar used some math and the date of bombing of Hiroshima, and a 67.29 year cycle to get things to line up with 2012. The final touch was a calculations of a fractal waveform known as Time Wave Zero, which with much fiddling, lined up with the 67.29 year cycle.

Like the Mayan calendar, the Time Wave Zero line ends after 2012. He originally had November 2012, instead of December 22, 2012. After finding out about the Mayan calendar, he was able to jigger the numbers to eke out another month of our existence. If there isn't enough coincidence, cheat.

Terrance did not stop there. Having figured out the coincidental date, to prove his point, he equated taking drugs to being a prophet. His theory was that 12,000 years ago ancient man was tripping on mushrooms and that let them see the future.

Terrance is conveniently dead. Coincidentally, most of his papers with all of his Time Wave Zero calculations were destroyed in a fire started at a nearby Quiznos sandwich shop. Love those toasted sandwiches!

Did we mention Terrance took LSD and psychedelic mushrooms?

Daniel Pinchbeck

Daniel Pinchbeck[39] is an author of several New Age books including two on 2012. Coincidentally, Pinchbeck also used LSD and those psychedelic mushrooms. Enough said. Sorry Pinchbeck.

Have Mayans Already Ended The World?

Mayan gods are not afraid of starting over. They experiment with different inhabitants of Earth and if something doesn't work, they just destroy their creations and try again. Because Mayan gods are picky and have destroyed the world many times.

First, the Mayan gods created animals for their amusement. Seems reasonable, but a god's needs is not met by cute little animals. Gods need followers. Followers should pray to you and thank you for creating them. Kind of like a kid saying thanks to his parents for all their hard work in the bedroom.

The animals were cool, but they had small brains. Not big enough brains to praise and worship their creators. If you can't imagine a magical being, you can't pray. Time to start over, but since the animals are cool, let them frolic in the forests while they try to create something dumb enough to be smart enough to believe in magical gods.

The first men were made of clay. This isn't like the Christian god building Adam out of clay. These were real clay people. Sadly, men made out of clay are not much better than animals

---

39 http://en.wikipedia.org/wiki/Daniel_Pinchbeck

in the praising-their-god department. Clay is, well, thick mud. Muddy clay people weren't too smart. It was a bad idea, so the god made it rain to wash away the clay people.

This mud people episode sort of sounds like Noah. Gods like floods and many have washed their mud people away. There are no new plots. Gods do seem to think alike.

The next destruction of Mayan men started when the god created the next version of men from wood. Sadly, wood does not test too high on standard intelligence tests. Again, bad worshipers. Time to wipe the slate clean again. This time the Mayan god was a bit more ticked off. Wooden men were chewed up like the fellow in *Fargo* looking real close at the guts of a wood chipper.

The Aztecs gods were a little more creative. The first time they ended the world, jaguars ate all the Aztecs. The second time they used the wind to blow man away. The final episode was when the Aztecs were conquered by the Spanish. The Aztec gods really didn't like Aztecs too much.

The New World gods are lousy at creating man. They were, however, quite good at cleaning up their mistakes. Jaguars, wind, fire, water, earthquakes, and finally with conquistadors.

Why are there no equivalent stories in Europe? You'd think someone would notice being eaten by a jaguar. Disasters are usually just for the locals, so the work of gods could be local too. The New World gods just didn't want to bother the rest of the world with their problems.

Quetzalcoatl depicted as a snake devouring a man – Codex Telleriano-Remensis.

The New World gods seem to be on vacation. Nobody has seen or spoken to one since the Spanish came. You may have noticed that there have been no appearances by Quetzalcoatl,[40] the feathered serpent since before Columbus. Is Quetzalcoatl shy? Did Columbus hurt his feelings and Quetzalcoatl is in a cave, moping?

You Might Want to Know

> *The Romans didn't mention Jesus when he was alive. They only started writing about the bothersome Christians many years later.*

Aztecs, Poltecs, Hopi, and all sorts of civilizations in the Americas have differing ways the world was destroyed many times in the past (like Noah's flood). The Mayans have a particular flair for world ending mythologies.

---

40 Quetzalcoatl is also called Tlahuizcalpantecuhtli.

Learn This Word

> ***Confusing:*** *Confusing means a set of information does not make sense. For example, almost all religions have creation and end-of-the-world stories. Even Atheists have the Big Bang and Heat Death. The stories are contradictory. We can't have all these stories be true. Your brain hiccups because Aztecs don't know about Noah and the flood and vise versa. Your brain upchucks on the contradiction, and we call this feeling, 'confusion.'*

All of this is **confusing** because they all can't be right. Even when there are similar flood stories for example, the sequence just doesn't add up. History, myth and that pesky evidence just wont add up so we can say the myths are history and find a pattern to discover our future.

The Aztecs [41] had, at last count, ninety-two gods. The Mayans [42] have 119. Have you seen one? We think the gods all packed their bags and left town. Probably too embarrassed about not protecting their people from the Spaniards.

Will Mayan gods end the world on December, 2012? Keep your eyes peeled because we bet a small village of Mayans in Chile will disappear. The gods will only do that to keep up appearances and set the stage for another History Channel special in a few thousand years when the Mayan calendar rolls around again.

Mayans Were Corny

Corn is the Mayan equivalent of Montezuma's Revenge. Corn, corn syrup, and ethanol are currently making the Earth a bad place to live (well, the air is a little cleaner, but that's all). Corn and its byproducts add up to being slowly killed. The corn and that oh-so-sweet syrup probably gave our generation type II diabetes. In 2012 we'll all just die of high blood sugar.

---

[41] http://en.wikipedia.org/wiki/Aztec_mythology. There are ninety-two gods listed on this wiki link.

[42] http://www.art-poster-online.com/mayan_mythology.htm

Ethanol has for the last ten years been a way to clean the air as an additive to gasoline. Now folks want to dump gasoline entirely and turn every square inch of fertile land to corn for ethanol. No room for real food, plus the fuel for your car will cost ten times as much and exhaust pipe smells like ranch flavored Doritos.

We'll starve ourselves to death as we convert food to gasoline. We will also go mad as corn syrup in our sweet drinks gets put in our gas tanks. Think of starving hordes of type II diabetic psychotics mowing down the rest of us with their corn-powered Hummers.

You Might Want to Know

> *If Quatzecoatl is real, then when the Mayan calendar ends in 2012, pigs won't fly, but feathered serpents will make stiff umbrellas very popular.*

Stopping Time

The Mayan calendar just stops. There isn't a little symbol depicting aliens landing or gods killing people. The calendar just stops and there is nothing more. Is this the end of time?

With the end of time, we will save a fortune on watches and calendars. We will lose all purpose excuse: "I couldn't think of a thoughtful gift, so I got you this Dilbert calendar." There will be no special dates to give gifts because dates will only be found on trees.

If we did have time, less of it would be wasted trying to find a Dilbert greeting card. Scott Adams will go broke because he can't make money off all the licensing deals or the newspaper cartoon business because there will be no daily newspaper.

There won't be anymore birthdays or holidays requiring lame calendar gifts (puppy calendars, not Dilbert calendars). There are very few downsides to ending time. The beginning of a golden age of enlightenment is upon us as people stop worrying about getting someplace on time and start doing something useful with their lives. Procrastination will be extinct!

Physics will lose a variable. Imagine how many students in high school physics will graduate with a B instead of a C. Milk will never go bad because it never expires. A "stitch in nine saves time" or "time flies" will be useless metaphors.

Imagine never being late for an appointment ever again. No more forgetting anniversaries or birthdays. The end of time sounds like a fantastic deal.

Summing Up 2012

Will the world end in 2012? The New Age lobby and the History Channel think so and so the people stocking their shelters. Imagine the inertia millions people believing just a little that Mayans really predicted the end of world. The panic around Y2K was nothing compared to a Mayan hysteria.

The end of the world in 2012 is not the only problem. Mayans are big on sacrifice. Avoid stone alters as the date approaches.

The evidence that the calendar is wrong (by 6,000 years) is not putting a dent in the festivities. The New Age machine is not going to stop just because archeologists, NASA, and Mayan witch doctors say it's all bunk. You'll still see Mayan apocalypse books on the shelves of your local spiritual enlightenment super store until at least 2014.

The one thing we know for sure is that the date is on the Mayan calendar. That's good enough for us to throw a party. If it doesn't work out, we'll at least have a wicked hangover to show for all the worry. You'll wish the world had ended!

Experiment: Pick a Date

Imagine a scientist has proven 2012 is the wrong date for the end of the Mayan calendar. Imagine the scientist's name is William Saturno and that he is from Boston University. Your mission is to create a new date to sell Mayan end-of-the-world literature, documentaries and movies.

Don't just pick a random date, do what other Mayan scholars have done to predict their dates. Learn the Mayan language, study all the Mayan artifacts, and join a Mayan cult. Use Mayan psychedelic drugs to follow in the footsteps of drug addled 2012 doomsayers. An excellent choice is the K'aizalah okox, also known as the "lost judgment mushroom" or by its scientific name, Psilocybe Cubens. It is very popular. At Fox News, all the pundits take it. Psilocybe Cubens mushroom pizza, yummy!

With your fresh Mayan knowledge, correct the Mayan calendar to predict a new end of the world. Don't worry if the date is correct, just make sure it's five years in the future.

Questions:

- ✓ How long did it take you to learn the Mayan language?
- ✓ Did anyone from the History Channel call you about creating a TV show about your predictions?
- ✓ When predicting the date, did you use any of the mythology of the Mayans to discover how the world will end?
- ✓ What evidence did you discover of aliens visiting the Mayans?
- ✓ When you joined the Mayan cult, how many ritual sacrifices were you able to perform before you were arrested?
- ✓ When you tried psychedelics, did you Guinea pigs start talking about the end of the world?

Are You a Doomsayer?

The word is full of doomsayers of all types. Only a few deserve to be called a capital "D" Doomsayer. What sets apart an official doomsayer from an unwashed bum carrying a sign that says, "The end is near?"

True doomsayers must have four of the following characteristics (the more the better). Add a point for each one that applies to you.

You know you are a doomsayer when...

- ✓ You live in a "compound" rather than a ranch.
- ✓ You have a following that listens to your every word.
- ✓ You have had sex with your followers (add a point for each follower that was younger than 18).
- ✓ You are the only savior and/or gatekeeper to salvation.
- ✓ Your sect/cult/religion requires supplicants to give their wealth to your organization. Add one point for every $50,000 spent on lawyers to make the 'donations' binding.
- ✓ Money changes hands … primarily from the believer into the doomsayer's pocket.
- ✓ Your converts are often targets of deprogrammers, the ATF, and local news reporters.
- ✓ You own more weapons than religious books.
- ✓ You have never succeeded in any other endeavor except this one
- ✓ Add one point for each time you have gone to prison for fraud.

Four points is good, but score seven or better and you are on your way to serving having a shootout with the ATF. If you are a doomsayer, good for you!

Are Doomsayers Con Artists?

Many doomsayers are crooks. They take candy from babies and slap little old ladies. They are con artists too.

Learn This Word

> ***Con Artist:*** *No, con artists don't draw convicts. Some con artists who have been caught by the law, have drawn portraits of other cons as part of their court mandated therapy, but that's just coincidence. The con in 'con artist' is short for confidence. Not purveyors of finger-paints, the confidence artist attains his victim's confidence to lure them into schemes where the rube (victim) gives the con artist their money.*

Smart con men use religion to stay out of prison. Lying is just free speech when dressed up as religion. Say whatever you want, lie, fleece your church members, it's not a crime when it's a religion. Nobody, especially the police, can say you're a crook when you are a preacher, prophet, or even a doomsayer.

It's impolite to question someone's faith. When you say angels talked to you, nobody questions the facts. Want to say you hear aliens? All you need is a good tax lawyer to make aliens a religion. That's right, even an Atheist con artist can make money from religion.

Some doomsayers become con artists accidentally. It's sort of like stealing cookies from the cookie jar. It's not your fault that you stole the cookies, it's the jar's fault. When you get away with the theft, it must be okay to steal cookies. Your god meant you to eat those cookies!

One moment you are expressing your irrational fears, the next you are selling a book and taking money from your followers. Suddenly you are thinking like an expert con artist.

The professional con artists are easy to spot. Not because they have criminal records, but they lack mental health issues found in normal doomsayers. When nobody is looking, a crazy person will still be drooling talking to the voices in their heads When nobody is looking at a con artist will still be talking to voices, but they will stop drooling.

Doomsayers are known to perform minor miracles, especially when they are doomsayers. A little faith healing helps sell the deal. Followers will write bigger checks when you seem like you are plugged into the specific almighty of your choice. Perform a magical feat of prestidigitation and your predictions of the end will suddenly be worth a listen.

Ancient con artists used to fake the miracles. Many of these con artists were killed or imprisoned when their tricks were eventually exposed. Faking a miracle isn't fool proof, especially when you are trying to fool a fool. Before you know it, somebody trips over a power chord or looks behind the curtain at the wrong time.

The modern con artists doesn't fake miracles anymore. It's simpler to tell people the miracle happened when nobody was looking. No witnesses to testify in court.

Faith healing is also a favorite con. Yelling and knocking people down is all you need to do. Like all good cons, the embarrassment of being conned is key. What's worse, admitting you were conned or coming back for a second dose of yelling and being knocked down? That's right, folks would rather be yelled at and knocked down again.

The religious con is less work than a normal con. In the traditional big con, you require many accomplices to help fleece the rube. With religion, people automatically believe your nonsense. Followers even have matching delusions!

Why aren't there thousands of criminals playing the end-of-the-world religious con? The simple fact is that it is hard to do without giggling.

Becoming a Doomsayer

Why are doomsayers so giddy? What makes them so passionate whenever **proselytizing** about the end of the world? Knowing the world was about to expire, we'd just give up and have a good cry. What possesses a doomsayer to take up the profession and begin a career that has a very clear retirement date?

Learn This Word

> ***Proselytize****: To proselytize is to convert someone's belief to another. In other words, we are changing people's minds about their religion, politics, science, and other subjects. The art of proselytizing is probably as old as human thought. From the moment we became thinkers we have wanted others to think just like us. We spend enormous amounts of time and energy just trying to make mental clones of ourselves.*

The simple answer is that we don't want to die alone. That's too simple of an answer. The real answer is that scaring people into believing the world is ending, gives you power over them.

How do you get more power? Fear! Fear is a great motivator. Do the accidental doomsayers cause fear on purpose? No, they just happen to mention something that scares the pants off people. These pants-less followers will worship anyone that will help find their pants. Followers are also more than happy to trigger the real end of the world at their beloved leader's command.

Power isn't strictly for the religious. Anyone can say the sky is falling. Scientists love the warm feeling of power they get from doomsaying. Tales of death from space are so frightening, we pee our pants in horror. A scientifically warm feeling is had by all.

Doomsayer Zoo

Doomsayers are not all alike! There are as many doomsayers and their are types of apocalypse.

In the doomsayer zoo, we have locked up the vicious doomsayers in soundproof cages without internet access. Nobody will be mentally mauled by a conversion or be motivated to join a cult. Children can learn about these creatures by safely reading a little placard in front of each cage.

Don't feel bad about these caged doomists. Doomsayers are not cute or cuddly. They destroy nature, not improve the ecosystem. Like wild pigs, they'll just dig up your mother's roses. Unlike pigs, they aren't looking for tasty, roots, just digging a bomb shelter. The world is safer and has cleaner underwear because we've locked up a few.

We captured these doomsayers in various locations in Dallas. We used modified badger traps baited with sour grapes. We had a little trouble trapping a paranoid doomsayer until we lined the cage with a soothing yellow wallpaper and hermetically sealed box of melba toast.

Get your peanuts and cotton candy, time to see the scary creatures. Please tap on the glass! They confuse the sound with the sky falling and it's fun to watch them scurry looking for a safe place to hide.

Religious

You were expecting religion, right? Religion-based doomsaying is part power trip and part sucking up to your god. You get status and recognition by adding people to the religion. Converts add brownie points redeemable in the afterlife.

The end is always associated with a final judgment. Doomsayers are hedging their bets. The more converts you have and optionally the more guns to fight the final battle, the better your chances.

It isn't enough to be kind, charitable, and loving of your god. Fighting on the side of good with a big army of fellow converts is the perfect ticket to the afterlife. Do it right and you get a first class ticket to salvation. You want to be in First Class Heaven, right next to God! Heaven is just Coach Class if you don't have enough frequent fanatic points.

The Job of being a religious doomsayers includes running a cult. It is similar to being the CEO of a multi billion dollar company. Executives don't sacrifice everything, why should a doomsayer. Why not fly First Class while on Earth as it will be in Heaven?

Biblical Math Geeks

A subspecies of the religious doomsayer has a pocket calculator. Their calculus of apocalypse adds up dates, number of horns on beasts, and other minutia to create a calendar of doom and identity key players like the Antichrist.

Calculator-doomsayers look for hidden meaning in their religious texts and in the world around them. These digital doom searchers have been at this for a long time.

Bible math is a little disingenuous. Right there, at least in the New Testament, Jesus says the time is unknowable. He didn't even imply that doomsayers use math or divine his exact meaning from reading between the lines. Note: Jesus never owned a calculator. Imagine math in Sunday school. We can't do math on a Sunday and we can't go to Sunday school either (both are against our religion).

Whatever happened to resting on the seventh day?

The Chosen

The "chosen" have inside information about the end of the world. The "chosen" see signs everywhere, even when they are not on the highway. They may be delusional, have recently been fasting, had a high fever, or missed taking their anti-psychotics. They are a Loonie short of a Canadian dollar coin.

The chosen-doomsayers hardly ever quote scripture. Their predictions of doom come from an unquestionable source: a voice in their head.

These doomsayers don't have witnesses as only they see and/or hear the voices and apparitions. The doomsayer gets all the attention because the folks they talk to wont talk to anyone else. Sort of like an imaginary friend with benefits. The invisible friend of course is very popular so the doomsayer becomes popular because everyone is lining up, hoping for an introduction.

There are two types of chosen people. Those that have a single visitation by the on-high spirit, and those that are in constant contact with the almighty because they can hear them speaking in their head. The single visitation 'chosen' are alway harping about that day they stood at an intersection of four Starbucks and saw God for a ten minute chat and a caramel mocha latte. No other visitations are reported and they milk the one they had for all its worth, even if it is fat-free skim milk.

The constant contact folks hearing voices are more fun. Those that have a direct connection are constantly getting updates from the almighty and their minions. Useful information, too, like who is evil or why a certain hurricane is the sign of the end. It's like having your god's Associated Press newswire service.

Paranoid

The paranoid are often lonely people, except for the paranoid doomsayer. Paranoia is contagious. Their delusions may sound crazy at first, but slowly seem plausible. Before you know it, your mom is posting on Facebook that driving with your lights on during the day will cause the Sun to explode.

Paranoid delusions also feed on each other. Kind of like baby guppies, eating their brethren so they can grow up and have baby guppies that eat their brothers and sisters. A batch of bad spinach leads to a belief that fresh food is only grown by terrorist farmers trying to kill us with a deadly strain of middle eastern E. Coli. A woman that a hairy upper lip becomes a bearded suicide bomber.

Scientists are studying the paranoid's doomsaying abilities to see if it's a self-defense mechanism. The theory is that doomsaying evolved naturally attract a group of followers as a surrogate for group therapy. Therapy is expensive! A paranoid leading an end-of-the-world cult gets free therapy. Of course everyone else is as crazy as the doomsayer. It's like monkeys that groom each other to rid each other of parasites. Unfortunately cults don't really cure each other and monkeys never eliminate their parasites.

Scientist

A scientist's motivation for doomsaying often starts and ends with fame. We don't want to be too cynical here, but there is cash and prizes that influences these scientists; it's just a fact. Independently wealthy scientists don't do doomsaying. Scientists don't take up doomsaying as hobby.

The average scientist needs grant money. The best grant money is fear-based. We are not saying that scientists think of the worst-case scenario and then build the science for the worst disaster. What happens is real science where all possible world ending scenarios area properly studied. The worst disasters are just much more interesting.

Scientists also study their mothers. Tales of doom that make mom shiver a bit in terror are worth writing a grant proposal. The successful scientist has a mother that is so frightened that she dies her hair weekly.

Fame comes from honest research. More fame comes from research that scares people. Watch scientists who study glaciers. They often do their work for a pittance. The average science jobs pay slightly more than illegal farm labor. Scientists are always looking for a little boost of their income. Call melting the beginning of the end of the world and you suddenly have a second income.

Scientists can't make big money writing reports about the melting of ice cubes the size of Rhode Island. If they sell the mind-numbing fear of a warming planet they put the fear of god into your average ice tea drinker. Imagine a world without ice tea. Say it isn't so, Joe!

Imagine being a scientists that studies polar bears. You are in big trouble if global warming is true. No more trips to the arctic and no cute pictures in National Geographic. No polar bears, no job. Imagine how creative you will become. No polar bears, no job. When a scientist says, "up to our elbows in melted snowmen" they get on Letterman. Selling the fear of global warming pays better and you don't get eaten by a polar bear.

They (usually right wing Republicans) say scientists shouldn't be out doomsaying. Scientists are putting good Christian doomsayers out of work! Scientists should just report on the ice-cube and polar bear shortage and stay away from the end of the world. Leave the doomsaying to the experts at church.

We believe in the free market. Let's not have any of that Tea Party socialism talk! We don't go around saying that the Tea Party is putting hard working Fascists out of work. It's a scientist's Christian-God given right to be doomsayers, even when they are Atheists.

This is still America — at least for a couple more weeks before something a scientist predicts kills us all.

Paranoid Nonscientist

There is a strange mix of the paranoid and the nonscientist. This is someone who thinks he knows enough about science to rub two sticks together and predict when the world will end. They become doomsayers because people really can't disprove a negative. Simply you can't prove that something can't happen. Not that it won't, because you can't disprove that either.

There are paranoid nonscientist doomsayers too. We'll call them "cranks," just to keep from creating a four-letter acronym like PNSD (doh!).

The best way to spot a crank is to look for a scientist standing alone in his or her field. You find them in every scientific field. Way out in the field, between the poisoned well, the burnt bridge and the electrified fence. Their doomsaying is the only way they get attention. Sort of a "destroy it and they will come" technique. The field doesn't get dead baseball players, just cult members.

Entrepreneur

The last type of doomsayer is the entrepreneur. The entrepreneur looks at the other doomsayers and says, "I've got to get a piece of that action!"

Anyone that wants to become rich and famous can be an entrepreneurial doomsayer. Everything you can learn in a business book will help. It is all just selling a solution to a common problem: fear so bad you poop your pants a little.

As intelligent humans, that fight-or-flight response is a little bit broken. Instead of running away from a doomsayer, we run towards them to seek advice, aid and expensive survivalist supplies.

Entrepreneurs may seem like every other type of doomsayer, but really they are just salesmen. Their aim is to make as much money as possible. Instead of laser pimple poppers and weasel deodorant, they are selling cult memberships, magical crystals, fallout shelters, and guns.

Doomsayers believe danger can be eliminated. This is particularly true when the danger is never going to happen – unless the rules of time and space are revoked.

The chance of an asteroid hitting your house is a trillion to one, but a bunker 50 feet underground doubles your survival rate.

Doubling your family's survival sounds so good that you find a shovel in your hand and you are in a deep hole before you discover you can't get out of this hole of imagined safety. You might think this smells funny (it's the dry rot of stupidity). Tell that to the millions that own guns, extra supplies and have cool safe rooms all for imagined disasters, fall of governments and the success of Democrats.

Entrepreneurs of doom are selling you hope. It's just like regular sales of hope, like a pimple laser or weasel deodorizer gives you hope you'll get a date or hope that your weasel won't stink up the house (it is darn hard to get a deodorant stick in a weasel's four armpits, so be careful). The hope for the doomed is just as important. We hope we survive. We hope our weasel, Betty, survives in our small and poorly ventilated survival shelter. We hope our pimple-free face will look handsome to the last woman on Earth.

Entrepreneurs can sell their excess pimple popping lasers by just repurposing as anti-doom products. Powerful enough to kill a zombie weasel! It's just good marketing.

The more you fear, the more hope you need and will happily empty the bank account for. Scaring the pants off the public is good business.

Fifty Percent Chance of Rain

As humans, we are statistically blind. Not blind as in, blind to the pile of bear poop you just stepped in, but blind to statistics. Scary statistics are frightening, just like bears. Statistics stick to your shoes like bear poop and smell just as dangerous.

You Might Want to Know

You might set this book down for a minute and look around for bears. Bear poop is nature's signaling mechanism. The scent of fresh bear poop is like a sex pheromone, only smellier, sticks to your shoes and has nothing to do with sex. You might say that humans don't have a great sense of smell. True! Always walk in your bare feet in the woods. Fresh bear poop is much more obvious when it oozes between your toes.

Look at gambling. It's okay, we'll wait. Back? As you can see, if you really did look at gambling, your chance of winning is always less than the house's chance of winning. They see that they could loose, but that's scary and they don't look at it. Gamblers are blind to the statistic that the house will win. Gamblers play to win, even though it is guaranteed they will loose. The possibility that they will be rich, blinds them to the fact that they will soon be poor.

Doom statistics are the opposite of gambling statistics. Instead of getting rich, we see the excitement of disasters, peckish aliens, and slavering zombie tax accountants. When the chance of dying is a billion to one, we believe in the one.

Doomsayers love to quote the odds. You never hear a billion to one odds though. Disasters either happen or they don't, and that's fifty-fifty. An example of this is high school physics teacher, Walter Wagner. Walter believes that the Super Collider Project has a fifty-fifty chance of creating a black hole. So far he has been wrong. Since there is still a chance, he has a web site at http://www.lhcdefense.com/ dedicated to shutting down the collider.

The logic sounds flawed, but there is real pseudoscience behind it. For example, Walter's web site has a video that states that scientists are divided on this issue of death by science. In other words, if 99% of all scientists say the collider won't create a black hole and destroy the Earth, that's half of the scientists (or high school physics teachers verses the scientists at CERN). This is simple division and translates into half the scientist agreeing with him about the danger – apparently Walter talks to himself and agrees with what he says. So, two theories, and thus a fifty-fifty chance that we will need to get used to living in a black hole.

Yes, there is only a one-in-a-billion chance of creating a black hole with the Super Collider or having the Sun tear off our atmosphere or even aliens deciding to eat us for lunch. These things are either going to happen or not, and that's a fifty-fifty chance.

Fifty-fifty is a two way street. Say you avoid a fifty percent chance of death by snowpocalypse by moving to Costa Rica, you still have a fifty percent chance of catching an antibiotic resistant form of cooties. Your new Costa Rica neighbor caught the Cooties while searching for Inca gold. He was bitten by an infected sugar squirrel that escaped from a Nazi laboratory hidden deep in the Costa Rica rainforest. The Cootie virus was being weaponized by a mad Nazi scientist from an original sample collected from a snotty little 8 year old girl from Chicago who contracted the deadly Cooties virus in a school playground altercation with something icky on the monkey bars.

An asteroid is going to hit your house in the next five minutes, or it isn't. When we only look at the 'happen' and 'not-happen' probabilities, the odds boil down to happening or not. After an asteroid does hit your house, please let us know.

Insignificant probabilities are not scary because we are not born statisticians. There is either a tiger in the next room or there isn't. Have you checked? Tigers escape from zoos all the time. Tigers are very quiet just before they kill you. Did you not hear that!

Learn This Word

> ***Rumination*** *is a cool word. We think about it all the time. Rumination is the act of thinking about the same thing repeatedly, like thinking about rumination all the time. Rumination is a symptom of several mental illnesses too. Psychologists say rumination is the direct cause of depression, anxiety, and paranoia. We think about rumination all the time. Rumination is the same as a cow chewing its cud. Cud is the stuff a cow kind of pukes back up into its mouth from its stomach so that it can chew on it some more. We think about rumination all the time. So rumination has a double meaning for worriers. Puking up a bad thought and then chewing on it again. We think about rumination... Yuck!*

Very smart people are predicting that nuclear war will happen in 2012. Cool! There will also be a flash flood in Sheboygan and a herpes outbreak in Walla Walla, Washington. Doomsaying has better inflation than a five dollar balloon.

Is your insecticide from China? Expensive ingredients that would normally kill wiggly grubs inhabiting your garden will be replaced with something that makes the innocent pest to grow bigger than your house. The super sized grubs also have a monster appetite for tasty human pancreas. Say it with us: There is a fifty-fifty chance.

Aliens will land near the President Jefferson Memorial in Washington D.C., because it looks like their mommy. Once they find Jefferson's statue inside, the aliens will assume they are orphans and get sad. The sad aliens will kill everyone on Earth. There is a fifty-fifty chance that it could happen (the memorial is really a UFO and the building was built around it by the CIA). |

If wishes were fishes, we would have had the apocalypse a long time ago. Sadly, we are usually on the wrong side of our fifty percent. The good news is that we could be on the disaster side of doomsaying at any moment because there is still a fifty-fifty chance!

You might think this is cynical. You might also think this is wishful thinking. We like to look at it as cynical wish fulfillment.

There is always a prize in the cereal box. You might just need to wait until you have eaten a few bowls before you find it. Just know the prize might be there, even when it's one of those adult healthy cereals that doesn't have prizes. A plague-infected mouse is inside, munching on those healthy corn flakes. This little mouse is not our hero, you are! You will be known as patient zero for a plague that sends humanity back to the stone age. Is your nose feeling itchy? Do you feel the sniffles starting? There is always a fifty-fifty chance.

Plug-in hybrids are becoming popular! All that pollution will disappear too fast for Mother Nature to compensate. Imagine the world freezing or burning to a crisp from the imbalance. Hey, that's two things that could happen, so it is better than fifty-fifty.

Statistics eliminates worry too. When it's a fifty percent chance of an apocalyptic disaster, we can't stop worrying and start running.

Experiment: Doom Time

Study the doom from your favorite doomsayers and choose a part of their doom and act it out. Don't do it for real, just make it look real. For example, paint a horse green and ride around spraying people with simulated disease. We recommend a Super Soaker filled with lime Jell-O. Emulate your favorite scientific doomsayers by simulating an asteroid strike by throwing rocks into the air when nobody is looking (small rocks, please).

Before you are grounded or imprisoned, conduct your experiments in several places like churches, the mall, and school.

Questions

- ✓ How long was it before the police arrived?
- ✓ Were people surprised, or did they just run away screaming in terror?
- ✓ Which location had the nest reaction?
- ✓ How are your sessions with your psychologist? Are you taking any anti-psychotics yet?

You Might Want To Know

There are times when formatting a book that you come to the end of a chapter with and uncomfortable amount of whitespace. This is one of those times. You might wonder why whitespace is uncomfortable. As authors, we strive for the perfect amount of whitespace for dear readers like yourself. You are dear! We need just enough blank space for you to have a tiny moment of reflection about what you just read. Too much and creativity kicks in and we are in big trouble. A reader might discover a new theory that allows humans to create faster than light travel. Sounds good at first, but then we'll meet an alien race that will enslave us. That would be bad. That's why looking at whitespace gives us the willies.

Good reader, we can see your thoughts and they say, "But I'm not a theoretical physicist. I don't even like Star Trek!" Whitespace can cause a burst of neural activity triggering you to go for a walk, watch Fox News, or vote Republican.

Oh dear, still more whitespace. A four year old could use this space to draw a bug with a crayon. We need to come up with something quick! How about pirates? Everybody likes pirates, especially Atheists for some reason. Why is that? First they start imagining teapots in orbit, then praying to the flying spaghetti monster, then carnally sailing the high seas with pirates. How does an eye patch and a parrot that's peckish for a cracker make you an Atheist? We don't understand.

Uh, oh. Too much, now we have another page and more white space to fill in before the next chapter.

Dam – as in the Hoover dam or rather as structure to hold back the damn water from drowning the damn people, not the curse word, which is spelled differently – got to go to the restroom! We'll be right back, so just move quickly on to the next chapter and skip all this wondrous whitespace. Put down that crayon and start reading the next chapter, please.

Not the First Time

This is not the first time the world has ended. We have many legends, religions teachings and scholarly books from scientists with tales of extinctions, ice ages, asteroids, wraths of gods, and even planetary collisions. These older apocalyptic events are important because they represent the toe of belief that keeps the door of apocalypse open.

The bad news is that not one of these apocalyptic events destroyed the entire[43] world. The wicked infidels of Noah were drowned, but Noah's family and select wildlife survived. Dinosaurs were destroyed while the faithful (mammals) are spared destruction.

For gods, this is "shock and awe" on their resume. It isn't necessarily about killing the wicked, but proving that you hate the wicked enough to do something about the problem. This destruction is also a warning that says you might do it again in the future. How can you believe a god will destroy the world unless there are a few examples?

The following tales are the documented tales, curriculum vitae, demos, and proof of god's and/or nature's world ending powers.

The Death of the Dinosaurs

Why are dinosaurs extinct? Nobody is exactly sure why because there are no dinosaurs to ask. We only assume some sort of dinopocalypse. The theories include climate change, evolution, huge asteroids, cosmic rays, explosive diarrhea, ice ages, or they were depressed and committed suicide before they could invent Prozac. No matter how Barney met his end, dinosaurs prove that no matter how big you are, you can be wiped off the face of the Earth – or be genetically converted to chickens.

No gods specifically take credit for the dinosaur extinction. A god could be responsible, but they are keeping quiet. Perhaps

[43] Except maybe the Moon hitting the Earth which sort of qualifies as remaking of the entire Earth.

their silence is to keep kids from finding out that a god destroyed the dinosaurs? It seems like good public relations. Would you worship a god that killed Barney the Dinosaur?

Our favorite cause of the dinopocalypse is that dinosaurs were drowned during Noah's flood. The theory is that Noah simply forgot and the dinos died along with the wicked. This theory is all wet, but a Christian thought up the theory so all Christians must believe it is true.

Here at Boys Books, we definitely believe in dinosaurs. We've seen the stone cold proof of dinosaurs **coprolite**![44]

Learn This Word

> **Coprolite**: Fossilized dinosaur poo is called coprolite. *Looks like poop, but has been fossilized. We've stepped in fossilized dinosaur poop, so we know its real. Luckily fossilized poop is easier to scrape off your shoes.*

A small group of Christians believe in dinosaurs. Some paleontologists even believe that Christians exist, although the paleontologists just have faith that Christians exist, not hard proof. Between the two groups you can rub a few fossils together and agree that dinosaurs don't exist anymore.

Scientists think we now live with a T-Rex descendant: the chicken. The theory is that chickens are descendants of dinosaurs. Through genetic evolution these thunder lizards evolved into the little processed nuggets in your happy meal.

The reason that dinos are now chickens is easily explained by evolution. If you don't believe in evolution, an unnamed god could have diddled with their DNA looking for a better omelet. Wipe out the T-Rex with its fowl replacement! Either way, somebody clucked up the dinosaurs. A pun most fowl!

A few scientists have been trying to reverse the genetic evolution of chickens to re-create dinosaurs. This would prove that chickens are really cool dinosaurs. We will also prove that Barney the dinosaur really tastes like chicken. Imagine the world's largest bucket of T-Rex fried chicken. Sort of puts a big

[44] http://en.wikipedia.org/wiki/Coprolite

hole in the theory that dinosaurs were destroyed when you create a fifteen foot McNugget.

Because dinosaurs were wiped out, along with the other victims of mass extinctions, we must assume a disaster of such magnitude will happen again. This also proves that life goes on and that you can't really kill off everything.

Noah's Flood

Noah's flood was a wet and wild Old Testament apocalypse. It was close enough to an end-times scenario for government work because only Noah's family and the appropriately paired animals survived and the wicked people were drowned.

One of God's greatest supernatural powers is delegation. God picks one of his believers to do all the work. Be it preaching, telling the world the end is near, or building an ark, God doesn't do the dirty work. God doesn't believe in backup plans or mass marketing. One quick meeting with a human is enough, thank you very much.

The neighbors were curious about all the hammering and stopped by to see what all the fuss was about. Noah told them about the coming flood and how it was all their fault for being wicked. Everyone laughed. Talking to God and building boats in the desert is knee-slapping funny.

Imagine Noah explaining this to his therapist. The large pet collection was okay, but the boating in the desert requires Prozac.

Sin and debauchery seems to cloud the mind and makes the devout Jew seem a little wacko. You would think that God would give Noah the power to convert the wicked rather than sailing skills. No, God doesn't play that game. Instead God purposefully makes his followers seem crazy so the sinners seem even more evil for laughing at the mentally deficient.

Using a flood, God is creating a clean slate to start over, wicked free. God is still paying the price for planting a tree of knowledge within arms reach of Adam and Eve. Why not cover up a few mistakes and invent boating at the same time?

God specified the size of the boat. No room for cool creatures like unicorns or dinosaurs (not one creature from the Triassic,

Jurassic Cretaceous, or the Ice Age. Just our current zoo of 30 to 50 million fresh water fish, fowl, carnivores, herbivores, spiders beetles, ants, mosquitos, flies, humans and other nasty creatures. No room for T-Rex, Saber Tooth Tiger and other creatures of delight. Imagine the children of Noah that had to settle for playing with plastic versions of these creatures like we do today. The sailing holiday wan't very fun.

You Might Want to Know

> *God made the second worst decision in the whole Bible by letting Noah and his family onto the Arc. Imagine how many fewer problems God would have with the wicked if He had simply ended humanity right then and there. Perhaps start over with monkeys?*

As the water started to rise, there didn't seem to be a "now I understand" clause for wicked folks to repent. When you are up to your neck in water and the only boat is owned by the only religious fellow in town, you kind of get the idea that Noah may have really heard Jehovah. Noah had not planned on the last minute believers. The space was already occupied by dozens of types of bears, crocodiles, and every form of poison snake. No space for the newly converted wicked as the water started to rise. Too bad. So sad.

Belief is worthless in the face of evidence. When the end comes, you are either a believer or you are not. Hedge your bets now and be religious before the sky catches fire. God isn't going to make an exception for a few new converts. It's too much fun for God to say, "I told you so!"

Jesus gave Noah an honorable mention in the Book of Matthew. We have the following quote, which is Jesus talking about the end-times and his return. Sort of odd that he is talking about his own Second Coming and the end of the world, but here it is:

> *"No one knows about that day or hour, not even the angels in heaven, nor the Son, but only the Father. As it was in the days of Noah, so it will be at the coming of the Son of Man. For in the days before the flood, people were eating and drinking, marrying and giving in*

> *marriage, up to the day Noah entered the ark; and they knew nothing about what would happen until the flood came and took them all away."*

The reason for Jesus mentioning Noah is to put across a couple of key ideas: First, the exact time and date of the apocalypse is unknowable. If you are not ready now, there is no makeup test and no boat to save you. Second, you can't convert at the last minute. Nobody believed the flood until they were already drowning and it is hard to pray to God for forgiveness when your lungs are full of holy water.

The Jesus quote also adds a couple pieces of new information not in the Old Testament. All those people were drowned because they were eating, drinking, and marrying. Holy smokes! God hates eating, drinking, and marrying!

We didn't learn that in Sunday school, did you? Guess we are all going to Hell. See you there!

At the end of Noah's tale, God says that the rainbow is a reminder that God will never destroy the Earth or even trouble mankind with a flood again. God even says to himself:

> *"I will never again curse the ground on account of man, for the intent of man's heart is evil from his youth; and I will never again destroy every living thing, as I have done."*

You might think that God was fibbing, given all the nasty smiting that follows in the Old and New Testament. All the destruction and all that will come, makes this a very false promise. There's more destruction to come with hurricanes, tornadoes, earthquakes, plagues, and flooding that we collectively call acts of God. Yep, a promise is. Promise.

This proves that God created man in his own image. The proof is that God had fingers to cross behind His back to invalidate any promise. Yep, God is just like us.

Sodom and Gomorrah

Sodom and Gomorrah were two ancient cities near the Dead Sea. God destroyed these cities for being full of wicked people. This occurred after Noah, but before the events of Revelation.

It's a diet portion of apocalyptic meat between two whole wheat world enders (with mustard, hold the mayo).

Debauchery at the time was concentrated only in these two cities and their suburbs. Unlike Noah's flood or even Armageddon, Sodom and Gomorrah was a sort of end-of-the-world surgical strike. Kind of like the LASER-guided missile of God.

Be careful about hanging out in the red light district, you might meet God or one of his angelic enforcers in a dark alley. God hates debauchery! The Lord loves smiting the adult entertainment district.

God tells Abraham that he is about to destroy these wicked places. Abraham pleads with God that if he can find any good people in these towns, then could God spare these innocents by not destroying everything? Abraham starts at fifty good men and worked God down to ten. This is the first Biblical account of haggling and began the Jewish tradition of getting a good deal. God walked away at ten because he gets innocents at a wholesale price.

Two angels were sent to look for the ten good men. They were headed in that direction anyway. The angels needed to save Lot, one of Abraham's nephews, who made a bad real estate investment by moving to Sodom.

Why send angels? Couldn't Abraham go to find the good men of the town? We don't trust angels. They are always up to no good. Satan was an angel, remember? Do you think there was just one bad apple? We're not even sure they have any math skills.

The next part of the tale, the rescue of Lot by the angels, sounds like a naughty joke told by our uncle Jack. Lot, being ever helpful, invites the angels to his house for dinner. The angels are very popular and a mob forms to — there is no easy way to say this — copulate from behind with the angels.

A good host shouldn't let their house guests get gang raped. To right this wrong, Mr. Lot, offers up his virgin daughters to be gang-raped in exchange for an angel-buggering moratorium. That's knee-slapping hilarious! You can't make this up. Here's the quote: from Genesis 19:5

> *They (the mob) called to Lot, "Where are the men (the angels) who came to you tonight? Bring them out to us so that we can have sex with them."*
>
> *Lot went outside to meet them and shut the door behind him and said, "No, my friends. Don't do this wicked thing. Look, I have two daughters who have never slept with a man. Let me bring them out to you, and you can do what you like with them."*

Unfortunately for Lot, the mob isn't interested in virgin girls. The crowd just doesn't swing that way. They do swing toward Lot and offer to party with him instead. The angels decide that this isn't good so they strike the mob blind. So, no debauchery and the people go blind. We wonder if their palms got harry too.

The angels are so grateful for Lot's hospitality, they offer to save his future sons-in-laws too. Lot invites the his daughters boyfriends to the house and they are told that God would be destroying the wicked cities and that they have a free ride out of town. The men laugh at Lot, thinking it was a really good joke. Offering up your little virgin daughters to gang rape and being a doomsayer, gives Lot the reputation as a comedian and practical joker. After a good belly laugh, the future husbands went home and were later destroyed with the rest of the town.

Are you starting respect Lot a little less? We drew lots to tell that pun, but none of us are artists. Lottery? Yes, they are bad puns. Quantity over quality! We have a lot more puns, as this is our *lot* in life.

We can hear you asking, "What about the future son-in-laws, weren't they innocent?" Why did they burn with the rest? They didn't believe the doomsaying of Lot, which means they didn't believe the angels, which means they don't take God's warnings seriously. They didn't appreciate Lot throwing their future wives to the crowd for carnal enjoyment, therefor they disapproved of being a good host, which is also bad. Add it all up and they must be wicked and perhaps Devil worshipers. Any shade of gray looks black to God. Innocents killed in Sodom. Do the math.

Curiosity is just as bad as debauchery. The angels warn the family to not watch the city's destruction. God's power shouldn't be witnessed (God didn't want witnesses that could turn him over to the cops).

Most people would rather be ignorant than a big pile of kosher salt. Lot's wife was a curious kitty and took a quick peek. The result is that she is turned into a pillar of salt. We sprinkle Mrs Lot on our French fries.

Lot's story does not end there! After the cities are destroyed, Lot and his daughters believed the whole world was destroyed. Apparently the angels weren't too clear about destroying a few towns. That's right, they thought they were the last three humans alive and the last man on Earth is dad! Lot's daughters decided to be fruitful and repopulate the world with their dad's drunken spermatozoa.

Oddly the omnipresent God didn't see this coming. The angels never hinted that just over the hill the rest of the world was doing fine. No warning voice of God, burning bushes, or stone tablets.

Let's summarize the destruction of Sodom and Gomorrah: Wickedness is bad, people love angels in inappropriate ways, salt is bad for you, and incest is okay as long as you keep it in the family.

Other Supernatural Ends

Egyptians, Greeks and other civilizations have gods that have destroyed their world in the past. They coincidentally follow the same patterns of deities getting mad at mankind and doing something really horrible. Some stories are like Noah where a few survive, and others hit the Earth's reset button.

Why is it that some god is always messing with us? Somehow things are just not perfect, too perfect, or we are a bit too sinful or too arrogant. The supernatural being's only response seems to be utter destruction.

Intelligent design is definitely not a good theory. Gods aren't that intelligent! No god seems omnipotent or smart enough to get the design right. The Biblical God created a mate for Adam with the brains of a BBQ rib that was gullible enough to believe the lies of a serpent.

Some of Adam's brains were in his ribs because he fell for Eve's coaxing at the dinner table. God, like any narcissist covering up their mistakes, blames Adam and Eve rather than himself for a poor design. Had God made Adam and Eve allergic to apples and deaf to serpents, we'd still be running naked through Eden.

All gods seem to make huge mistakes and are always disappointed with their creations. The New World gods of the Aztecs and Mayans used dodgy material like wood or clay. Each creation worse than the next and erased from the world each time.

Evolution apparently sucks too. Problem is that gods are too impatient to wait for evolution to work. Evolution selects for intelligence which screws things up for most gods by allowing us to dispel belief in the face of cold hard facts. Gods don't like facts! The only way to get rid of facts is to destroy them.

Don't forget nature. We could be the best god lovers and the world will get flattened by an asteroid. It doesn't matter what your religion is when the sun puts off enough radiation to bury us in fifty feet of microwave popcorn.

The moral of the story? There isn't one. Put a smile on your face and stop moping.

Experiment: Repeat Performance

Study the end-of-the-world myths and legends. Find a particularly juicy end and then give it a modern twist. Write up a summary and if you are artistic, draw up some scary pictures. Make sure you back up your story by saying you had a vision or you found a golden book. Post your vision on Facebook.

For extra credit, take out a full page ad in the local newspaper announcing that the world will end in the manner you have discovered.

Questions

- ✓ How long was it before the History Channel called you to star in a special about your vision?
- ✓ From the Facebook messages, compare the number of responses of people that believe in a vengeful god and those that don't. Are you surprised by these numbers?
- ✓ If you advertised, did the newspaper have any questions about your beliefs, or did they just take your money?

Surviving Apocalypse

There are many ways civilization can survive most end of the world scenarios. Even if the world is ultimately destroyed, we need to survive long enough to see the show. Think of the joy of representing the last bit of humanity on Earth.

Biological Weapons

Biological weapons kill us with biology. No messy explosions or radiation, just a natural death available from any health food store. Biological weapons reduce the cost of making weapons because you grow them instead. Biological weapons include bacteria, viruses, fungi, or biological toxins from biological sources.

Biologicals are the creative alternative to traditional weapons. Traditional weapons have a small list side effects: explosion, fire, and you might glow in the dark before your hair falls out. We need more options! You can die instantly, slowly, from bleeding out every poor, be sterilized so you can't reproduce, go crazy, get covered in lovely spots or ugly bumps, and have random body parts that fall off.

A key advantage of biologicals is that there are far more possibilities than there are methods to defend ourselves. How do you plan for an itch in an inappropriate place and a disease that rots your brain?

There are different timelines from a slow death from dementia to a quick and embarrassing death from projectile diarrhea. Either you are dead faster than you can find a cure or the thing that kills us has been killing us for years before we realized what happened. An example of slow death is diabetes. A Communist scientist invented the perfect poison; the joy that is fast food. They did it so long ago that even they forgot about how poisonous and addictive that stuff is. Makes sense now, right?

First up on our list of deadly biologicals: Toxins! You may not catch a cold, just eat food or breathe the air full of poison created by mother nature. A great toxin is botulism which is the result of little microscopic creatures pooping poison. Botulism kills by paralyzing you, but you'll look younger because it also reduces wrinkles.

The second type of bio weapon is the viruses. Not the common cold, we are talking about the nasty stuff like the plague, ebola, or smallpox. A virus bio weapon is easily created in a laboratory or a badly maintained refrigerator with unlabeled Tupperware containers.

Finally, fungi. That's right, mushrooms are biological weapons! We are not talking portabella, but things like Cryptococcus gattii which kills by setting up a mushroom farm in your lungs. Other branches of the fungi family tree can create all sorts of nasty toxins from poisons to hallucinogenics to athlete's foot. Imagine a world where everyone thinks they see pink ponies and has itchy, smelly feet!

Biological weapons are the latest plaything for your up-and-coming terrorist. Biologicals are more stylish than the explosive vests, shoe bombs, and less embarrassing than underwear bombs. Terrorists are fashion conscious and the bulky bomb vest isn't flattering and underwear bombs make your butt look big. Biologicals let you wear the latest fall fashions.

There is a slight problem with biologicals like viruses.Though viruses are small, it's easier to spot the biological terrorists. Just look for someone with a runny nose that touches doorknobs a lot.

Surviving Biological Weapons

Stay away from people, don't open your mail (pesky anthrax, the spore, not the heavy metal band), use credit cards instead of paper money, and stay upwind of tall buildings. You may not be safe, but you'll feel safer.

People are the biggest problem. Once they figure out they are doomed, they start roaming the streets, sneezing and then touching door knobs.

Living in a cave like a hermit is your best defense. Caves also don't have doors, so no door knobs.

Canned soup is always good for when you are sick, but there are other uses. Soup cans make great weapons to throw at infected neighbors. If you miss, that's ok because the target will assume you are being polite and will go away to have a soup dinner.

One remedy for dust-sized particles of spores like anthrax is to use Lemon Pledge and a Swifter. Don't use Duct Tape to seal your home. Germs, Anthrax and Cooties stick like crazy to Duct Tape!

Don't do any of these things unless CNN is broadcasting the news with limited commercial interruption 24 hours a day. There could be a conspiracy. You need to take defensive steps now! We suggest you start taking your anti-psychotics again – Being medicated is your best defense!

Learn This Word

> ***Terrorist:*** *Terrorism is a type of debate. In a debate, each side has a counter position that they argue. Each side in the debate uses logic and persuasion to win. In an example of such a debate, the terrorist begins his logical and scholarly argument by blowing you both up. The terrorist goes to Heaven and you go to his version of Hell. The terrorist always wins the first round of a debate.*

Muslim Terrorists

We are sorry, we need to talk about the *Muslim Terrorists*. Like a bandaid, let's rip it off quick. Yes, *Terroristic Muslims* can destroy the world.

We should apologize in advance to our many good friends who are Muslim. We have been to a mosque, on Meet Your Muslim Neighbor Night, and loved the food. Sadly, Muslims have a little history of attacks and suicide bombers despite scrumptious the Middle Eastern cuisine.

Muslim Terrorists are an obvious choice to be implicated in the end of the world. Why? Do we have to spell it out for you? Ask your dad for an advance on your allowance so you can afford to buy a clue. Quite simply, Muslims need to eradicate the infidels.[45]

You Might Want to Know

> *We capitalize and italicize Muslim Terrorist to set these folks apart from your common Muslim. We also wish to acknowledge that we have yet to be threatened in any way by the often confused Muslin Terrorist and their religious cause of lightweight cotton cloth.*

Who are infidels? Anyone that is not a specific part of their sect of Muslim belief. Everyone else is a target. The Koran does not pull punches when it talks about killing infidels. Neighbors, friends, family members, and even children are classified as infidels.

When Muslim kills an infidel, they are usually killing innocents too. Their defense is that the good Muslims will go to Heaven. When a *Muslim Terrorist* triggers a biological weapon, no more cute little puppies, even Muslim puppies. The whole world could be destroyed as long as one infidel is inconvenienced and the terrorist's conscious is clear (also too busy with virgins to care).

The Muslim end, as described in the Koran, is a rather simple affair with shaking of the world, darkening of the sky, and burning of the ocean. Basic stuff that sorts out the believers from the unenlightened and them the world ends. You might say, "Why would *Muslim Terrorists* destroy the world with wars, bombs, or disease? None of those look like what is written in the Koran." The answer is simple, like all religions, *Muslim Terrorists* don't really read their own book too closely.

You may have heard that Muslims generally condemn terrorists and that the Koran does not condone that sort of thing. Unfortunately *Muslim Terrorists* believe such beliefs are blasphemy and will kill these Muslims infidels. Isn't religion fun!

---

45 http://en.wikipedia.org/wiki/Infidel

You Might Want to Know

There are no known cases of an arsonist who was not also a virgin. Of course we are referring to your standard vanilla arsonists — not mob arsonists, who do such things for money or advancement. Apparently the flames of passion are a good sublimation for the more literal flames of an arsonist. Did you know most terrorists are also virgins? We see a pattern.

Surviving Muslim Terrorists

Like most religions with an end of the world, the faithful are in a hurry to get to the end. They see wicked infidels on every corner.

Muslim Terrorists are not hard to spot. Just look for nerdy teenagers. Teenagers are usually sexually frustrated virgins. Their recruiters hook them with a promise of girls in the afterlife and a cure for acne and that's all the convincing they need to strap on a vest of explosive.

Christians caught in the Muslim's final reckoning will be able to plead brainwashing. The Koran mentions Jesus over thirty times, so they know who he is and that the Christians have got it all wrong. Your defense: You were misinformed by your Christian upbringing and Mohammed, blessed be his name (don't forget that), will let you cop a plea.

Fundamentalist Christians

Fundamentalist Christians are angry and in a hurry to end the world. They are worse than *Muslim Terrorists* because they don't have to be frustrated teens, though it helps. All they expect is that their actions will put them in Heaven, a little closer to God.

Oh, and that all their enemies get what's coming to them. The key word for fundamentalists is always "revenge."

Learn This Word

Fundamentalist: *Remember an earlier vocabulary word,* ***terrorist****? A fundamentalist*

> *is like a terrorist. Fundamentalists believe whatever they want, but usually there is a group of fundamentalists called a congregation or a mega-church who all believe whatever their leaders tell them to believe. In the debate, you argue for science and freedom of thought. The fundamentalist says you are going to Hell for your sins and ends the debate by marching out of the auditorium. Fundamentalists don't win many arguments but because they believe so hard in whatever they want, they also believe they always win.*

The Book of Revelation promotes fundamentalism because there is and army that is supposed to fight for God. These are the Christian soldiers. Oddly there is no mention of country bumpkins, country music, or pickup trucks. As close as you get is the Four Cowboys of the Apocalypse.

Fundamentalists are willing to destroy the world because of Sunday School. Look at all the nasty violence in the Bible: Noah, Sodom and Gomorra, Battle of Jericho, David and Goliath, and of course the killing of Philistines. There are even battles at Meggido, which is of course the same place as Armageddon.

Fundamentalists stand out in the crowd because they are always trying to convert the crowd to their religion. Fundamentalists dangerous because almost nobody but a few wackos join their church. They slowly go mad because they think most of the world is against them. Easier to end the world early and they get to say, "I told you so!"

Fundamentalists are not born, they are born again. This explains why they are generally against abortion because it can happen at any age.

Before they became fundamentalists, these people were lost, had no hope, no friends, ostracized from family, and probably on more than their fair share of drugs and alcohol. Down on their luck, looking up from the gutter they find themselves in, they are easy converts. If you were depressed, you'd believe almost anything to make your life better too. Once converted, these fundamentalists try to convert new members by looking for more hopeless people ready to believe anything that could change their sad lives. Here is and average conversation with a potential convert:

> ***Fundamentalist:*** *Hi, did you know Jesus died for your sins? He is going to come back soon and kill everyone that doesn't believe in him. I'll talk with you for five minutes so you'll be a believer too.*
>
> ***Convert:*** *Have you been a practicing fundamentalist all your life?*
>
> ***Fundamentalist:*** *No, just recently.*
>
> ***Convert:*** *When you became a fundamentalist had you been poor, stressed out, on drugs, out of work, or had a loved one recently die?*
>
> ***Fundamentalist:*** *Yes, how do you know that?*
>
> ***Convert:*** *Before you became a fundamentalist, were you depressed? Would you believe anything that provided a shred of hope?*
>
> ***Fundamentalist:*** *Ah, yes. I guess I did. I'm starting to feel a little dirty, please stop.*
>
> ***Convert:*** *Did you know that the Nazi Party came into power when Germany was in a depression, and millions were hungry and without jobs? Germans would have believed anyone with a shred of hope, and followed them to the ends of the Earth (including killing Jews and Gypsies?).*
>
> ***Fundamentalist:*** *Oh. Ah, I see what you mean. I need to go home... Sorry to have bothered you.*
>
> *A fundamentalist will end this conversation by yelling repeatedly, "You are going to Hell!"*

Many conversations go like this because there aren't that many hopeless people. Look around, there are not that many people ready for conversion. Eventually fundamentalists realize that it is easier to destroy the world than go knocking on doors.

Surviving Fundamentalist Terrorists

Your best defense is to simply join the party. These guys sweat good-old-boy politics. Join the fundamentalists and you will be part of God's army. The food is good and you will learn to shoot automatic weapons.

Barring becoming a card-carrying member of the Religious Right, you can always follow their lead and invest in abandoned Minuteman missile silo.

Another way to survive is to convert fundamentalists to your religion. Just kidding. Once they become fundamentalists you can't get them to change because fundamentalism causes brain damage. The logic centers of the brain have been destroyed from sitting in church too long waiting for someone to get saved — why do they always try to save people 'at' church? The best thing to do is get them hooked on something crazier and a little more harmless, like watching hoarding documentaries on The Learning Channel.

Financed Apocalypse

Imagine pulling out your checkbook to finance the apocalypse. Your checking account is divine intervention with overdraft protection. This is another apocalypse enabled by the Fundamentalist Christians. They're using their wealth to pull the plug on the world within their lifetimes and are spending millions of dollars to be sure.

Why would fundamentalist Christians write checks to help God destroy the world? Is this a biblical tax shelter? Will the end times send the tax man to Hell? No, the money is an insurance premium to ensure a prime spot in Heaven!

Buying your way into Heaven has been happening ever since money was first minted. Why money is mint flavored is a mystery, but purchasing salvation through bribery is a universal truth. You can bribe a man, so if a god created man in his image, you can bribe a god. We love logic!

Sacrifice is a good example of heavenly bribery before we had credit cards. Sacrifice a chicken and your god comes to dinner. Ever notice that most holy men are overweight? Gods worry about their **own** weight and let the local holly men eat the sacrificial leftovers.

The rich Christian's shopping list includes blowing up a building in Jerusalem. Doesn't sound like the end of the world, but it's an important building. The building is the mosque at the

Dome of the Rock. The Christian God doesn't like this building because nobody living there likes Him. They are not bad neighbors. They mow their lawn and their dog doesn't bark until 3:00 a.m., but they aren't good Christians.

One of the many signs of the Christian apocalypse is a new synagogue built at the Dome of the Rock. The Ark of the Covenant was first stored at this lovely real estate location (not where Indiana Jones put it). The Romans evicted the Jews and destroyed the temple when God didn't pay rent. The Muslims are just squatters.

The devout Christian investor's portfolio includes cattle genetics, blue dyes, and soldiers of fortune. All are required to fulfill prophecy. Destroy the temple at the Dome of the Rock, check. Genetically create a perfectly red heifer, check. A blue dye to dress up the Rabbi, check. All tax deductible!

You Might Want to Know

> *The Dome of the Rock is next to the temples of Paper and Scissors. This explains why wars fought between the three religions seem so silly.*

Why would Christians want to help Jews build a synagog? Seems strange given that Christians think Jews are missing the point of the whole Jesus episode. The loophole is in the Little Apocalypse in the book of Mark. Jesus, a nice Jewish boy, predicted the Romans would be punished for beating up the Israelites and destroying their best synagog. The revenge would be followed by a Jewish savior (Jesus is of course talking about himself and his travel plans in the third person).

You Might Want to Know

> *A funny thing happened on the way to the apocalypse. The Muslims kicked the Romans out of Jerusalem and built the Dome of the Rock. This is hilarious because Muslims are really a sect of Judaism 'and' Christianity. They just believe that Mohamed was Jesus and Jesus was just Jesus. This means that a Jewish temple was built where it should have been as predicted by Jesus. During the Crusades the*

> *Dome of the Rock was turned into a Christian church, but that too was destroyed. After the six-day war in 1967 a rabbi made the Dome of the Rock a Synagog for a few hours. So many signs, so little prophetic follow through.*

Fundamentalists are also funding war, famine, disease, and plain nastiness. Good times are bad when you are a Fundamentalist Christian. Where there is general nastiness, there are signs of the apocalypse.

These filthy rich, religious, fanatic, zealots are buying brownie points and box seats for the final battle between good and evil. We've met a few of these guys and they are nuttier than a nut factory. One moment they are shaking hands on a million dollar deal, and the next they are talking about how pleasant it will be when the world ends and all those nasty non-Christians heathens and Democrats are sent to Hell. No more competition and they win every election in the afterlife.

Surviving the Financed Apocalypse

Get rich. Really, it's that easy! The only way to fight is by investing in the anti-signs.

Take red heifers as an example. Christians are investing in a perfectly red cow for sacrifice at the new synagog in Jerusalem. Why not counter this by buying up all the farms and genetic research companies. Better yet, create a genetically better cow that is small, pink and tastes like butter.

Counter the financial apocalypse with tax incentives. Run for congress and tax red heifers. Give bunny farms a huge tax break. To get the crazy doomers to do the same, start a rumor that Jesus will come back if every child gets a bunny for Easter. Hop to it!

The rich prefer a good deal, so raise the price of doing doom. Hire mercenaries at a premium rate. This inflates in the cost of private wars. Give the mercenaries jobs guarding bunny farms.

Evil Scientists

Why would a scientist be evil? The biggest reason is the postdoctoral process. This is a process where people with enormously silly amounts of education and intelligence are forced to work for a narcissistic professor to prove to the world they are smart, but dumb enough to work for a narcissistic professor.

This postdoctoral process is similar to indentured slavery except that slaves are treated much better. There is verbal abuse, mean spirited pranks, and a cast system worse than India's. Our friend, Mr Revenge (or Doctor Revenge in this case), leads these scientists to search for retribution and a permanent solution to their torment by ending the world.

Republicans believe all scientists are evil. Scientists don't believe in creationism, gods, miracles, intelligent design, or poisoning the Earth in the name of profit. Republicans believe in all of these things, so are suspicious of the motives of those that don't. Anyone that does not believe in what you believe, must be evil, right?

Learn this Word

> ***Cast System***: *A cast system is best described with the cast of Gilligan's Island. Gilligan is at the bottom because he is poor and had the lowly job of first mate. Thurston Howell the 3rd was at the top because he was born rich. Cast systems are based on birth, but also rank. The upper cast (or upper crust, if you are a rich baker) abuses the lower class physically and verbally. For example, the Skipper is always whacking Gilligan with his hat. Many post doctoral candidates have a status between nematodes and Physarum (a rather intelligent slime-mold that is similar to a Gilligan).*

Surviving the Evil Scientist

Spotting an evil scientist is the first step. Luckily the evil scientist is easy to spot, especially when you work in the fast food industry. Look for someone with thick glasses and a lab coat that doesn't understand your no substitution policy. Please be careful and be very friendly. All it will take is mayonnaise instead of mustard and they will push the button that will end the world.

Once you have identified the evil scientist, introduce him – evil scientists are always guys – to your friend Karen. Curing the evil scientist of his virginity usually works. If this fails (Karen isn't as caring as we thought), become his lab assistant and carefully foil his plans to end the world.

Spoiling an evil scientist's plans are surprisingly easy. All scientists need supplies and your job is to disrupt the supplies without the scientist figuring it out. It just takes little things like calling in an anonymous report to the authorities that hazardous chemicals or equipment is being mishandled. Suddenly there are government inspectors hovering around the lab and big fines piling up.

Buying supplies is also easy to disrupt. Just share the scientist's credit card and bank numbers with Facebook. Soon there won't be any money and the evil scientist is spending endless hours talking to tech support in Creditcardistan.

When the business of evil is cash based, you can fix that too. Get some florescent ink and write the scientist's plans on the bills. Denominations like $50 and $100 are usually checked at the bank under florescent lights for authentication. This will get the authorities interested quickly. If the suppliers are bad guys too and testing for authentic bills, write bad things about them and howe the scientist plans to kill them in an especially painful way.

If you can't disrupt supply or money, time for a little sabotage. Sand in the gears of the killer robots, sugar in the jet fuel of the drones, and itching powder in the hazmat suits. Anything you can do to slow down progress. Our favorite is food coloring other ingredients (we love the stinky stuff in fly traps that smells like something dead) in the biological experiments. Imagine an evil scientist attempting to create an invisible poison gas and having it come out hot pink and smelling like roadkill.

You Might Want to Know

Itching powder has been used since ancient times as a practical joke. The simplest itching powder is made from ground rose hips. Any product that contains the fine hairs found inside rose hips can be used or you can grow them in your end of the world hydroponic garden.

Super Criminals

Super criminals are fun. They have all the power of an evil scientist with an evil laugh. Mwaahaahaa!!!

Super criminals will hold the world hostage with threats of cataclysm in exchange for cash and prizes. Their threats include big bombs, super-diseases, and great toys like nipple lasers. If we don't pay, the world will end.

Super criminals don't really want to end the world, just threaten it for power and money. Why end the world when you're rich? Then why would we say super criminals can end the world? The world ends because someone accidentally leans on the wrong button. There's always a button you shouldn't push.

Surviving Super Criminals

The best way to survive is to be henchman. Even though their ultimate goal is money, they like to feel rich and safe while they do. That means surrounding yourself with henchmen, hench-women (henches) and opulence where they are safe from their own weapons is characteristic.

Opt out of the drug experiments unless you like pressing buttons and want a prehensile tail. As an accomplice, your compensation package includes three meals a day and accommodations at end-of-the-world survival colony. As an extra benefit, there are beautiful women to help repopulate the world, though you are not allowed talk to them–you are too young anyway and it is the best way to avoid a nasty case of cooties.

The super criminal will have a secret island with dozens of beautiful women. If you sell skimpy bikinis and get a large order from a private island with a fake volcano, give us a call. We need to call Mr Bond right away.

Super Volcanoes

Imagine a super volcano that could end all life. The lava lamp of doom. Super volcanoes have already caused large extinctions, luckily in our distant past. There's even evidence that various dinosaurs were wiped out by the Earth's belching. Ancient super volcanos explain why Caesar Millan is know as the Dog Whisperer and not Dinosaur Yeller.

Super volcanoes are not just a single volcano, they are a group of volcanoes going off all at once. There are large weak spots in the Earth's crust, like Yellowstone where thirty square miles could blow up. Black holes, asteroids, planets aligning or a god could command the Earth to crack open too. All have the same result: a venti cup of lava.

Doomsayer visions include earthquakes, fire, endless night, and other phenomena that could be confused with a super volcano. Scientists, usually agnostic or atheists, rationalize such ravings of doomsayers as super volcanos. Much easier to believe in vulcanism rather than an angry god called Vulcan (the Greek version, not Trek). Of course by doing this rationalization, these scientists are admitting that doomsayers are predicting the future.

Beyond supernatural or natural influences for volcanoes, the Earth could crack open because of the excess weight of the junk we have collected over the years that now chokes our closets and garages. Could the combined weight of your grandmother's fifty years of *National Geographic* magazines be too much for the Earth's crust to bear?

Learn This Word

> ***Rationalization**: Rationalization efficiently replace nonsense with better nonsense. All you need to do is replace the laws of cause and effect with imagination. We rationalize because it takes too much time and money to hire a scientist to do our thinking.*

Super Volcano Warning Signs

The good thing about volcanoes is that they are relatively slow about getting on with their business. Look at Mount Saint Helens.[46] Took years before the geologist started calling a well deserved, "Wolf!"

When you see a suspiciously large number of giddy geologists, you know there is a super volcano in the neighborhood. Geologists will be mucking about with their gas analyzers, drills, GPS movement sensors, seismometers and pizza. The pizza is used to compare the heat of the lava to the heat of the pizza sauce to indicate when the volcano is hot enough to burn the roof of your mouth and the roof of your house.

---

[46] http://en.wikipedia.org/wiki/Mount_St._Helens

Learn This Word

> *Seismometer: The seismometer is a lie-detecting polygraph for the Earth. Just before the eruption of a volcano, the Earth starts telling little lies. Geologist use this tool to see tremors caused by the volcano's nervousness when fibbing. When a volcano is caught in a big lie, it blows its top. The USGS has a website with a weekly report on the Earth's lies.[47] Keeping up with possible super volcanoes has never been easier.*

Here are a few super volcano candidates:

Mount Shasta

Mt. Shasta, situated in the center of California, isn't a super volcano though it does have potential for a spectacular eruption. We include Shasta because it is rumored to be where descendants from Atlantis live. The Atlantans moved to the mountain during their war with the Lemurians. At about that time, Atlantis was accidentally sunk during a weapon test, stranding them in the bowels of Mt. Shasta.

The destruction of Atlantis was so powerful that the History Channel can't find its location during a two hour special. The Atlantan descendants are rebuilding their continent-sinking super weapon in the center of Shasta right now. North America will soon be destroyed by someone leaning on the button of the Atlantan super weapon – or an Atlantan will flush an ancient toilet one too many times, causing Shasta to erupt with more than lava.

Yellowstone

Unlike lightning, super volcanoes definitely strike twice in the same place. Yellowstone looks cool now with its majestic geysers. The tourist photos hid a past when Yellowstone was like a failed cork in the back side of a well fed pig. Just like the last great eruption, Yellowstone is bulging and shaking as all that pressure builds up. Even a minor eruption will create a

---

47 http://www.volcano.si.edu/reports/usgs/

mini ice age. The economy will collapse as the ice-maker market collapses.

Mount Hood and the Cascades

Mount Hood is just down the street from Mount St. Helens. The rumbling Mount Hood rises into the sky like an ice cream cone dropped by a god. Hood is in the Cascade range which includes Helens, Rainier and many other volcanoes.

Hood and these other volcanoes are caused by the movement of the Juan de Fuca Plate. A Mexican plate causes volcanoes? Yep, it's all the spicy food. The Cascade range is part of the Pacific Ring of Fire, a chain of over 450 active volcanoes.

The biggest problem is Starbucks. When Starbucks' corporate headquarters gets buried in fifty feet of molten lava, the world will end a few days later when we run low on double shot mocha cappuccino soy lattes.

Mount Redoubt

Mount Redoubt at the time of this writing is starting to show signs of life. In the shadow of Mount Fuji, it could be signaling a chain of events that causes Japan to become a lava theme park.

Because the volcano is in Japan, we need to worry about our supply of cool electronics. Sure, everything is made in China, but it's the Japanese who figured out how to add the cool blinky lights. What happens when the guys that wrote Donkey Kong and the Super Mario Brothers sink into the Sea of Japan?

You Might Want to Know

> Krakatoa *blew its top in 1883. The explosive force was 13,000 times greater than the first atomic bomb. This created a mini ice age and spectacular sunsets. The bloody sunset in Edvard Munch's painting, The Scream, was caused by Krakatoa's ash. The scream itself was caused by the depressingly cold winter. Super volcanoes will have much prettier sunsets and a lot more screaming.*

Edvard Munch (1863–1944), The Scream,[48] painted in 1893. Suspected to be a self-portrait.

How to Prepare for Super Volcanoes

First thing to worry about is poison gas. The effect of poison gas depends on how close your nose is to the volcano. Too close, only a well protected Bubble Boy will survive. If you

[48] Image is public domain except Norway until 2014 (unless the world ends earlier). *Taking this book into Norway may result in confiscation because this image, no matter how weird it is, it's still under copyright in Norway.* See http://en.wikipedia.org/wiki/The_Scream

have plenty of warning, just get out of town. Beyond that, stock up on food, water, and Bubble Boy bubbles.

Surgical masks or those dust masks at the hardware store are good for volcanic ash. In a pinch, a good bra will do. Padded bras are better, but make sure they are advertised as breathable. Bras are washable (delicate cycle only), with the option of a built-in second filter and stylish lace trim.

Hoarding of face masks is a good thing. Hoarding bras is good too, but seems a little creepy. Bras also double as good barter when banks are covered in lava. A couple of cases from Victoria Secret are expensive, but an investment greater than gold.

Global cooling comes with volcanoes. Even small volcanic eruptions cause a mini ice ages. Super volcanoes might put us into a quick freeze. Think frozen wooly mammoths and replace that with a business man caught in mid-stride walking out of a Starbucks. Instead of a daisy on your tongue, future scientists thawing you out will find you sipping a latte with cranberry muffin on your breath.

You Might Want to Know

> *Looting is generally hard because everybody is looking for the obvious food, drugs, and weapons. Target lingerie stores will be relatively free of fellow looters. You will be collecting a highly valuable product in the barter economy. The market for kinky underwear will not go away just because it's the end of the world.*

Alien Invasion

Aliens, love them or hate them, they probably hate us. Aliens love us, but only when served with garlic mash potatoes. Alien invasions come in several flavors (like humans); instant sterilization of life, mind control, people as food, and hunting humans for sport. Even friendly aliens will give us a worldwide epidemic of Deep Space Runny Squirts s bad that we'd die of the smell before our butts fell off.

Don't assume millions of aliens are going to show up in the skies all at once. The aliens are going to send an advanced group to get things ready. A few humanoid robots will come down and subjugate humanity. They seem to already here and running Fox News. That's right, aliens are Republican.

There are signs of aliens everywhere. We aren't talking about fuzzy photos of UFOs or anal probes in Oklahoma, but the explosion of fast food. Aliens are fattening us up for the big invasion. Earth's obese people are the only rare thing in the universe. We are juicy too!

Aliens are synonymous with rectal probes. The probing is alien research[49] aimed at curing hiccups. The aliens are also installing plastic pop-up turkey (human) timers.

Aliens also want to destroy us because we are irritating. They are sending death rays and killer robots the size of houses to stop the insanity of reality TV. This is why SETI has never found intelligent life. The first sign of intelligence is that you don't watch *So You Think You Can Dance*.

Enslaving humanity seems a little silly. We haven't been good slaves for more than a few thousand years. It's even worse in the last couple of hundred years with rebellions, religions, unions, and commercial advertising. Imagine us fighting our alien overlords for comprehensive health plans, 20 minute breaks, and two weeks of vacation.

Aliens who were here during the times of Egyptians, Mayans, and other ancient civilizations, are in for a surprise. All our stone chipping skills are gone. What are aliens going to do with a world full of people that drink lattes and post comments about their cat's toiletry habits on Facebook?

Surviving Alien Invasion

There's no forewarning of aliens invasions. Nobody gets an email or a phone call from E.T. One day things are fine, the next you are reporting to a people-processing plant to be ground into human-burger and strawberry flavored people-pops. The world will be clueless. The only sign something is happening is fewer Facebook friend requests.

Aliens visiting Earth for its natural beauty are going to turn right back around without ever saying hello. Politicians will see

---

[49] http://www.theregister.co.uk/2006/10/06/ig_nobel_awards/

this as a good thing and a reason to pollute more. It will be used as an excuse to fill in the Grand Canyon with radioactive medial waste. We will all die a few years later. No surviving that.

Aliens need proper communication to your brain to make you their slave. Shield one room in your house against mind-control. We recommend the bathroom. Aliens prefer our stink stays at home, not in the overlord's chambers. The mind-control will drop at the time as the poo. Remember to put on your foil hat when you are awake enough to smell the roses.

To dodge the aliens completely, build underground community. Look for large underground areas that are far from your alien overlords. Basements, subways, and abandoned missile silos are all good. Avoid locations under your alien overlord's noses, if they have noses. Natural caves are good, but avoid famous caves like Carlsbad. Aliens watch the Travel Channel.

Making people-burgers and fries shouldn't be a full time job. Unlike the movies, aliens are not going to send teams of hard working hunters out every time they feel peckish. It's robots herding humans into pens for slaughter. Keep out of sight and off the menu.

Don't think you are just going to survive on your back yard garden. Growing your own food in a garden of tomatoes and strawberries sounds good, but such crops are too easy to spot from a flying saucer. Combine hiding underground with farming mushrooms. If you have a little spider hole, just eat the spiders. You'll be amazed how good they taste after not eating for a few days.

A great way to survive the alien apocalypse is the Dr. Smith or Gaius Baltar[50] approach. Just be the worst of humanity. Strive to be the best self-serving worm you can be. Lawyers and politicians have the advantage!

TM

[50] http://en.wikipedia.org/wiki/Gaius_Baltar

Experiment: Survival 101

Sign up to teach a continuing education course on apocalyptic survival at the local senior center or YMCA. Offer a complete course on surviving zombies, demons, Republicans, death from space, and other dooms.

Be sure to advertise in church newsletters, twitter, fliers in Laundromats and on your Facebook page (Google+ if it's still working).

Questions

- ✓ How many people showed up?
- ✓ Which parts of the course were more popular?
- ✓ Were you able to get students to give you money?
- ✓ Are you surprised by how eager the students are to learn?

Zombie Apocalypse

Zombies are great source of apocalyptic doom because they spread quickly. Zombification is like the flu. Unlike the boring flu, there is the extra excitement of the zombie trying to eat your brains, not stalking you from a snotty door knob.

Where do zombies come from? The good news is that almost anything can create a zombie. A scientist could overturn a beaker in a lab, we breath comet dust, a disease mutates, or old-fashioned black magic. With all these possibilities, a zombie apocalypse is going to happen at any moment.

The spread of zombies is what makes them especially cool. Zombies can infect the living through blood born disease or satanic animation. No matter the cause, the more zombies attack, the more zombies we get.

During the initial days of a zombie apocalypse, the government declares a worldwide emergency. Like a snow day! Imagine being ten years old and hearing that school is canceled because of zombies. Cool!

Unlike a snow day, zombie days are not as fun. No making zombie-snowmen or zombie-angels in the front yard. No homework, but you are going to spend time barricading the doors and praying.

Zombification

Zombies don't come in one flavor. They all like brains but they are created in different ways. Zombification, or the process of creating a zombie, is important because it gives us clues to avoid becoming a zombie and give us clues for defending ourselves.

There are many books and movies that give you a good idea, but you may not have time to study, so here's the short list:

Animation Ray — Aliens use zombification ray at the cemetery to animate the dead to be their slaves. We recommend you watch the enlightening documentary on the zombification ray, *Plan 9 From Outer Space*. The good news is that the zombies don't seem to be infectious and are not very smart.

Unfortunately, aliens and animated dead can only be battled by scientists that moonlight as heroes. Just in case there are no heroes in lab coats, dig a hole and take up mushroom farming.

Biological accident — Biological waste is dumped at an indian burial ground causing a long dead tribe to rise and take their revenge on the local population. This is a very unpredictable form of zombie. They may be infectious or just be hungry for brains. We suggest you have a scientist study the zombies to find out which. If the scientist becomes a zombie, you'll know right away. On the other hand, you will be safer if you dig a hole and take up mushroom farming.

Cosmic rays — Radiation from space zombifies almost everyone. These are the worst as most of the population is zombified. Just dig a hole and take up mushroom farming.

Disease mutations — Disease is great for zombies, bad for people, dogs, sheep, badgers, and sugar squirrels. The best news is that you can become a zombie as easily as you can catch a cold. The only good news is that zombies can't figure out how to use a doorknob. The really bad news is you need hazmat armor to protect yourself from stray zombie cooties. We suggest you dig a hole and take up mushroom farming.

Cursed — These are the spiritually raised undead. Sort of like Christians with a desire to eat brains. You need to burn these zombies to properly kill them. Hacking them into little bits will just create animated bits of zombie. You don't want to wake up and find a zombie kidney gnawing your leg off. There is an exception for dusty zombies we will cover later. Your only defense again is a hero but in this case someone from the other side of the cursed street. Best defense: Dig a hole and take up mushroom farming.

Remember that some zombies dig themselves out of their graves. Use those holes to your advantage. Happy mushroom farming!

Generic Zombies

These are the most common zombies. They are created by one of the many types of zombification we have already covered.

Generic zombies are definitely contagious. Some need to bite you and or just transfer their zombie disease with a little blood splatter or saliva (avoid chainsaws, tongue twisters, or zombies that spit when they say words with the letter P). Although beheading will kill these zombies, the inevitable spray of bodily fluids will infect anyone within five feet or so. Killing from a distance is advisable.

Constantly monitor friends and loved ones. There is usually a gestation period and a few warning signs. For example, they might start getting giggly when they smell brains. We recommend good airlock style quarantine vestibules on your home or your post-apocalyptic enclave.

You Might Want to Know

> *We have uncovered research that zombies can catch a cold. Runny nose zombies will be infecting everything! The only good news is they can't sneak up on you when they are sneezing.*

Spiritual Raising of the Dead (the bad type)

Zombies raised for evil purposes have goals to their actions. Goals in life are good, but goals in the undead are destructive. Evil zombies are raised to do a job. Their job varies from revenge, eliminating the heretics, or destruction of civilization so that aliens can put in a parking lot. As mostly brainless zombies, they don't complain, so they are the perfect minions, though not very smart. These zombies only get distracted by something juicy and a need to stop the screaming of their victims.

Raised zombies have rotted flesh (or none at all) and diminished brain capacity. They are your garden variety shambling zombie. Their spiritual curse makes up for their handicaps by making them hard to kill. There isn't any biology, just magic that keeps them going. Shooting them is a bit pointless. Hacking off body parts is useful, but could backfire if the magic is strong enough to keep the parts animated.

Dead raised by evil have an extra spiritual oomph that allows them to blatantly ignore biological rules. They don't need beating hearts or even a functional brain to do their master's bidding (you'll find them lurking on eBay). Even without a head, the nasty spirit inside will still be able to grab you. Severed hands are quick and strong enough to kill or maim.

The malevolent zombie does not transmit it zombieness with snot, spit or blood, so battling them is relatively safe. A chainsaw works quite well, if you can stand the mess. On the downside, when you die, you will be raised as a heinous zombie, bite or no bite. Take special care with the mortally wounded (as you should with any zombie type).

Burning the freshly dead is the best solution. Please, do not start cooking your friends! Just because Fred would taste great with BBQ sauce, does not mean you should become a cannibal. Proper cremation of the dead is despicable if you are wearing a Kiss The Cook apron. Yes, if Fred were cooked well-done, you might kill any zombie infection or evil intent–but there is always somebody that likes his meat a little rare. The Zombie Steak House is NOT open for business.

Spiritual Raising of the Dead (the good type)

Zombies rising from a divine intervention are very different from those we've covered so far. These zombies are raised from the dead by a god, high priests, accidental triggering of a long-forgotten religion, and by building track homes on sacred burial grounds, just like the bad type, but they are friendly. With the rot of the grave, perhaps not cuddly, but at least they aren't trying to kill you.

In the Christian religions they say that the dead will rise from the grave, like Jesus Christ. We get something similar to spiritual animation. Let's explore that for a minute (sorry, Mom).

Jesus seemed to still have all his mental faculties. This is great! Your Uncle Harry will still tell those old jokes and want to play a game of checkers. You might want to buy some scented candles to mask the rotting smell and keep him in the back yard until the embalming fluid drains (it stains carpet). Be carful that your uncle doesn't bite you for a fun little joke.

Jesus went to Heaven after running around to speak with a few neighbors and friends. That's really good news for us with loved ones about to rise from the grave. Even though Uncle Harry has been fun after he "rose," he is just hanging around for a bit before he takes the next bus to Heaven.

There are inconvenient details about the resurrection that also could mess up the raising from the dead experience. Jesus got out of a mausoleum-like cave by pushing a big stone away from the entrance. Fine for a son of a god, but what of normal folk?

Uncle Harry was buried under six feet of dirt and encased in a stainless steel coffin with brass plated bolts holding the lid closed. That's good news and bad. Should Harry dig out past the fancy casket and six feet of earth, then you know he is strong, persistent, and probably mad. If uncle Harry isn't able to get out of his coffin (pay extra for the heavy duty coffin locks), don't worry. The knocking and screaming will be muffled by the dirt and a premium coffin insulation.

Jesus was anointed with oils before being laid to rest. We generally pump grandma up with a few quarts of embalming fluid. Not good. A lack of animated blood in an animated body would be a problem. The freshly raised dead will be running around with gaping wounds and about three quarts of embalming fluid oozing out.

Jesus still had wounds in his hands from when he died. That means that resurrection does not include fixing of previous wounds, just a zombie-like animation. Think about modern embalming techniques! Then there was all that messiness when Aunt Dorothy was accused of poisoning Uncle Harry. The medical examiner didn't find anything, but Uncle Harry's brain is in a jar at the county morgue. No jokes, he can't tell any.

When it's all said and done, we can't say how well the dead will mentally handle resurrection. Imagine an atheist resurrected by a very forgiving Christian god. Those that believe in reincarnation will be doubly confused coming back to life as themselves! Things are worse if you are raised from the dead by the Devil for his final battle. Post-resurrection therapy will be in demand!

Be careful about killing the resurrected undead. They may have been animated by a good-guy god. They may not want to hurt you and are just waiting around a bit before being taken to Heaven.

Use extreme caution with any zombie because it is easy to confuse the good with the bad kind of undead. Mention brains to see if you get a reaction. Your best investment is one of those brain shaped jello molds you see at Halloween super stores.

Anyone salivating when you cut into jiggling lime the jello brains should be asked to play a round of hide the shovel in the brain pan.

Body armor is best when zombies sneak up on you with a quiet shuffle. Shark-proof chain mail is very effective at preventing a nasty bite. A good stiff motorcycle helmet will help protect your brain from nibbling. You can also wear motorcycle leathers to avoid an accidental bite. Finally, when you don't have access to any of these, tie a baby bottle nipple to your head. The zombie will try to suckle on your brain matter like a hungry infant, use this time to mount an escape.

Examine clothing for fresh blood. They may have been snacking on human flesh. Don't be fooled when they say it was catsup. Do not believe them! The undead don't use condiments!

Other Zombies

Why limit things to *people* zombies? Anything could become a zombie.

Pets

Fluffy isn't much of a pet when she prefers the taste of human flesh to a bowl of kibble. The zombification could be caused by bad Chinese pet food or a PETA scientist's revenge fantasies. Suddenly we are going to the gun store instead of the pet store.

There is nothing worse than a gerbil with glowing red eyes and a thirst for blood. Mr Sprinkles could get a zombified just as easily as a human. Don't laugh — there are millions of pet gerbils.

Zombie gerbils grow to the size of houses and their IQ is a respectful 85. Big, smarter than a politician, cute, and peckish for human brains.

Dusty Zombies

Can somebody's ashes become a zombie? Cremation is very popular and an untapped resource for zombification. Imagine uncle Leo rising from the urn on the fireplace mantle. Grab the vacuum cleaner, time to clean up a few dusty zombies. Better yet, before Leo gets any undead ideas, get the duct tape out and seal that urn right away!

It's not just the dusty urn-American zombies swirling up your nose to eat your brains. With all those candles and incense in churches and temples (not to mention fiery sacrifice). Ashes to ashes has a new meaning as soot is reanimated. Millions died un-buried and withered away to dust. Ashes have been dumped at sea, from mountain tops, and at the ballpark too. Think of the tons of potential zombie dust in the air.

Someone that should not have played with matches could be lurking in the dust on your book shelf. Their ashes are everywhere, spread with the wind. What do you think dust bunnies are? That's right, dust bunnies are people.

Imagine a zombie dust bunny with sharp teeth. After you stop giggling, start thinking about how unsanitary a zombie made up of dusty dead people, dog hair, and your dad's toenail clippings. Maybe a dust zombie won't rip your arm off, but that's disgusting, repulsive, sickening, nauseating, stomach-churning, stomach-turning, off-putting, unpalatable, distasteful, foul, nasty, vomitous yucky, and very gross!

Feel like vacuuming some dust bunnies?

Woodland Creatures

Imagine Bambi, R. J. Squirrel, and Smokey the Bear becoming undead. You'll get the first hint when you see a cute little bunny sitting down to a meal of forest ranger tartare. It's best to head back to the city, as the twittering of the robin is drowned out by the screams of Boy Scout Troop 12.

Fish

Imagine watching a Bass Fishing show on ESPN 6 when things get a little bloodier than the usual hook in a finger. As with most woodland creature zombies, fish zombies are triggered by a need for revenge. That means the first to go are bass anglers. Beware, sushi lovers are next!

Fish zombies don't seem too bad unless you are in the water, right? Not so fast. The first place they strike might be in the seafood restaurant. Nothing worse than a Trout Almondine ripping out your date's throat.

Because they are undead, these Jacque Cousteau zombies don't have to stay in the water. They'll flop right out of the ocean or your aquarium. On land, Nemo Zombies will be easy to avoid because of the smell. Zombie fish flesh will rot just like their terrestrial cousins. Watch for herds of cats nearby to avoid running into a school of the flopping undead.

Another method to avoid zombie fish is to listen for music. These are the only undead that that can play the scales. There's something fishy about that pun.

Defense against aquatic zombies is difficult. They are slippery and hard to grab. They don't need water. Don't let the lack of legs fool you, either. Fish flop out of the fire onto your brain pan.

The zombie fish are not easily defeated. Chopping off their heads is difficult, unless you are an expert with fillet knife. Trapping the finned undead could be simple. Just bait some hooks with human brains (use a politician — they literally won't mind).

Revenge is good motivation for animal zombies, and fish are no exception. Any animal that is lower on the food chain has a high probability of going zombie and feasting on the new lower rung of the ladder. Stay out of harms way by avoiding a diet of fish. Not smelling like fried catfish dinner will give you a stealthy advantage. Hang a raw calf kidneys off your belt for extra protection. A diet of chicken or beef might help, but they feed most livestock a mixture that contains ground up fish. There's a reason rich people eat expensive free range chicken and grass fed beef.

We can't be complacent just because fish oil is good for your heart. When zombified, they'll eat your heart out! Invest in an ichthyology zombie defense like frying pans and fishing equipment.

You Might Want to Know

Laser used to be spelled with capital letters because it stands for Light Amplification by Stimulated Emission of Radiation. 'Stimulated' should be replaced with "Zapped" so that it would be spelled 'lazer.' Don't you think laser should be spelled with a Z instead of an S? Anything seems more powerful when spelled with a Z. Muztang, eggz, zylophone, fauzet, butterflyz, zkyzcraper, and our favorite, lazer.

Zombie Insects

Think that flies, mosquitos, and cockroaches are annoying? Imagine insect zombies infesting your apocalyptic life. Zombie insects like brain-flavored craniums are hard to kill because they are already dead.

There are trillions of dead flies that could suddenly rise from the dead. That annoying buzzing in your ear would be much more annoying when super-sized to a few million zombie flies.

Zombification includes weird side effects like growth spurts. Super-sized zombie termites could eat your home in one bite. Not that they still like wood, they'll eat the house for your juicy brains in the center. Giant mosquitos could become the new vampires. No-see-ums[51] would be visible and their bite lethal instead of just itchy. The normal household infestation will be reduced to just one roach Two roaches if you have a two car garage. Imagine when crickets become super-sized. The world going deaf from millions of massive crickets making that terrible noise. The lowly fruit fly could become dangerous when it becomes the size of a Ford Apocalypse GT coupe and starts liking human flesh more than rotten fruit.

Learn This Word

> ***Plague:*** *Plague has a couple of meanings. First, is the disease type. Simply a disease that quickly spreads and kills people. We used the word plague to represent a large number of insects or other creatures that upsets civilization through spread of disease or destruction of crops, for example, a plague of insects, frogs, clowns, or other nasty creatures. Zombie bugs don't need to get as big as houses to cause problems. All we need is a proper plague of zombie insects to destroy humanity. Bugs in large numbers are as bad or worse than super-sized bugs. When they are small, shooting a missile at them is both unsatisfying*

---

[51] http://en.wikipedia.org/wiki/Ceratopogonidae

and ineffective.

They say that when you see one roach in your house, there are hundreds more hidden in the walls. Imagine seeing a zombie roach at the dinner table. When you see that one, there are a thousand red-eyed, drooling brethren sneaking up behind you.

How do you fight a plague of bug zombies? Well, aiming a shotgun at their heads is not going to be very easy. Chopping off the head of a bug isn't too good either. Roaches will stay alive for a long time without their heads attached.

The only defense against the zombie insect is squishing. Buy some stout boots and a good fly swatter.

Appliances

A great thing about zombie appliances is that they are already dead. Inanimate objects just need a little psychotic animation. The good news is that appliance zombies have uncontrollable drooling which will short circuit them fairly quickly.

Zombie toaster ovens, are scary. Think about the choking cloud of burnt bread crumbs a as the attack begins. Did you know the first sign of a brain tumor is the smell of burnt toast?

Don't think you are going to be safe because of the length of the power cord. The only life force that your waffle maker needs is your little grey cells and some maple syrup.

Cloudy With a Chance of Zombies

Zombies are the most likely way the world will end. There are just too many ways to create zombies. If you are betting man, seeing a zombie in your lifetime is greater than winning the lottery (see the following graph).

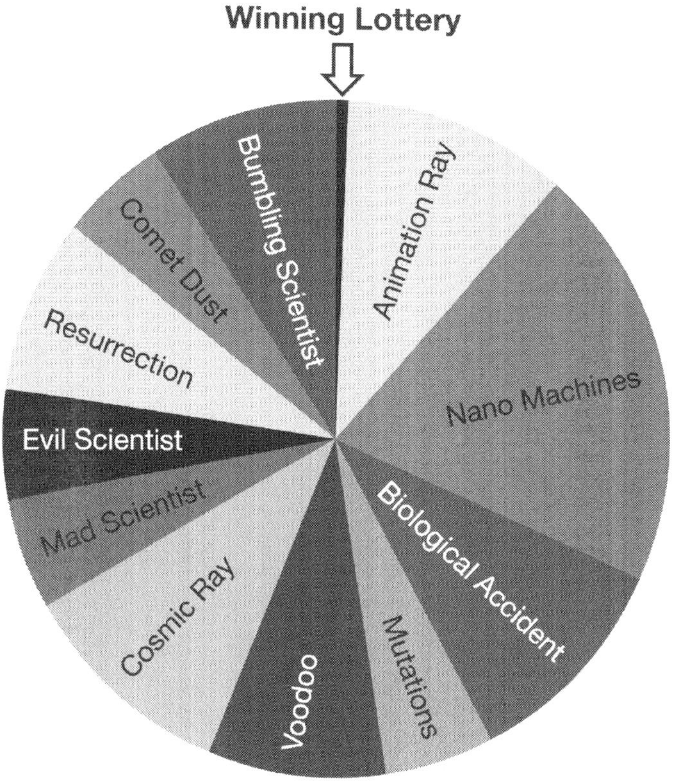

Zombie cause versus your chance of winning the lottery.

With all these zombies, it's possible that you get several types at once. Why not? Zombie party! Undead palooza! Of course 'palooza' means partying at one place with a ton of people like there's no tomorrow. That's it, except the other people want to eat your brains and there is definitely no tomorrow. Good news is that you can't have a hangover after someone eats your brain.

Surviving Zombiegeddon

Can you fight against zombies? Sure you can. The most important rule is to decapitate. Decapitation works for every type of zombie except certain cursed zombies and cockroach zombies. Amputated parts roaming about are bad, so burn any animated remains that are still wiggling. Fire trumps all other methods and a well-done zombie tastes like chicken.

There is only one problem with killing zombies, there are always more zombies. Why not join them? Brains are considered a delicacy in some cultures. Becoming a zombie transforms you into a brain gourmet. There's good with the bad, like a shambling walk. The only two words you are able to string together in a sentence are 'brains' and 'brains.' You can have dinner with your friends, but it's your friends that are for dinner.

Experiment: Create a Zombie Survival Kit

The Centers for Disease Control and Prevention, affectionately known as the CDC, publish instructions on how to survive a zombie attack. No, we are not kidding. Here is the web address:

http://emergency.cdc.gov/socialmedia/zombies_blog.asp?s_cid=emergency_002

Create you emergency preparation kit according to their instructions and add any additional items you feel are necessary for the various types of zombie cataclysm. For example, torches for burning the desiccated (that means less water, dried out, and very flammable, dead people), risen zombies, holy water for demonic zombies, big boots for insect zombies, lemon and butter sauce for fish zombies and bladed weapons for beheading most zombies.

Questions

- ✓ Are you surprised that the CDC believes in zombies?
- ✓ What types of weapons did you add to your zombie prep kit?
- ✓ Why doesn't the CDC didn't list weapons in their emergency preparedness kit?

Top Religions: Improving Your Odds of the Hereafter

Betting on the afterlife to survive the apocalypse? You have some serious choices to make. Most religions have tough rules to follow for eternal life that are not very pleasant. Following a religion is much harder than surviving a god given apocalypse. You can't be sure you've picked the right one until the very last moment. There's not even a 90 day guarantee!

Knowing your religious choices lets you make an informed decision. It's also good to know your gods, because you might need to worship a new god at the drop of a hat or a hail of brimstone. Be ready to seek alternative absolution.

Christians

Starting with the obvious, Christians have the edge. This is especially a good bet when the Book of Revelation incontrovertibly comes true. They wrote it; they own it; they survive it. Sadly you need to be a Republican too. Survival requires sacrifice!

Unfortunately there are too many different types of Christianity. Odds are low that you will pick the right sect. The Christian God isn't too clear about who to specifically follow. He won't start getting too clear until the killing starts.

When the world starts falling apart and you see colored horses, look for who is surviving the plagues and winning the battles, and then switch to their religion. Hedge your bets with a radical fire-and-brimstone church. God favors crazy followers.

Buddhists

Being a Buddhist is reasonably good for the apocalypse. Buddhists aren't bothered by such things. Buddhists are like an atheist that does yoga. Unfortunately, your only apocalyptic defense is to contemplate your bellybutton and hope enlightenment happens before a demon eats you.

You don't need to be a 'good' Buddhist. Buddha never talked about an afterlife, so there is no place to go and no entrance fee. If you are generally lazy and hate rules, you've come to the right place because when you are dead you are dead. No afterlife! Just sit back and decompose.

Some Buddhist sects unfortunately do have a heaven. Do your research before you sign the membership forms! For example, Thai Buddhists have a heaven populated by gods, weird creatures, and monkeys. Lots and lots of monkeys! There's a hell too! You need to be a "good" Thai Buddhist because there are really bad monkeys in Thai hell that you don't want to meet.

Buddhists blur other religions so much that you should get your eyes checked. Buddhism does not care what your religion is, only that you seek enlightenment and follow its precepts to do so. Buddhism is a philosophy, not a religion, except when it's a religion. Buddhism is seen as a religion because most Buddhists have not abandoned their Eastern-based religions. Most Buddhists follow Hindi traditions and add a little time contemplating their bellybuttons.

Why don't they abandon their old religion? Because no Buddhist would be so unkind to say your religion is silly when you are naked. Oops, that's nudists, not Buddhists.

In the West, we see Buddhism as a philosophy, not as a religion. We are also a bit single-minded. Most Americans can only keep one golden figure in their heads at once. In the rest of the world Buddhism has dozens of Buddhas, plus minor and major deities. In the West, a Buddhist is just an Atheist who drinks Karma Cola. In the East, its reincarnation instant milk.

Is Buddhism going to save you or get you into Heaven? With most apocalyptic scenarios, Buddhism will let you die with a smile on your face. Death is the end of suffering. When the end is a Christian Armageddon, well, you are toast too. Just die with a smile on your face, like the Laughing Buddha. You're going to need the sense of humor when you get to Hell.

Agnostics

An agnostic does not outright disbelieve in the existence of a god, but is willing to be convinced. It's certainly possible for an agnostic to be accepted by whatever god happens to be true. Agnosticism is a religion that waits until the last moment to figure out which god to believe in.

Agnostics have faith, just like other religions. They have faith that after they die, all the mystery about gods and religion will all be clear. Joining this religious cult is a sure ticket. Why would a god fault you for being open minded, but sticking with your principles?

There are meetings here and there of like-minded agnostics, but no church. Usually they show up at atheist meetings. For some reason they usually meet in New York style delicatessens. Oddly, they never talk about religion.

Prayers of the agnostic are only in times of imminent death or a nasty hangover. It goes like this: "If you are real, sorry for not believing in you sooner." When it's a compassionate god, you are headed to whatever afterlife is promised. In the likely event that it's an angry god, you may be better off because you don't want to buy anything He/She/It is selling anyway.

UFO Cult

Aliens are smart people, with all their spaceships and medical device probes. UFO cults are in contact with these aliens, and that means access to that technology and a ride out of town when things get bad.

Be careful with aliens. UFO cults will willingly walk into man-sized toaster ovens. When part of worshiping your alien overlords includes slathering yourself in butter… Run!

Reincarnation Instant Milk

Your actions in this life determine if you are coming back as a pony or an ill-tempered wolverine with male pattern baldness. Karma is always in force, so don't do silly things.

Eat chocolate covered grasshoppers and in your next life you will die in a vat of warm chocolate. Be good and good will befall you. Give money to book authors, especially us, and in your next life you will be given great wealth.

For any end of the world, reincarnation is unfortunately a poor survival tactic. You can't expect to come back as an eagle or a cow when the world no longer exists. Reincarnation is a little hard to do when the Earth is a pile of smoldering rubble.

What happens when only humans die out? Not too bad when come back as a monkey or a cow. Not so good when you come back as a slug.

When humans are extinct, you can't get promoted past fish or fowl. It becomes impossible to add good karma as a creature without free will. You'll keep dying and coming back next rung down on the karmic ladder. No promotion for you! The position of human has become redundant. Please wait a few million years for intelligent life to evolve.

The only people who will be happy are the Hindus who get reincarnated as cattle. Sadly though, cattle are dumb because of domestication. Cattle will quickly die out as a species because they can't care for themselves in a world without humans.

Karma is like Murphy's Law or the Law of Gravity. Karma seems to be an eternal truth of the universe. Too much bad karma and you'll be the first person hit on the head by a rock from space or be the first bitten by a zombie. Don't do bad things. Pay it forward.

Other Religions?

You might ask about Aztecs, Sun Worshipers, and the many ancient but defunct religions. Suppose all of this end of the world business is just because Zeus is getting sick and tired of only being acknowledged in high-school mythology classes and by Joseph Campbell reruns?

It's just throwing the dice. Worship the wrong lowbrow or forgotten god and you are the first to feel the correct god's wrath.

You could worship all gods. Most of us hated mythology because there are too many gods. Imagine worshiping that many gods, on purpose! Our society is too lazy for that kind of work.

Hints of the old gods showing up will be a voice from the sky, say Zeus, talking about punishment (yes, Greek hell is a pun contest). The return of Aztec gods is simple to spot when you find a twenty-two pound bird poo on your car and you keep seeing feathered serpents out of the corner of your eye. At this point start studying the Aztecs at the local library.

Picking a religion is hard! The key is to be flexible. You never know when you'll need to switch sides at the last moment. Be very flexible!

Murphy's Law… Obvious choice for the religion of humanity, right?

Experiment: Join a church!

Join every religion in your neighborhood. Ask for pointers on how to survive that religion's end times. Compare these religions and the opinions of several of their members for consistency.

Questions

- ✓ Are the members of the religion surprised they have a new convert?
- ✓ Does anyone question you about joining purely for survival?
- ✓ In the same religion, do the survival tips vary?
- ✓ Are any of the survival tips similar among the different religions?
- ✓ When you told your psychiatrist about your latest ventures, what was his or her reaction?

Throwing an End-of-the-World Party

The party is a constant in all end-of-the-world tales. They partied while it rained on Noah's Ark. They made merry when Sodom and Gomorrah burned. Even Y2K had its parties to celebrate our computers upchucking because of the calendar ticking over to 2 and triple goose eggs. Raise a glass and sing a tune. It's the end and our last chance to celebrate!

We recommend you have a shelter and supplies for your guests. Nothing worse than being at a party without a place to crash when fireballs are falling from the sky *and* a hangover. Be a gracious host, as it may be your last chance. Be aware of possible harbingers of death crashing your cataclysmic cotillion.

Security is a necessity when the world starts going wacky. The apocalypse is not a job for rent-a-cops. You need highly trained mercenaries. Pay them well and guarantee accommodations in your survival shelter too. Everything will go pear-shaped when they see zombies and no room at the inn. Remember the little people, especially the ones with weapons.

A fun party is a safe party. When there are biological toxins or radiation in the air, have your guests strip down to their birthday clothes and try your new detox shower. Scrubbing naked people with rough brushes is a fantastic ice breaker.

Wearing hazmat-suits aren't the best way to throw a party. Just a little too hard to mingle. Wine sipped through an antibacterial filter has an aftertaste of tin and cat urine. When your home is properly equipped with filtered air, you will party in your lucky bowling shirt and Bahama shorts.

Rule #1: It Hasn't Happened, So Not Now

Odds are that the world will not end. Look at Y2K and most religious predictions of Second Comings and global doom. Throw a party. Party hard. Don't worry. The hangover will be the only reason you'll wish the world had ended.

Keep your guests at ease. Avoid displaying your 'just in case' preparations. Guests should only fear the five-layer bean dip and the five dollar wine. When you have essential supplies like guns, holy water, yack spit, razor wire, keep them in the bunker and away from the curious kitties.

It's okay to ask guests to bring a side dish. Don't ask guests to bring ammo or canned goods. Just beer and a side dish. We recommend banning mayonnaise-based foods just to avoid any thoughts of panic.

Rule #2: It Could Happen

It never hurts to be prepared. When the world is really in danger, a party is good to relieve the tension and pool resources. When an asteroid is blotting out the Sun, even when scientists say there's no danger, panic in the streets could still happen. Be vigilant when the scientists don't seem to be available for interviews the day before. When scientists disappear into government sponsored bunkers.

A proper host should guarantee guest survival. Set up some razor wire to stop the zombies, a few crosses to dissuade fanatic religious followers, and a pit of spikes to kill wandering lawyers (bait the trap with a runaway Toyota accident). Have a good array of weapons for all occasions and teach your guests in their proper use. Duct-tape windows, keep a ton of freeze-dried food in the basement. Invite at least one doctor to the party.

Avoid all forms of risky foods. If it stinks or causes irregular bowel movements, don't put it on the buffet table. Just say. "no" to five-layer dip or those wonderfully stinky cheeses. Not even garlic (unless there are vampires). You might be stuck in a small shelter with your guests when the effect of the beans hit. Little known fact, shelters filter outside air, not the air inside.

A potluck is great for end-of-the-world parties. It's a great way to get your friends and neighbors preparing for the end too. Avoid gate crashers by making the price of entry a donation of a ton of nonperishable food or a medical degree. The golden rule is that paper plates and some store-bought cookies isn't going to get you in the door! Partygoers must supply the proper end of the world supplies and a few bottles of whiskey.

A party for end of the world should also be held in a proper place. If you have a cabin in the country, perfect! When the world does end, you don't want to be in the city.

One of our favorite books is *Lucifer's Hammer* by Larry Nivan and Jerry Pournelle. The book is about an asteroid that hits the Earth and smartly ends life as we know it. The book is great survivalist fiction.

In Larry and Jerry's book, we learned that when a rock from space hits the ocean, it makes waves, big ones! Avoid party crashers with surf boards. Party on the high ground.

Rule #3: Poo Happens

Forget the predicted disaster. No matter how dire the end of the world scenario is, people panicking in the streets will be much worse. Panic will end the world a lot faster than a real disaster.

Expect idiots. Idiots are a dime a dozen and we have an awful lot of dimes. We speak not of a deficient IQ, but people who have lost the capacity for thinking once the hysteria from Fox News begins to flow. There does not need to be a real disaster, just enough people assuming there is one in progress. These nuts are happy to kill their neighbors for food and shelter when there are rumors of apocalypse. When the common man panics, everyone looks like an evildoer or competition for food and shelter.

There is no such thing as idiot-proof. There are however a few ways to prepare for the general types of pudding-heads. Visible security, a couple of German Shepherds, and a few plastic guns poking out the windows, will deter most crazies looking for easier prey.

Belief in the end causes panic even when the end doesn't happen. Think about what happened with David Koresh[52] of Wacko Waco fame. People do weird stuff because they *expect* the world to end soon.

Religious zealots will be running up and down the street trying to kill one more nonbeliever. A good end of the world party host should take such roving mobs into account and be ready to protect the guests. Pass the ammo with the appetizers!

---

52 http://en.wikipedia.org/wiki/David_Koresh

Manners for End-Times

An end-of-the-world party should have a few extra rules for guests. Anything could happen and we need a few house rules to keep our guests safe and happy. Even if you don't think the world will end, the world may not be as cooperative. Things could go udders up while you and your guests are munching on little cocktail wieners.

Manners originate from ancient times when life was a bit rougher and a little politeness could prevent death and dismemberment of guests. The rules were created to keep people alive, not just for polite tea time. A good example of this is washing your hands. Scrubbing up before dinner could be the difference between life and death, or at least a night without the rude sounds of dysentery.

You Might Want to Know

> *It is believed that Vikings were the first society to enforce the rule of removing your hat as you enter a home. With their pointy horned hats, Vikings had a long history of goring injuries at parties. Sven "One Eye" Johanson was credited with creating the hats-off etiquette for his nights of post-raping-pillaging knees-up, bunfight, and merry alcohol poisoning. Historians also believed that One Eye also invented cocktail weenies, saving even more lives by preventing the spread of germs by serving perfectly shaped mini weenies on hygienic toothpicks.*

Important rule: Guests must report when believe (or know) they are a carrier of a disease, recently irradiated, bitten by a zombie, or a recent alien probe of their nether regions. Inviting someone into your home should be a pleasant experience and not spoiled by inappropriately possessed or otherwise contagious guests.

Imagine engaging in spirited conversation when you can't tell someone is salivating over the cheese plate or the wondrous bouquet of live brains. Guests shouldn't worry about demonic possession while playing Pictionary, zombie bites at the snack table, or forced into quarantine after a game of spin the bottle.

When you're in the middle of your dinner party, sipping on fine wine (or that fine box of wine), the pretzels should not glowing! The host should have decontaminated everyone from the dirty bomb. Pass the lead underwear and iodine pills, please!

Provide wet-wipes because there is nothing worse than having bits of a demonic evildoer's rotted flesh on your hands after a long battle. You should have clean hands before you start getting grabby with the bowl of corn chips.

Protect Your Guests

It's your obligation as a host to provide security. Party games are more fun when guests feel protected against roaming demons. Guests should feel safe even when the world is more exciting, in a bad way, than a game of charades.

There is nothing worse than Truth Or Dare and have the 'dare' be the teasing of gatecrashing zombies. Instruct everyone to aim for the head of zombies and only use the silver bullets exclusively for the werwolves. No horsing around with the squirt guns because holy water is only for the vampires.

You Might Want to Know

Flying demons are a problem. With evil harpies crashing through the windows, it's difficult to keep guests interested in your amusing stories. We recommend little stick-on gothic cross silhouettes for your windows.

Experiment: Party Time

The world is always ending. Don't just sit there, time for a party! The best time for a party is on the date predicted by a doomsayer. Look around and you will probably find one. If there isn't a convenient date, just make one up.

Questions

- ✓ How many people said they couldn't come because they were in their own bunker?
- ✓ What types of survival supplies did your guests bring?
- ✓ Are your neighbors getting paranoid that you invited your friends and not them to party in your bunker?
- ✓ Take a pole and see how many really think that this is their last party?
- ✓ Did your psychologist come to your party?

Revelations in Marketing: How to Sell Your Apocalyptic Products

Commerce will never stop. There will be demons at your door one minute and then a kid selling magazines the next. People need food, shelter, and the trappings of useless status symbols. Why not go into pre and post-civilization commerce?

Sell before, during, and after the apocalypse. Adjust your marketing spin to appeal to fear, uncertainty and gullibility.

Don't just sit there! It's been days-from-the-end-repent-now for centuries. Get ready to make some money!

The End of Marketing

How do you drain the bank accounts of people who believe in the end of the world? How do you take advantage of irrational behavior? We believe paranoia is the new wave of marketing and it's worth billions!

The best customers are religious fanatics. They are required to think about the end of the world by their religion. When you are part of a religion who's god is about to flush their creation, you're worried about surviving Hell on Earth just long enough to get a ticket to Heaven. You will also be a little paranoid that you aren't perfect enough to deserve that ticket too.

When there is uncertainty, we need insurance.

Sure, Mom probably thinks her children will go straight to Heaven when the trumpets blow, but she isn't so sure about herself. There was that one incident with the potato salad at the church picnic. Before the pastor's wife started turning three shades of green and spewing like a demon possessed by Linda Blair, well, Mom should have followed her instincts and threw herself on the potato salad like a Marine on a live grenade. Instant rapture is out of the question!

Why not buy Mom the piece of mind that comes with a battle axe for slicing and dicing the demon hoards during the final battle of good verses evil? You love your Mom, right? Buy that axe now!

We want to live! There is a fortune to be made by delaying death. Link longer life with the impending predictions of world-ending events to make the cash register to ring!

Deep down we might not believe in an afterlife. Uncle Harry hasn't come back from Heaven. No pictures, no boring travelog, so Heaven seems a little improbable. A perfect afterlife just doesn't seem as good a deal when nobody you know has pictures of their trip. A few stolen towels and an ash tray with Heaven's logo would be extraordinary evidence that James Randy, magician and skeptic, would approve.

Pleasing your god is like gambling in Vegas. The house is against you. The dice are loaded with original sin and free will. Betting your eternal soul by trying to be like Mother Theresa is crazy! Why not survive forever with medical immortality or be downloaded to a robot body? If you are rich, please invest in these two paths to immortality. The robot is the better option because you can stay in your shipping box until the shooting stops.

The Stock Market

The stock market's middle name is Fear. Our formula is simple: People who believe in the end of the world will sell their stocks at bargain prices within a few weeks of doomsayer predictions. End of the worlders will then sheepishly buy back their beloved stocks at a premium when the world does not end.

Metals like gold could be sky high weeks before a predicted disaster and then affordable a few days before. That's when you should buy. Dragons are not really going to come out of their holes and eat our souls, but the gold market isn't about rationality.

A related way to make money in stocks is to follow the terrorist alert rumors. Various governments are always reporting on terrorists and their targets. Most are false alarms. You can make embarrassing amounts of money speculating on the disinformation by buying stock low when the rumors are at their highest. Sell high when rationality of the market begins to rise.

Target Your Customers

Go for do-it-yourself kits versus individual pieces of gear. Choose disaster scenarios that are popular. Aliens, second coming, volcanos, solar flares, Democrats, its all good. Zombies might not be probable, but they are popular. Global warming is too slow and boats are hard to sell, so avoid them.

A knife advertised for its effectiveness against zombies, is only good when customers are afraid of zombies. Label the knife as good for filleting fish, stabbing terrorists, opening beer bottles, and decapitating zombies. Sell with a 20% markup!

Time to open an apocalypse superstore! Divide your merchandise into the respective disaster scenarios. Instead of menswear, ladies unmentionables, sporting goods, and kitchen appliances, your sections of doom will be biblical, political violence, disease, alien invasion, and ladies unmentionables — remember padded bras doubles as a volcanic dust mask.

Your super store should be designed like any other big chain, with a maze. You shouldn't be able to run in and just buy ammunition. The customer should be frightened by a dozen different apocalyptic scenario on the way in and on the way out. Even as they check out at the counter, be sure to have a few crosses and bottles of holly water for that last impulse purchase. Educate them on what will kill them and what is on sale that will save them.

Fringe groups may be small, but they have discretionary cash to stock their enclaves with supplies. This is also a good reason to start an internet business. Be prepared to ship to a post office box because most enclaves are secret and don't have a mailbox out front.

Study your clients' paranoid delusions. Be ready with helpful advise and of course expensive gear. Delusional crazies are your best sales representatives as they are always telling their friends about surviving the end. Invite doomsayers to speak at your store too. Don't go to the cult; let the cult come to you! Use good judgment — not doomsayers off the street — just the ones with good hygiene and book deals.

The Faithful are Paranoid

The faithful are not as sure of salvation as you might think. Remember this is all about faith. All it takes is stubbing your toe and taking the Lord's name in vain and your all-access pass is revoked.

Chip away at their doubts. Sell your products with little labels, "Just in case you sin."

Permission Marketing

Permission marketing is just a way to get people to beg for your advertisements. Not ads like, "Ammo, 50% Off!" No, we need stories where a little extra ammo saved someone's little girl — stuff that is scary and promotes an automatic reaction. Customers will gleefully sign up to hear your tales of doom. Then they will buy ammo at full price!

Feed your customer's paranoid delusions. Appeal to their sense of survival! Mix doom with anti-doom. When their fear be asteroid-based, talk about how it will all be okay if you only owned a special bracelet with a magnet to ward off the space rock. When they shake in there boots at the mentioning of aliens… We believe a special bracelet with a magnet is the perfect answer because it scrambles the alien's antennas. Famine, zombies, demons, Buddhist presidents hypnotizing the masses? All be solved with a special bracelet with a magnet.

You Might Want to Know

Crystals are out, magnets are in! The reason is obvious; magnets are modern! Do they work? Sure! Search Google for magnets and you will find they will improve your health, ward off spirits, and lower your taxes. Don't search for magnets and pseudoscience because the articles will be a little negative. Don't worry, we are fighting negativity against magnets with the Boys Book of Pseudoscience — in book stores soon!

Remember the old saying: You can catch more flies with honey than with vinegar. Well, the saying is wrong. Truth is, you attract more flies with vinegar. Flies think vinegar smells like stinky feet and you know how flies like stinky feet. Marketing end-of--the-world products with fear, uncertainty, and doubt is paranoid's vinegar.

Remember the J. Peterman Company? Elaine on Seinfeld, worked for J. Peterman on the show. Despite being on a comedy show, the catalog is real, though Elaine isn't real, just Seinfeld himself and the J. Peterman Company. The Peterman catalog has flowery descriptions of products, and lures the buyer into a world where they must have the product to live the story. We can do the same with tales of doom. Here's an example:

> *Our practical collection of luxury weaponry from shiv to broadsword are perfect for demons of any size or other doom befalls intrudes your home or in the battlefield. We guarantee the evil-dead will be quickly and easily dispatched with any of these weapons. Forged in the tradition of King Arthur's Excalibur, the handles are a work of art. Manufactured from the rarest rose wood, carved by an obscure tribe of Brazilian pygmies, polished to a mirror finish then wrapped in buttery Corinthian leather. The metal of the blades are a work of metallurgical art. The recipe, discovered by a Nobel Prize winning materials scientist, Dr Joseph U. Smith of the Detroit University of Metals and Fasteners, created with a specialized mixture of iron imported from Chilean mines high in the Andes, scat from the very rare aye-aye Lemur (for the perfect carbon and trace minerals), then mixed with Gibeon meteorite for its rarity and out of this world strength. The blade is forged by hand, using the secret techniques passed only through bloodline from father to son of the great Damascus blacksmiths. Hand sharpened to an edge of only 10 molecules across, the blade has the durability to decapitate a rampaging zombie with the finesse to delicately dice a tomato!*

Please hire us Mr Peterman!

You are Not Paranoid, Unless You Are!

The best marketing is paranoia and conspiracies are the best sort of doomsaying, especially when selling products. Here is a list of some of the best sellers:

Currency Swap

The United States (or insert your own country) will exchange currency at one-hundred to one value for a new type of money. This will reduce inflation and decrease the national debt. Of course this also means you are 1000% poorer. Do the math yourself (we were just guessing).

The second part of the currency swap conspiracy is that gold will always cost as much as gold. After the swap, sell your gold for 100% what you paid for it.

Rumors of currency swaps are everywhere. They are started by gold merchants and backed by the currency of paranoia. Start your own rumors of currency swaps and you can do the same with wonderful margins.

Scarcity Scare

Scarcity sells. Tell people that you are going to stop selling original Coke and suddenly people are buying cases of the stuff at double the price.

Scarcity is about marketing, not how important a product is to survival. Look again at classic versus new Coke. The classic wasn't important to keeping people alive. It didn't even taste better. People who had never even tasted the new Coke saw classic Coke as scarce so they bought cases of it before it could be discontinued. Just being scarce was all they needed to want more, even if they drank root beer.

Play Classic Coke versus New Coke to create an artificial scarcity panic. It is even better when the fans of the products are doing the marketing for you. No fans? Pretend to be a fan! Problem solved.

Market the future scarcity of your goods. Nothing is in abundance when civilization ends. Sell the belief the end is coming and they will seem scarce.

If people aren't buying, stock less on the shelves to make it look like people are buying. A great strategy is to close for lunch and move half your goods to the back room to make it look like it is a good day to stock up for a disaster. Spend the rest of the day grumbling about canceled shipments because of rumors of government hoarding while you restock the shelves.

Rumors of rioting came just before Obama was elected president. The far right (and Fox News) put out rumors that African Americans and Hawaiians would riot in the streets when Obama lost (or won). The net result was a huge amount of profit as the paranoid bought guns, ammo, and canned pineapples.

Boost your sales with plausible rumors. No reason for them to be true, just imaginable. Anything will set off a panic buying. Start a rumor that cigarettes are about to be banned or that everyone will be forced to buy American cars. It could happen!

Like all con games, the rubes are too embarrassed to ask for refunds. The gullible will fall for such rumors and will then invent new rumors of panic to justify their silly hoard of survivalist weapons and food. In other words, they will sell more of your products! This is the same as Apple iPhone remorse where iPhone buyers pay 10 times the cost of a cheap phone for a phone that is slightly better. Because the phone doesn't live up to the hype, they instead over sell iPhones to cause their friends[53] to buy an iPhone. Eventually we all are happy with our poor battery life and dropped calls because as cattle, chewing our cud is more important than truth. We love word-of-mouth marketing!

Population Reduction

There is supposedly a group of people trying to reduce the world's population. One theory is that flu shots are the delivery mechanism to kill off 90% of the world. Only the rich, famous, and their gardeners will survive.

This is a general purpose scare. Riots or the collapse of society are easy to imagine. You can sell anything with this rumor from guns and ammo to cases of vitamin C.

---

53 We own an iPhone! We love it! Buy one!

Colloidal silver is another great seller as everyone knows, ingesting heavy metals is good for you. Fight flu and vampires. Silver won't cure disease and vampires require a steak, not water with traces of silver, but who cares? Note: Vampires can only be killed by a well-done T-bone to the heart.

Buy Now!

You can't get blood from a stone, and you can't get dead people to pay their bills. The time to sell your survival goods is never better than right now. Don't wait for more signs of the end. Use those fiction writing skills you learned in school to write your own end-of-the-world scenarios and jack up your prices.

People buy more groceries when they visit the supermarket hungry. Your job is to make your patrons hungry for survival. Decorate your store with scary things. Chat with patrons about the latest conspiracy theories. Be creative and be sure to mention how safe you feel with your hoard of supplies and weaponry bought with your meager five percent employee discount.

Here's a great idea: show Fox News on several big screen televisions. Customers will be reminded almost constantly that the world will end soon.

Show a few History Channel favorites that depict the end of the world. The closer the customers feel to the end of civilized society, the more they want to prepare.

Don't decorate your store with trophies of deer. Deer are too cute. You want wild boar with big tusks, mannequins dressed as ninjas, liberals, or liberal ninjas. Customers should feel that you have the weapons for the worst that nature, society and politics will throw at them.

Remind your customers of the extended family. Usually their is one psycho per family and they need to protect their sons and daughters as well as their wives, husbands, and their kids. Everybody in the extended family needs a gun to hold. Preach that more is better when it comes to survival of the family.

Price Gouging

Overcharging in disaster zones is an art form. It goes by many names: privateer, parasite, opportunist, profiteer, merchant of death, scab, exploiter, black marketer, bloodsucker, vampire, shark, and of course, lawyer. Who cares if they call you names? It's about the profit!

Exploiting a disaster is a challenge. There's the low-hanging fruit, like plywood to cover your windows or clean drinking water, or even low-hanging fruit (important when there is a plague of scurvy pirates).

Gouge early, just as the panic starts. The end is likely not real, so everybody is going to be alive and have lighter wallets when the panic starts to become reality. By gouging early, you have time to skip town before the rubes get wise to your no refund policy.

Mobs are Bad for Business

Price gouging is illegal. If you are too blatant, mobs will start to form. A very angry mob. Mobs have a memory; so even temporarily dodging an angry mob is only putting off the inevitable.

Avoid the angry mob with good planning and the following checklist:

Price Gouger's Checklist

- ✓ **Keep prices competitive**: It's not profiteering when everybody is selling water at $5.00 a bottle.
- ✓ **Look big & scary**: A good sign like "Our Prices are High Because We Employ Snipers" will deter troublemakers, even when it's only your 8 year-old with a Daisy pellet gun.
- ✓ **Walk the talk**: Justify your price with tales of inflation and economics theory (this will bore your clients enough to reduce the urge to riot).
- ✓ **Protect your stock**: High walls, razor wire, gun emplacements, security cameras, etc.
- ✓ **Think crowd control**: A narrow alley or feeding goods through a slot will insulate you from Joe Mob.

- ✓ **Quality inventory**: Don't make crowds angrier with poor quality. No food poisoning or tetanus from rusty products. Quality must also survive the end of the world.

End-of-the-World Case Studies

The following are case studies selling apocalyptic goods and services. Why case studies? Business people expect case studies! We need this book to show up when precocious young entrepreneurs search Amazon. It's like putting lipstick on a pig to make the pig look sexy.

Buy Your Caskets NOW!

People are going to die, so why not get things ready and do all your burials close to home. Do you think the funeral home is going to be business as usual when the world ends?

Key selling points:

- ✓ Funeral homes will be crowded.
- ✓ Burial is easy when you know how.
- ✓ Laws about burials at home will be void at the end of the world.
- ✓ Many people live alone. Make it easy to bury yourself.
- ✓ Use web-based instructions to save on printing costs. Sell nothing for more profit!
- ✓ Send consultants to the client's home so they can plan grave plots in the back yard.
- ✓ Apartment dwellers need help too! What about prefab mausoleums?

Going the extra mile for the customer:

- ✓ Grave digging services (remind customers to book early)
- ✓ Biodegradable caskets
- ✓ Self-cremation kits
- ✓ Do-it-your-self embalming kit, with instructional DVD

- ✓ Self-burial kits — Drops the dirt on your grave when you're the last one in
- ✓ Easy to store, easy to assemble caskets
- ✓ Got a pool? How about a mini burial at sea?
- ✓ Do it yourself grief counseling training videos
- ✓ Don't forget personalized grave markers!

Pull on the strings of their heart and desire to feel secure:

- ✓ Care for your loved ones as they would expect
- ✓ Imagine the peace of a proper grave
- ✓ Be "safe" in your grave
- ✓ Know you have prepared for the end in the most natural way
- ✓ Have the benefits of a funeral and all the trimmings at home

Easiest selling tool — Fear:

- ✓ Imaging rotting in your home
- ✓ Think of your loved ones rotting in your home, when you are still alive
- ✓ Imagine your neighbors knowing you and your family are rotting in your home
- ✓ Stop the mutilation of corpses by demons with proper burial technique
- ✓ Would you rather be properly buried or be your neighbor's protein?

Books, DVD, Magazines

Books are a great way to make money from The End. Regardless of whether this is our DVD, our magazine, the eBook, or audio book on iTunes, whatever, it sells. We are proving that even someone as intelligent and good looking as you will pay good money for something written by a team of amateurs.

People listen to experts, but that means you need to start pretending to be an expert. Start writing! You'll eventually get used to the dirty feeling of being a scumbag as the money replaces your guilt with sports cars and box seats at the ball game.

What to Write About

There are no limits. Preach against sin or talk about the god of your choice. *We highly recommend that you do not sell humorous books on the end of the world.* This book has already cornered that market as will its many sequels. Instead, here are a few titles that don't have us as direct competition:

A Few Book Topics

Zen and the Art of Bomb Shelter Maintenance — *A ripping good tale of renewal and change in the face of the end of the world.*

Chicken Soup of the Soulless — *Tragedy, as long as it happens to other people, is heartwarming.*

Teaching your Dog to Hunt Zombies — *Don't ignore the specialty self-help books. Pet lovers are survivalists too!*

Understanding the End of Time — *Reduce confusion, even if it gives your readers the willies.*

Religions of the World, and How to Guarantee Your Soul — *One of our favorites (too bad it's already a perfectly good chapter in this book).*

Cooking for the Left Behind — *In the world of chaos and death, you still need to cook great meals for you and your family. More than 50 recipes, from road kill to picking wild plants or scavenging from bombed out neighborhoods. With a special bonus chapter, "From Vegetarian to Cannibal." Whip up a* *scrumptious post-apocalyptic menu. Special bonus: "Transforming Sawdust to a Dessert Topping."*

The Web

The power of the web in the end-times is god-like. Really! There is so much potential for starting a new internet business that could make billions from The End. Imagine a Left Behind Facebook! What about a twittering service for prisoners of the alien overlords? Potential lies in every brimstone scented bit and byte when the Antichrist comes to Earth.

Global Warming and Real Estate

With global warming and the threat that California will shake itself into the sea, you need to be thinking real estate. While avoiding killer tsunamis from killer asteroids to being as far away from civilization as possible, you'll make silly amounts of money in pre-cataclysm real estate.

They say the average world temp will go up several degrees which means Alaska will feel like Bangkok. Great news for the colder climates. Rain forests are headed to the poles!

Scientists say, 'global warming' and 'deserts' in the same breath. They talk about the death of forests. Look around where it's really hot and you will see that miles and miles of forests in the tropics are doing just fine in the heat. Friends, the tropics are going to move a bit north.

With change, comes opportunity. Oak and Pine — Out! Mango and Coconut — In! Global warming changes fear into a passion for shrubbery and landscaping. Global warming is creeping up on us. Pine trees and their brethren are firewood. Tropical plants are in! Alaska is the new tropics. A tropical paradise! The cabana boys are stacked like chord wood.

Time to rethink landscaping. Change your landscape from pine trees and perennials to tropicals. Mangos, coconuts, dates, bananas, rose apples, dragon fruit, durian, and many more tropical edibles will also help sell the home.

You Might Want to Know

Be careful where you plant coconut trees.

> *Coconuts are great, but they are one of the number one killers in tropical climates. A coconut will hit your head at about 50 miles per hour. Ouch!*

Don't worry about water. That's another silly fib from climate scientists. With more of it not locked in glaciers, there is more water for rain. Yes, there will be new deserts, but new lakes too. Good drinking water will be scarce, but only because the amount of water used by each human will increase because of the increased popularity of Japanese toilets with butt sprinklers.

Shifting Real Estate

Did you know that the melting of the ice caps will change the tilt[54] of the Earth? Sure, it will take thousands of years, but you need to plan!

The low lying ground will be under water because there's not enough weight from glaciers, so Greenland pops up, causing a huge rise in ocean levels. Jack in the box continents. Who knew?

Everyone is planning to be fifteen feet under water, but what should you do when it's twenty-five feet? Hedge your bets! Buy or build buildings with lower floors as parking. This way when the water rises higher than expected, nothing gets damaged.

Altitude is important. Forget the coast. Mountains are the in-thing. Altitude will increase your property value for many types of apocalypse from tsunamis caused by asteroid impacts, sea levels rising, diseases in crowded cities, or even zombies (they prefer open fields, as shuffling uphill is difficult for the undead).

Location, Location, Location

In your real estate listings, don't just crow about the number of bathrooms and the cool media room. List the things that owners will find important when the world is about to snuff it. Here are a few things to put in your listings to guarantee a quick sell:

- ✓ Convenient access to fallout shelters

---

[54] http://tinyurl.com/c3yn2b

- ✓ Valuation, as beaches get closer after ice caps melt
- ✓ Distance from the beach (killer tsunami survival)
- ✓ Nearest survivalist enclaves
- ✓ Ease of conversion to a defendable fortress
- ✓ Distance (away) from high value terrorist targets
- ✓ Lack of or density of neighborhood fanatics
- ✓ Devout neighbors and fanatics that will help protect you against the Antichrist

Target the fanatics too. Make the property shine for someone willing to pay top dollar for an investment that meets their fanatical leanings.

Think of that last bit again: fanatical leanings. Hold out for the fanatics. They spend more money for anything that meets their fanatical ideals. A worthless property is worth ten times more when you put a fanatical spin on it. Fanatics equal silly profit, plain and simple.

What about the ease of security? Are the windows the same size as sheets of plywood? Homes on hills are easily defended from everything from demons to floods. Show the buyer how easy it is to put razor wire on the fence.

Know your audience. Write for the survivalists and publish in the fanatical rags, like gun magazines, survivalist web sites, or the Sunday flyer at the evangelical cult.

Did you know new pools and homes with pools sold better just before New Years 2000? It happened because people were afraid of a Y2K disaster and a pool increases the amount of the drinking water. A three bathroom, two bath house only has enough water storage for about a week (assuming tubs are filled just before the Devil disconnects the plumbing). A pool is great for entertainment and leisure, but adds a backup water supply for months! Swimming pools can also be converted to post-apocalyptic aqua culture (homegrown catfish for dinner is yummy).

The apocalyptic housing market is already picking up as we get closer to 2012. The value of abandoned missile silos is taking off like a nuclear tipped rocket! The closer the end-times, the sooner you are making a killing in real estate!

New Land Rush

Fly over Siberia. It is all ice, snow, and more ice. No cities for hundreds of miles. Doesn't seem like a good spot for a vacation home unless you like making snow angels when it's 30 below. Global climate change is about to thaw out the real estate market in these winter hinterlands.

Right now icy land is cheap. Look for the right land that won't be swamp in five years. When you end up with swamp land, sell quickly. You can always fall back on the buyer-beware laws. Use fine print plus a good lawyer to keep out of trouble.

Once you have good land, look for government handouts or folks that already have their share. We expect buckets of government money to be paid to people that loose their homes to seas rising. Governments love giving away money to people that decided to live in a disaster zone!

As an alternative real estate strategy, consider buying low lying land in Louisiana. Eventually another storm will flood the area and there we be more government handouts. Being an idiot can reap great profits.

Promoting New Communities

Why are there so many people in California? The Tournament of Roses[55] parade. Imagine you are living in Buffalo, New York, one of the coldest places in the USA. Imagine watching a parade in sunny California while there is twenty feet of snow waiting to be shoveled out of your driveway. A few weeks after the parade, there are hundreds of new immigrants headed to California.

Buffalo is quickly becoming a balmy paradise because of global warming. Girls in Buffalo are going from pasty white to healthy tans. Californians are tired of having their lawn chairs catch fire each summer and are running to Buffalo.

Well…. Not Buffalo. Not until they get a better parade.

---

55 http://en.wikipedia.org/wiki/Tournament_of_Roses

Plan a celebration that will help promote your community. When continental ice shelves fall into the sea and flood coastal cities, you should be ready with a parade. Spin the celebration as an invitation for refugees to resettle in your new community. Invite refugees with a party, with free drinks, and low interest loans.

Farther north, where the permafrost is now not so permanent, there are other opportunities. We'd call our new community Mammoth or Wooly. You don't have to find an ancient beast in the permafrost. Make up a good story about daisies on a baby mammoth's tongue. It will help sell the image of a tropical paradise returning — minus mammoths mucking up your garden and sabertooth cats eating your little dog, Fluffy.

Psychological Counseling

The stress of The End is going to make people a little bit crazier. There will be enough screaming, bodies slathered with peanut butter and jelly, and even normal people roaming the streets with a butcher knife in one hand and a copy of volume three of *Left Behind* in the other. What we need is a little therapy.

World wide cataclysm will create a golden age of the mental health industry. Patients lining up to get absolution from someone paid to listen.

Even normal people will think they are going crazy. Your best bet for fame and fortune is to buy a therapist couch and store it in the garage until the right apocalyptic moment. Beware: You need a strong stomach and some plastic furniture covers resistant to the sort of stains caused by fear-based bowel movement.

Therapy sells better when patients have options to choose their specific flavor of crazy. Have a menu! Nobody wants to eat the same crazy every day. Here are a few specific therapies to serve:

Pre-End Therapy

First up are the stressed out pre-end worriers. Tension builds up every time they start to hear about possible horrors and rumors of signs of the world ending. When Fox News is advertising survival backpacks and gold, patients will begin the march toward fear, uncertainty doubt and run-around-naked-in-the-streets panic.

The doom-crazy don't hide their fears. Almost anything will set them off. Hang out in the book store and wait for a little scream when they see the cover of this book. It is easy to find them, the skill will be to get them to pay high fees to get someone to listen to their fears.

Want to find patients? Frequent the local Army Navy surplus stores and clap your hands loudly every few minutes. The apocalyptic nuts will either jump at the sudden noise or ask you if the clapping keeps the voices under control.

Approach prospective patients slowly, don't just whip out your business card. Start slow and ask if the family is worried about the end of the world. The goal is to sell multiple hours of lucrative talk time to the family members affected by Mr Crazy Pants. Mr Pants will be happy to go because he craves someone to talk to.

What do you think when your spouse suddenly starts digging a shelter in the back yard? Crazy, right? That's free money when you are a therapist. Families don't always see eye-to-eye on imaginary disasters. Need your significant other to buy into your fanaticism? There's couple's therapy for the fanatical! Specializing in end-time delusions is sure to fill the waiting room.

Nobody wants a therapist to help them disbelieve. It's hard work to believe in the end times! They want to feel better about their beliefs, not get rid of then! It's perfectly legitimate to pretend you are in the same boat (or perhaps ark). The delusions are useless unless they bring others into their imagined reality. Lure them in with seminars on *The End* or Facebook groups for survivalists.

Pre-end therapy doesn't require our world to expire. The patient just has to believe the Earth will be udders up at any moment. The only sure cure is that the world ends, so you'll have a patient for life until people start rising from the grave (another source of therapy clients).

You Might Want to Know

Nothing is unethical when you make enough

money to pay your lawyer.

End Therapy

As the end is happening, people will seek help. You'll have two types of patients: The ones who were already worried but now see it happening and those that don't believe it's happening and now think they are crazy and imagining it's happening.

People believe just about anything when they are seeing real live aliens, Yellowstone becoming a hundred mile wide volcano, dead rising from the grave, or the pointy demon tails poking out their neighbor's Bermuda shorts. Add antidepressants and perhaps a little dramatic voodoo Kabuki theater and you are the only therapist driving a Hummer as the world rots.

Patients need some help to cope with the terror of the Earth opening up and the Sun standing still. Sell *Find Your Inner Calm* subliminal hypnosis tapes. No need to really create subliminal jibber jabber. Just print new labels. Nobody can hear subliminal messages, so why should you record them? It's also a good way to dispose of your ex-girlfriend's Barry Manilow CDs.

Left-Behind Therapy

When the world ends and the dregs of humanity are still clinging to existence, it's time for talk therapy. There is no need for lawyers, accountants, gardeners, or hotel clerks. The biggest job now is making people feel good about surviving and becoming one of the *left behind.*

There could be billions of people on the edge between being taken up to Heaven or who only sinned a little too much to make the cut. Many are called, but few are chosen, as they say. These confirmed sinners need to examine their lives for why they were left behind (note: you were left behind to make a profit). As a self proclaimed and semi-qualified and properly compensated professional therapist, it is your meal ticket–especially since you aren't Heaven bound anyway.

Therapy essential when the zombie badger poop starts to burn your sinus. When you can feel it oozing between your toes, therapy becomes as necessity as a pedicure.

As a self-proclaimed therapist, you've got the skill to barter for food and shelter. Aim high and look for a survivalist enclave with the best benefits. You may not be able to contribute in meaningful ways, like scavenging for food or sacrificing virgins to the Antichrist, but by being a therapist, you'll keep folks from going ape poopy crazy.

Convincing an enclave leader that they need a psychologist on the staff is the only tricky bit. The end-of-the-world enclave is run by a psychopath and already missing a screw and a few other parts–which is how they got the job. Leaders of enclaves are already sensitive to being called wackos. The reason these leaders are in charge is because they were already prepping for a world that was going look like a pig farm the day after port was declared okay. One wrong word and you're one of the 'evil ones' and you won't get paid.

Take precautions when meeting your patients. When the world is running low on food, roasted therapist tastes a lot better than mud pies. Use barbed wire and steel doors to separate you from your customers during therapy sessions.

No-End Therapy

When true believers miss an apocalypse, they don't simply wake up to reality. No, they get depressed. Imagine waiting for demons, aliens, volcanoes, or fire from the sky and having a date roll by with nothing happening?

People who expect an end might be a tad more suicidal than others. Look at the cults who had vodka and pain killers or the cyanide and cool-aid. They were so disappointed.

We are not certified therapists, but we watch therapists act on TV. We've learned a lot from watching Oprah. Laughter is good medicine, and you should buy doom cult members this book. Make them laugh. It's a first step.

The worst cases are the true believers that also have university degrees. So smart, but so dumb. It takes hours of very expensive therapy to cure that kind of dumb.

Smart people are so smart that they convince themselves of anything. Even with direct evidence they will stubbornly stick to their guns and find excuses. "We misread that calendar. The world has to end sometime, right?" It's your job to stop such nonsense in its tracks. Prescribe expensive drugs and three sessions a week plus group therapy. Let your heart be your guide when you need to pay for your second home in the Bahamas.

The milder psychotics will live in trailer parks. A therapy session will start like this: "I didn't see any aliens last week, so I guess they decided to call it off. I figure they didn't like our beer. Thought they'd like Bud, but they is picky little green men." The notion that aliens don't like our beer will be the only focus of the therapy. Group sessions should be avoided as your clients will become competitive and start showing everyone their anal probe scars. Therapy can't repair the damage from seeing a group of trailer trash residents dropping their drawers and winking at you.

End-Proof-Homes™

There is money to be made in the shelter business. Shelters aren't just for the cold war anymore. Sell doom-proof housing and accessories for every scenario from a Democratic presidential election, to aliens, to terrorists, and Chinese food additives that cause global constipation. Whatever the disaster, there's a custom hole just right for your customers to put their head into until the smoke clears.

Use caution when you install the features. Some end-of-the-worlders are very paranoid. Egyptian Pharaohs would kill anyone who knew their secrets. These guys are like Egyptians except they have guns and a pit in the back yard. Never ever meet the client in person and use blind labor.

Do-it-yourself Shelters

End of the worlders are into self sufficiency. They love the feeling of building IKEA furniture, even though it looks like a pile of pressed wood trash when they are done. The paranoid also want to limit the number of people who know about their shelter.

The gravy on tart apple pie of do-it-yourself end-of-the-world shelters is the low overhead. Sell the plans, not the materials. Even better, sell the plans online! Nothing better than collecting[56] money for designs that cost you nothing to print. No need to hire an architect. Just resell old blueprints from ICBM missile silos.

Nobody successfully builds IKEA furniture. Sure, we love the feeling of building our Billy bookcases with our allen wrench and a Swedish to English dictionary, but all the furniture at our office leans a little to the left. The cat keeps throwing up. Learn from the big guys (IKEA of course) and rent out cheap labor with battery-powered screwdrivers.

Don't forget about the procrastinators. Herds of TV-remote-button-pushers don't want to do things until it is really obvious — not just the sky turning red, but grandma-gnawing-on-your-arm obvious. For those folks, create designs built from scraps and splinters of a war zone.

The key to a great kit or plan is the title. Here are a few good ones that have already been tested on residents of our local psych ward.

- ✓ How to Drain and Decorate a Cesspool or Sewer
- ✓ Remodeling Abandoned Silos
- ✓ Adobe Brick Homes: The Miracle of Turning Mud and Grass Clippings into Civilization
- ✓ Using Minions to Build Your Pyramid
- ✓ Scavenge Your Way to Security and Shelter
- ✓ How to Build Your Road Warrior Fortress

Equipping Homes and Apartments

To the entrepreneur, the doom-minded survivalist apartment dweller is ripe for profit. They have credit cards and don't expect civilization to survive long enough to send a repo man to collect. They are ready to buy! Here's their shopping list:

- ✓ Surveillance cameras
- ✓ Radios for dating the last man or woman on Earth

---

56 Sorry, no refunds for eBooks.

- ✓ Duck tape (not *duct tape*), the ultimate in home sealers
- ✓ Blackout curtains so zombies can't tell you're home
- ✓ Bulletproof glass and steel doors
- ✓ Plywood and nails
- ✓ Anti-mind-control barriers (works for aliens and CIA)

Air Purification Doesn't Suck

When there is pestilence, infestation, or the smell of death, filters are in. Be in the business of smells, stench, rotting neighbors, airborne pathogens, radioactive dust, or the bad breath of alien invaders. Each make living deadly, significantly deadly, or so nauseous that buzzards can't keep a meal down.

When things get bad, sell charcoal and a wet rag, or jars of Vics VapoRub to make things smell less "I just puked in my mouth a little."

Mind Control Solutions

Everyone has mind control. Aliens, secret organizations, supernatural beings and even scientists have a device that can bend your mind to their will. Devices can make you see God, become irritable, or even make you believe someone is standing behind you. Fox news has the biggest mind control antennas in the world, just outside Dallas.

Mind control comes in many forms, so sell various types for different scenarios. Protection from the otherworldly versus the run-of-the-mill alien may take something stronger than aluminum foil. We recommend Lithium, holy water and protective saint medals. An excellent defense is an iPod with annoying advertising jingles. Jingles stay in your head long after the iPod's battery goes.

It's hard to get a premium price for simple tin foil hats. Go high-end with wire mesh beanies, priest-blessed ear plugs and Faraday cages. All of these are guaranteed sellers and as long as your customers aren't psychotic, you can offer a money back guarantee.

Anti-mind control is a multi purpose product! They also block cancer-causing cell phone radiation. Such radiation has not been proven scientifically, but it does seem to affect how people drive, why not be paranoid?

Your customers are the ones that want to protect themselves from mid control. Many are already victims. This is good news because you can hire them to do your sales and marketing. They know what sells to the paranoid and you get extra help for free from the extra voices in their heads. Employees can be found at www.hearing-voices.org.

Survivalist Farming Supplies

Fresh-farmed food is a godsend when your god has destroyed everything but juicy grubs scavenged from the neighbor's corpse. Farming isn't easy, especially when all you have is a stick. You need supplies for proper farming.

Biological war or other nastiness like flying hell hounds means it is a lot safer to stay inside. Being inside also means that you customers need to bring their survival farming inside too. Lucky for you, the medicinal marijuana industry is a great source of at-home farming supplies. Here are a few more things to sell:

- ✓ Anti-radiation fertilizer
- ✓ Magic beans
- ✓ Anything that can be fermented into alcohol

Don't forget about the pests. A good scarecrow dressed as a Catholic priest will keep away the demons. Use holy water for irrigation for protection and a heavenly flavor.

A perfect survival crop is mushrooms. All you need is fresh poop and a dark place. When the world ends, there will be tons of fear-based fecal matter too! Mushrooms don't require grow lights, so they are the best crop for your dark hiding place.

Radiation and cosmic waves are the only enemy of the mushroom farmer. As we all know, a little bit of the wrong radioactivity will mutate a portabella mushroom into deranged killer. Use the mushroom's tendency to mutate to your financial advantage. Sell radiation detectors, flame throwers, and semiautomatic shotguns too.

Maggots are at the top of the survivalist food pyramid. Yes, eating maggots is disgusting! Who would want to eat cute little baby flies? It's all about survival. Grind them up, form them into the shape of chicken nuggets, coat with crunchy fly wing batter, then fry them up. Yum!

Restraints

What happens when your family becomes mindless zombies? What do you do if your sister is possessed by evil? You don't want to shoot your loved ones in the brain stem. Why not have a set of restraints to safely care for your subhuman, zombified, or otherwise demon-possessed family?

Restraints are also legal to sell and own without a license or messy background check! Few laws have ever been written to restrict the sales of restraints. Sure they are illegal to use on your mother in law, but only if she isn't possessed.

Restraint (of others) has its pleasures and privileges. You're the guy in charge and dictate terms when you hold the keys. Did we mention restraints are legal? No gun permit and no waiting period! More money in the bank, sooner!

Self-expanding packing foam is a great restraint. A bucket of that stuff could immobilize a whole slobbering hoard of shambling brain eaters. When the world doesn't end, it's also great for packing all your useless survivalist gear and selling it on eBay.

Think big and small. You never know when you'll be up against a seven foot devil-may-care demon or very small evil pixie. Sell your customers all the options. Sell the joy of restraint.

Don't limit yourself to physical restrains. Restraints come in many forms. Holy water-soaked twine or silver cloth or blessed baggie ties, sell it all. Sell salt and chalk so customers can defend against whatever supernatural attack they are irrationally afraid of meeting in a dark ally.

Remember, it isn't what's real that we are afraid of, its what we imagine is real. Same goes for your defense products. It's what you imagine will work. If you sell it for twice the price, it works even better!

Magic supplies are also good restraints. 'Magic' chalk with a booklets detailing the best way to draw pentagrams the perfect Christmas present. The 'magic' in 'magic' chalk, tis of course just chalk. The instructions however are as authentic as you can make them seem. We highly recommend a creative fantasy writing workshop at the local junior college.

Disinfectant Systems

Germs are big business. Look how Bird Flu caused people to flock to the drug store. Ultraviolet lights, misters, clean room air purifiers, soap dispensers, all are loved by the anyone that is afraid of germs. Your best customers have Mysophobia (not to be confused with Germaphobe, which is a person that is afraid of Germans).

Decontamination showers are wonderful devices. They wash off everything from anthrax to radioactive dust and zombie spittle. Even super volcano ash is washed right out of your hair with one of these high powered body-washing systems. Go for the ones that don't require a team clad in anti-contamination suits and wielding bristly brushes (though institutional sales should not be ignored).

Decontaminations showers are an easy sell to moms. Tired of your child tracking in radioactive waste? Wash the messy killers off at the door before your child ever steps foot in your shelter's airlock.

Home Security

Having a shelter is worthless if you can't keep the riffraff out. Think razor wire and gun emplacements. Make a comfy home a fortress. Sell heavy duty stuff that would make a soldier of fortune jealous.

Quiz your customers for hints on what to stock. Here is a shopping list from a church member in Dallas:

- ✓ Lucky charms (voodoo, not the cereal)
- ✓ Guard dogs/cats/rats/zombies
- ✓ Pope-crow (a scarecrow with a pope hat)
- ✓ Blessing of ultimate protection (from the popular god of the moment, of course)

- ✓ Rubberized plague victim decoys
- ✓ Faux gun nests
- ✓ Fake security cameras.

Survival Food

Food at the beginning of disasters is as important as a change of underwear. The end does not come between lunch and afternoon tea. The world is going to devolve into chaos on its own schedule, so you need to be prepared to wait months and even years before you expect to end your life on Earth. There is nothing worse than dying of starvation when you could be properly killed by whatever calamitous, dreadful, fateful, ghastly, and gloomy apocalypse is coming your way.

You're going to need to eat in conditions that are beastly, creepy, dire, distressing, fearful, formidable, frightful, ghastly, grievous, grim, and grody. If you expect to live for a while, especially when you're itching to fight for good (or evil), you need calories.

Freeze-dried food is good, but it has the disadvantage of requiring some cooking. Sell a device similar to the ones used on the International Space Station or Space Shuttle. Brand your products with astronauts giving a thumbs up and NASA logos!

Survival food should be compact, have a shelf life of twenty years, be simple to prepare, and taste at least a little better than sawdust. Considering these simple requirements, most snacks found in vending machines will work. Speaking of fast food, sell puke buckets too. Apocalyptic cuisine is hard to keep down. Why waste a good meal?

Mixing survival food with wild game will also stretch the client's dollar. Sell a good survivalist cookbook at the same time you sell the freeze dried corn and assault rifles.

Why not add a personal touch by writing your own cookbook? Adding bugs and grubs for protein is good for you and adds a little crunch. Maggot chili is just as good a meal as Fritos chili when you keep your eyes closed and suppress your gag reflex.

Survivalists Gear

Survival is the key to marketing when the world ends. Despite all the gloom and doom, only a few disasters will kill off everyone. Selling survivalist gear is also a well established marketing concept and a very profitable business. What you need to do to really sell is target additional buyers from the lunatic fringe of doomists.

Survivalist gear is just camping equipment. The key to making sales is that customers don't buy the gear for family outings. Everything is labeled with the worst-case scenario and a Bible quote or two.

Have outings where you teach customers how to use their equipment. Simulate invasions and disasters. This is great because customers use up their supplies and need to buy more.

Customers need to feel special. Have a special phone number for customers to hear a recording of the latest world-ending threats? You can also announce the literally last minute opportunity to buy fresh supplies. Customers appreciate a good sales and a head start to begin running and screaming off to the mountains.

"Survivalist gear" often goes by the code word "camping." When you are at a camping store, the clerks will often ask if you want to buy a two foot long Rambo-style special forces survival blade of death (compass built into the hilt) for "camping" — and they usually say, "camping" with double finger air quotes and a wink.

"Camping" stores do twice the business when they sell army surplus, silver bullets, and the odd crucifix dagger (works with vampires and demonic squirrels). Your sales pitch should be filled with concern for your customers welfare. Be a story teller too. A good tale of an encounter with unpleasant wildlife, like biker gangs will sell your premium weapons.

"Camping" stores often have a locked display case behind the counter with interesting items like butterfly knives, nun-chucks (if you were raised catholic, you would understand why these are a necessity), and throwing stars. In the trade these are called martial arts supplies. They are rarely used for any kind of art, but are especially meant for teenage kids who watch martial arts movies. Cash in when the fourteen-year-old kids get their allowance.

Many weapons are classified as outright illegal. For example, switchblades, sword canes, and other concealed mayhem. How do you sell them? It's easy, just label them as art, memorabilia, and as a collectible. They are illegal to carry, not to sell. A good shiv knife belt buckle is good for cutting rope and keeping your pants up — nudge, nudge, know what we're talking about (knowing wink and double air quotes)?

Apocalyptic Franchise!

Owning your own business is a fool's game. You work and slave to make and sell your anti-demon charms, but you get no time off. You are your own boss, but your boss is a slave driver. Time to franchise!

One of our favorite books is *The E Myth* by Michael E. Gerber. In this wonderful book the author shows that owning a business, although fun, is hard work. The better business is selling dozens of copies of your business. Think golden arches or unreasonably priced coffee. Ideal franchises are lucky charms, water purification, anti-Antichrist balms, and do-it-yourself-cult kits.

Document your business. How do you make those anti-demon charms? Write it all down. The secret of the franchise is selling the instructions.

The sign of a successful franchise is consistency. How do you greet your customers? Do you simply greet them with a blessing or spit on them to ward off evil? What do you chant as you roll your cart down the street? "Get your anti-demon charms! Keep demons off the doorstep! Blessed and approved by our spiritual leader!" What keeps the franchisee safe from the angry mobs? Their safety will keep those franchise fees rolling in.

What is it about your cart, signs, and things that set the business apart from the others? Is it the charms that give a customer a sense of service, or the beheaded demon in a jar? What about your uniform of leather and spikes? Write it down!

Franchise are more than just the instructions. Profits come from selling the trappings of your business. Signs, carts, and the raw materials for your demon charms. Supply them slaves, minions, or properly charmed demons to do the hard work. Customers will always be impressed by happily zombified employees, even when the world knee deep in wildebeest poop.

Next, make up rules and procedures for your franchise operations. Rules are important. You want your franchisees to follow the rules to the letter to protect your brand and assure consistent service. A magical ward against evil should work and feel the same no matter where you buy it, just like consistently crunchy French fries at one of those Irish clown fast food restaurants (note to self: trademark Witch-in-the-box McWarlock and Witch-in-the-box).

The trick will be to enforce rules when aliens are busy probing or demons are biting. There are no lawyers to sue people during the end-times (they will not survive the first rabid mobs). Hire a voodoo priestess to curse a violator when they step outside the prescribed lines of your franchise guidelines. Use a curse to prevent them from selling at a discount or substituting cheaper materials.

Call in an enforcer. There are out of work minor gods that can be had for a low payment of a sacrificed virgin. This will be much easier when the Earth opens up and finding lava is just down the street. Find a virgin, toss her in – or him, because nerdy and awkward virgin teenagers are more plentiful. In fact, you might not even need to throw them into the lava as they will probably trip and fall in if you distract them with a box set of Firefly videos.

Visiting your franchisees is important. Keep a watchful eye on quality. A real ever watchful eye will do when the world slips into weirdness. Know when a franchisee's charms are not as effective or customers are getting eaten by slobbering red-eyed zombie wolverines. Take action quickly when the poop is hitting the fan and blowing in the wrong direction.

Make an example of the offender so others know you weren't kidding. Public floggings and rumors of a curse of oozing herpes sores are effective motivators.

Chicken feet and bat entails will be expensive as civilization crumbles. Economize by using human nature and environment to control your franchisees. Inform the franchisee that they'll get explosive diarrhea for even thinking about breaking a franchise rule. Add a contract written in blood to ensure the level of gullibility is set on eleven. The power of suggestion and dodgy end of the world hygiene will keep them thinking you know their every thought.

End of the World Reruns

Plan for the world not ending. Doomsayers disappoint and asteroids fail to kill us everyday. A failure to end the world is just plain inevitable. The best time to strike is soon after nothing has struck. When their predictions fail, believers will be confused by a world that's no different from the day before. They'll have no resistance to a sales representative who is ready to sell them a brand new apocalypse.

Selling Your Survivalist Cache

World still here? Got ten years of freeze dried food, 500 gallons of diesel, 20,000 rounds of machine gun ammo, and a gallon of anti-demon yack spit? What are you going to do with all this stuff when the sky doesn't[57] fall?

Another end-of-the-world cult is always in the wings. Sell your stuff to the cults that have a date for the end of the world later than your old cult. These cults have all the proof that your cult's end of the world is the "false end" because it hasn't ended. Q.E.D.: their end is the "true end." They need to stock up with guns and yack spit!

Sell your cache to the competition. Sell "like new" yack spit and all the dressing. The trick is quickly getting the word out to the cults of doom that still have a date in the future. Start a bidding war between cults.

When 2012 proves Mayan pants are on fire, there'll be cults still praying that 2012 is a bust. Get your listings up on eBay an hour or so before 2012 and have the action end in a few days.

Sell your shelter/silo/cave as fully furnished and stocked. Unloading your secret base, weapons and goods all at once is a great strategy.

---

57 There are no cases of a cult that wakes up alive after an end of the world prediction and suddenly becomes Atheist.

When selling your property, be careful. Remember how paranoid you were when you bought your little slice of anti-apocalypse heaven. Take precautions and avoid death and dismemberment by your paranoid buyers. Some of the mixed nuts buying shelters don't want anyone to know where they are hiding out. Imagine being the first estate agent of missile silos listed as "Missing" on milk cartons.

For Sale; 3 Bedroom, 2 bath Minuteman missile silo. Completely furnished with rebuilt class-one biological and radiological filters, blast doors, 3 new remote controlled .223 full-auto machine gun nests covering entrance, 50,000 gallon water and 5,000 gallon diesel, 10 years freeze dried food for a family of 5. Great price!
– Call box 3078, ask for Bob

Experiment: eBay #1

This is an experiment in fear. Sell two identical pieces of jewelry on eBay. In one description, be honest about the jewelry. In the other, say how the jewelry is really an ancient charm that will protect the wearer from the coming apocalypse.

When you are inevitably successful, start up your own eBay store specializing in protective charms and retire to your own private island.

Questions

- ✓ Does it help to name the specific end-of-the-world scenario?
- ✓ Did you promise protection from demons, better health, peace of mind, or wealth? Does this help sell more or affect the bid price?
- ✓ What percentage of your sales were delivered to trailer parks?

Experiment: eBay #2

Create and sell your own anti-mind control hats. Extra credit if the hats become a fad!

Questions

- ✓ Does it help that your hats can be hidden under a real hat or look like a real hat?
- ✓ Do your customers appreciate quality materials?
- ✓ What claims did you use to sell your hats?

    a. Protects against CIA mind control
    b. Psychic proof
    c. Tested by aliens
    d. Proof that you test each hat
    e. All of the above

Experiment: Start an End-of-the-World Garden

Get dirty! The result should be to have more information on what to sell the paranoid for their end of the world gardens.

Build a defense system to protect your crops. Note: In place of real weapons, use squirt guns (use holy water — don't get too creative). Also, use twine or rope with twisty ties to simulate barbed wire.

Questions

- ✓ What is the difference between a fruit, a vegetable, and a mutant killer vegetable?

- ✓ Why is it that vegetables are always the mutants, and not fruits?
- ✓ Describe the best techniques for growing mushrooms in a bomb shelter.
- ✓ Are there any radiation-resistant crops?

Post-World Entertainment — Entertaining the Left Behind

When the world looks like a Mad Max, we need own Thunderdome of entertainment. Live entertainment will never go out of style. Entertain the last few people on Earth and make a mountain of cash.

Professional Wrestling

Think masks, capes, and cool names like The Crusher. The only problem with professional wrestling is that it's fake. Fake wrestling is hard to learn, and the pay is rather high for such faux skill. Instead, have no-holds-barred death matches instead of the fake stuff. You eliminate the high-cost talent and save money on fake blood. Your audience will also appreciate the honest violence and the satisfying crackle of broken teeth.

Getting talent for a death match isn't as hard as you would imagine. The desperate are willing to trade a chance of death for a can of peas. They have a look that says: So-hungry-I'll-eat-rats-and-like-it.

Don't just have battles between people. Take advantage of demons, aliens, zombies, Baptists, and lawyers. The crowd will love to cheer for the home team too. Mr. Rogers versus Demon From The Seventh Level of Hell!

Zombies are entertaining too! Why not have them fight over a bit of brain on a hook? You could make a little extra cash by selling lottery tickets to be the one that donates the brains.

Stand Up To Comedy

Comedians let us forget our worries, our empty bellies, poor economy, death form the skies, and missing loved ones being served at the dinner table of our alien overlords. Laughter will heal the soul, even when your eternal spirit is destined for damnation.

Comedy is hard. People think they are hilarious, but rarely do they deliver. When the professional comedians killed by the opening volley of the calamitous, cataclysmic, catastrophic, and cruel end, you'll need to look for whatever funny remains in the rubble of humanity. In the beginning you will need to have competitions before you find the true comedians. A comedian death match is will pack the house, sell popcorn and have a few laughs too.

Comedian death matches are twice as entertaining. Two comedians compete, with the loser being fed to a mutant poodle as big and mean as your mother in law.

Entertaining Alien Overlords

A great way to survive an invasion from space is to entertain your alien conquerors. Knowing what's humorous is a challenge, especially when you are trying to make an alien laugh. Even figuring out when aliens are laughing is hard to do. It may seem like laughing, but it could be bad gas from eating a fatty human liver. Hard to tell with human babies, but with an alien, the baby gave it gas.

A good way to judge an alien's entertainment quotient is to observe them. It's doubtful that they'll like normal entertainment, so keep an eye out for what they think is intellectually stimulating. Look for people the aliens don't eat right away. Perhaps they find these people entertaining. It could also be that they are saving a particularly tasty human for a holiday meal. Be observant or be dinner.

Snacks and Refreshments

Snack food is important as a part of your entertainment dollar (or barter). Popcorn has a very good shelf life. Once the popcorn is gone, you may need to get creative. We recommend deep-fried mutant chitlins[58] liberally salted with a homemade hot sauce.

Keeping Entertainment Technology Ticking

Electricity, cable video, and the internet will not survive the apocalypse. Imagine a world without *Dancing with the Stars* or *American Idol*. Yes, the world will be better for the loss, but we will lose reruns of *Gilligan's Island* too!

---

58 http://en.wikipedia.org/wiki/Chitlins

You Might Want to Know

When a person is said to be 'going to Hell in a hand-basket,' they are in an extremely bad state and becoming worse. Those who watch Dancing with the Stars are a good example. Note: Dancing with the Stars is a sign of the end-times.

The horror of losing electronic entertainment is right up there with the fear of public speaking. Most people couldn't go five minutes without entertainment. Imagine having to hear yourself think? Feels like a three year old screaming and with a runny nose! That's incredibly scary for anyone who owns an iPhone. You are at the peak of entertainment… Then nothing but the sucky Dyson vacuum of your own mind...

What are we to do for entertainment? Start with disaster-ready solutions for traditional electronics. Think rentals of solar panels, bicycle generators, rather than video player rentals. Everybody has a Blue Ray player. Nobody has a 2000 watt Honda generator.

When your neighbors are twiddling their thumbs and telling old jokes by the fire with their children, your kids can be watching *SpongeBob* marathon and be out of your hair while you and the wife are out hunting demons.

Bicycle generators are perfect solution for most disasters. Customers can justify a purchase to their loved ones as a way to loose weight before the asteroids hit.

For the post-apocalyptic entrepreneur, think video rental. Remember the old days when we could rent a new-fangled DVD player from the video store? With the end comes a new opportunity to rent a generator! Imagine the cash you'll bring in with the extra income from black-market gasoline!

Methane power generators are another great power source for electronic when the world goes to, well, you know what we mean. As an added bonus, you now have a place to poop when society's toilets back up.

Experiment: Media Focus Group

Design a new form of post-society entertainment. Use a focus group to test your ideas. Unlike normal focus groups, you will need to get your participants into the apocalyptic mood. Instead of the normal array of coffee, donuts, and popcorn, use Spam, popcorn maggots (when they pop they make their own butter), and dirty water. While your test audience is watching the entertainment, have external sound effects, like people screaming and random gun fire.

Questions

- ✓ Does violence sell in a post-society world?
- ✓ What are your ideas for protecting your patrons while they are being entertained?
- ✓ How many people in your focus group believed the world had ended?

The End and Your Pets

We have dogs. We love them. There are cats too… What happens to our beloved pets we get taken up to Heaven? How will our dogs survive on their own? The cats, less of an issue, but the dogs! Is there a trusted heathen to take care of your beloved pets?

If we are left behind, will our dogs become Fluffy The Vampire Slayer or will their eyes start glowing like coals from Hell? Will they get hungry for human bacon bits? Is there a proper collar for a man-eater? Is there brain flavored kibble?

Most dogs will do okay in the end. There will be more than enough vermin and wild game. Even when all the humans are wiped out by a super plague, they could survive a long time on your flesh.

The really small dogs need a bit more care at the end. The teacup Chihuahua and other yappy lap dogs will need to be taken care of. They'd probably get eaten by a rat rather than catching one for food.

For small dogs, we suggest one of those automated dog feeders, but replace the three-day supply bin with several fifty-five-gallon drums of kibble.

Do All Dogs Go to Heaven?

We're often asked, will my dog go to Heaven? Of course the answer depends upon your dogma. After ducking the shoe thrown for such an obvious pun, we give the following advice: Do you live in fear of losing your pets when you get taken up to Heaven, try a religion that's pet-friendly. Take that last walk to Heaven together.

Most religions don't take pets seriously, especially Christians. This is quite odd, given that God created pets before he created man by a whole day. The only pet created after that was Eve. We'd not want to be a member of a church that excludes pets — it's barking mad!

The Catholics will give your pets a blessing that has an implied guarantee of a ticket to Heaven. The other religions are not quite so pet-friendly. Sometimes you have to risk a religion that could pose a higher risk of personal damnation, but will get your pet into a furry pair of angel wings.

When your religious neighbors and your pets are missing one day, you may have not literally bet on the right horse (or Golden Calf). The good news is that your pet is in Heaven. The bad news is that you won't be. This is one of those things that would make us believe that our god was a smart cookie. Not that we'd be happy to be stuck on Earth, just happy for Scruffy.

Learn This Word

> ***Catholic:*** *From the Latin, Cat-Holics, or the drunk cat people. Pets became a part of the Catholic religion, when Saint Francis of Assisi gave away all his wealth to become a hermit. His only possession was a pet pig (honest truth, you can't make this stuff up). The pig turned out to be a poor choice because Frances liked ham. Francis vowed to never eat a friend again. His second choice was cats, but they breed like rats. Saint Francis of Assisi's brother-in-law, visited his cave to find dozens of cats in residence and coined the moniker Catholic. We lost the meaning of Catholic when 'cat lady' became the preferred label.*

Best Pets for the End-Times

If you are smart (we assume so because you are still reading this book), you will have a good companion for the day when civilization is crushed into rubble. The evidence is in most post apocalyptic movies. *A Boy and His Dog,* or the remake of *Omega Man*, *I Am Legend*, or even *Mad Max* (known as *The Road Warrior* in the U.S.) has dogs (not cats) that rise to the challenge of a rotted civilization.

Don't settle for a mutt. You need a purebred that has hundreds of years of breading for specific skills and instincts. Mutts have their place, but only if they get a mutation that makes them smarter than you. The breed is important depending on how the world ends. Here are a few pointers (and non-Pointer breeds):

Terriers

Any breed that is based on Terrier stock is great for when society has checked out. The terriers are fierce hunters and good alarm systems.

Terriers are great intruder alarms. They will yap at any intruder, even friends. They won't stop until they can get a good lick or sniff to confirm identity. Be careful though, because most terriers can be bribed with treats or a good game of fetch.

Terriers are good at keeping vermin at bay. They won't be much help against hell spawn. The prey needs to be the size of a demonic squirrel. The cute little baby spawn of hell spawn are definitely in trouble from the tenacious terrier.

Toys and Other Small Breeds

There are uses for little bitty dogs. They serve as low maintenance alarm dogs. They will yap at anything. Unlike terriers, they are not smart enough to be distracted by a game of fetch. Yapping is good and bad because some of these dog will bark at "anything." An alarm is no good when it goes off all the time.

Most toy breeds are versions of bigger breeds. Miniaturization causes a few changes from the original. For example, the toys have more puppy-like behavior.

Puppy-like is not all bad. When you need sympathy, drag out the toy. They'll let you get close to enemies with their puppy-like looks will melt hearts. A scratch the dog behind the ear and you can put a knife in a kidney. This is useful when dealing with henchmen or mooching a meal from a rival gang.

Toy versions of Dobermans will cause someone to think Daddy is nearby. The only drawback is that Toy Dobermans have a small and yappy brain.

Toys bred from Terrier stock are an exception. As you shrink a Terrier all you are doing is concentrating their personality into a smaller package. A toy Terrier will take down a wolf, given the chance and given the stupidity of the wolf to get within range of an angry Toy Terrier.

Toy Terriers can be trained to attack an assailant by jumping and biting important male anatomy. No need to have them learn how to attack women, as these Toys are so cute that defenses long enough for an attack or start a long-term relationship.

Zombies and the Herding Dogs

Wht is the best dog for a zombie apocalypse? The best dog for zombies are *not* attack dogs like German Shepard. Biting is bad because your dog could catch the zombie's disease.

Yappy dogs are bad too because they attract zombies. A Pointer breed is useless because zombies are easy to spot and smell. A lap dog is going to end up on the wrong lap.

The best dogs for a zombie apocalypse are hearers like Sheep Dogs, and Collies. These dogs are bread to avoid getting bitten while herding a flock. A single herding dogs control whole flocks of sheep and herds of cattle. Herding a George A. Romero of zombies will be a normal day for these hard working animals. It'll be a piece of cake or at least a dog biscuit.

Training for zombies is easy, but you need a few friends. Have everybody watch *Day of the Dead* and go play in the park with rotted meat around their necks. Use all the whistles and commands of the sheep herder[59] to control your dog. Make sure your friends moan and chant, "Brains!" This is especially helpful should your friends become zombies — the dogs are already primed to heard them out of the house!

Herding animals are good at protection too. They are fierce protectors of their masters. When a demon from Hell appears from the myst, Scooter will nip at its heels while you grab the holy water.

You Might Want to Know

The unit of measurement "George A. Romero of Zombies" is a recently proposed scale for a group of zombies that equates to about three dozen zombies. You might see more, but they are computerized special effects.

---

59 http://dogplay.com/Activities/Herding/herding.html

Bloodhounds and Other Trackers

When hunting monsters or tracking down raiders, a Bloodhound is essential. A Bloodhound is also useful for finding food and survival essentials like gasoline.

Train your bloodhound for the scents related to survival and tracking. Gasoline, explosives, weapons (gun oil is a good scent marker), tubers, and small game are easily found by the well trained hound.

Training your dog's sniffer for hellish creatures is as easy as using a little rotted meat and dousing it with some sulfur. We recommend ammonia and other strange smelling chemicals to train a bloodhound to track aliens. This is not because this is what aliens smell like — we won't know until the saucers touch down — but because we expect they will smell mighty weird. Ammonia (small amounts, just a dab will do) will get your dog used to tracking something odd, rather than possibly delicious.

The Guard Dog: German Shepherd

There are guard dogs and then there are guard dogs that look like guard dogs. German Shepherds will fiercely protect their owners by ripping their enemies to shreds. Everybody knows it and nobody is willing to challenge the fangs of the fierce protector.

When it comes to the attack, the Shepherd won't stop until the prey stops screaming. There was that one thing that killed a Shepard, but that was only in the movie *The Thing* and it was a special effect.

German Shepherds are immune to diseases that would affect humans. They are generally immune to demonic possession, bird flu, and there are no tails[60] of Shepherds being probed by aliens. Your only disease they seem to have an issue with is related to zombie bites. If you love your dog, don't let it out to fetch a zombie.

You can spot a German Shepherd from a distance. Their fierce reputation will keep everyone out of range of those scary teeth.

---

60 Was that pun wagging the dog or the tail wagging the tale? The pun wasn't intended, despite the pain of its bark.

Should your Shepherd be an old softy that would lick a perpetrator to death, he still looks like he'll kill the average intruder.

Hounds from Hell: Rottweilers

The Rottweiler[61] is by far the breed used most in movies where people end up as dog food. We at Boys Books do not own a Rottweiler because we already have nightmares.

When the Antichrist comes for a visit, these dogs should not be your first choice for a pet. If there is an Antichrist, this is his dog. Watch for their eyes to glow red and a habit of eating guests. Bad dog!

For a non-Christian end, we don't see an issues with Rottweilers and heartily recommend the breed if you can sleep at night without nightmares. Rottweilers make fierce guard dogs and can rip a man's arm off.

Rottweiler are especially scary for anyone that's watched any movie about the Devil. Rottweilers look like they'd survive a 44 Magnum. Most people wouldn't even waste a bullet on a Rottweiler out of fear of pissing it off and the inevitable mauling. No, you don't shoot at a Rottweiler and live[62] to tell the tale.

---

61 http://en.wikipedia.org/wiki/Rottweilers

62 If you hated the last pun, don't worry. We won't do the tale/tail joke because Rottweilers don't have much of a tail to tell.

Experiment: Zombie Dog

Teach your dog to herd zombies! The goal is herding, not attacking. They should never bite or they will be infected. That also means no fetching anything like an amputated finger or other body parts.

To simulate zombies, get your parents to wear bloody cloths, shuffle, and moan a lot. When your parents are busy, look for a Fox News commentator in your area.

If you have a mutt, take advantage of each of the parent breed's instincts. When your mutt seems to have no redeeming qualities, use green hair dye to make your pet look like something that would take a leg off.

Questions

No questions! This was just for fun!

Really Strange Ends

There are as many interesting and amusing ways the world could end as there are stars in the sky – especially the ones that could kill us with radiation when they explode. Aliens could stop by for a midnight snack and pig out on humanity. The Sun can stop in the sky and mankind will slowly be eaten by carnivorous Aztec cats–that's far more interesting. Without further ado, let's tickle your brain cells (the ones related to paranoia and fear) with the creatively bizarre ways our world will end.

The Dreaming Butterfly Wakes Up

Remember the old saying: "Am I dreaming of being a butterfly, or am I a butterfly dreaming I am a man?" Simple idea. Butterfly wakes up and contracts permanent insomnia. The end.

We are a Simulation

In another universe (the one simulating us), they have a really huge computer that simulates the world. A cleaning lady kicks out the power cord and we cease to exist.

Boiled to Death in the Horton Universe

The great theoretical physicist, Dr. Seuss, put a theory into the public eye in his 1954 paper, *Horton Hears a Who!*[63] The theory is that our universe is just a small bit of fluff that makes up a spec of dust in Horton's universe.

The theory is based on the mathematics of fractals. A fractal is anything that looks just as complex at any magnification. Universes when magnified, are made of clusters of stars, stars have planets and a sun, suns and planets have molecules which have electrons and neutrons that in turn are made up of even smaller stuff whizzing about. Coastlines are fractal too because they look just as wiggly from space as they do up close.

[63] http://en.wikipedia.org/wiki/Horton_Hears_a_Who!

Our little corner of the universe, is lodged at the edge of a clover flower of the fractal dimension one level up in the vicinity of the Jungle of Nool. Because we are a noisy bunch, an animal with very large ears by the name of Horton can hear us. Because he likes us, Horton protects us.

Dr. Seuss posits that our universe survives being boiled alive in a Beezelnut oil apocalypse. Like many doomsayers, the residents of Nool don't believe Horton and cannot live on faith that we exist. We ultimately save ourselves by being so loud that everyone in Nool can hear us.

Dr. Seuss discovered two more theories that make this possible. The first is the inverted inverse square law for sound amplitude. This allows the smallest Who in Whoville to communicate with the inhabitants of the Horton universe. The second and greatest discovery of Dr. Seuss: A person is a person, no matter how small. Combined, this lets the whole jungle of Nool hear our cry for help.

There's a great deal of controversy about Seuss's theory. For example, Fox News assumes a person is a person and so is a company and the more money a person or a company has, the more they are a person. Fox scientists have proposed a modified law, called the Theory of Relativity to Republicans. It is formulated thus: A person is a person, no matter how large, unless they are a Democrat.

A second problem with the Seuss theory is that a person, no matter how large, cannot protect something so small. Our ultimate fate is simply postponed. One day soon, Horton will sneeze on us. We'll all die in a horrific deluge of elephant snot.

Death by Catalyst

Catalysts[64] have a great potential for ending the world. A catalyst is a five-dollar word for a chemical or other entity that facilitates a reaction without itself being destroyed or consumed.

Catalysts are important as possible ends of the world. Politicians are catalysts because they cause a reaction without being destroyed (mostly), as are cult leaders.

---

64 Alternate definition: A cat that cat that lasts a long time.

On the chemical side of the periodic table (the periodic table side, not the back side which has instructions for River Dance). Let's say you had a catalyst that could convert water into hydrogen and oxygen. Sounds great for the energy industry! Finally a cheap way to create hydrogen! Unfortunately, such a catalyst will end the world.

Here is how it will happen: An American conglomerate creates a device based on the catalyst to split water into hydrogen and oxygen which is in turn used to generate electricity for home power generation. Wal-Mart buys millions of the devices, but because they are Wal-Mart, they hire a Chinese company to make the devices. Dozens of giant container ships are used to transport the devices to America. Then pirates show up.

Somali pirates hijack a shipment of these Wal-Mart water splitters. The pirates, not exactly rocket scientists, make a mistake by starting up a few of the devices to charge their iPhones. Because the devices are manufactured by child labor in to save money, the pipes are not as tightly connected as they would be if built by burly workers in America. A pirate accidentally sinks the boat while toting on a joint and ignites a cloud of hydrogen leaking from the device. Down you go to Davy's Locker.

Once in the ocean, the catalyst material in hundreds of generators becomes supercharged by the vast pressures of the deep. Trillions of tons of water get split into hydrogen and oxygen and form a vast cloud over the Pacific Ocean.

The end comes as vast clouds of perfectly mixed hydrogen and oxygen ignite around the world when it intersects with a medicinal marijuana pharmacy where a bong toting patient lights a flame.

The explosion is sort of like Coke and Mentos,[65] but on a grand scale. All the forests burn, the world is thrown into a new ice age, and we all die. A pirate and a patient that smokes marijuana to reduce the nausea from playing XBox light up a few buds of pot and everyone dies. The world goes to pot.

How about: The bong heard round the world? A catastrophe? The coming cataclysm? A bowl of Purina Cat Chow? A catalyst

65 http://en.wikipedia.org/wiki/Diet_Coke_and_Mentos_eruption

for the end times? No, those are really cat puns, how about Super*catalist*fragilisticexpialidocious?

Seed Crystals

A seed crystal is a single crystal that promotes other crystals to begin growing. A simple experiment is to take supersaturated sugar water, just add a few crystals of sugar and the sugar in the water starts latching on the seeds and then more sugar attaches to the new crystals until you get a pile of rock candy.

A different type of seed crystal not only causes more crystals, but changes the nature of the chemical reaction. Ice only freezes at zero degrees Celsius, but what if you had a seed crystal that did this at normal temperatures?

An excellent example is a gun toting Republican at an anti-Democratic rally. The gun nut is a seed that causes a change in the temperature that Republicans become psychotic. Suddenly there is a wave of good Christian Republicans that are buying guns to kill Democrats. Don't believe us? Just before Obama got elected, gun stores could't keep ammo on the shelves. If your mom is Republican, ask to see the gun safe.

We've seen this theory in several scholarly works. Our favorite is Ice-nine,[66] from Kurt Vonnegut's, *Cat's Cradle*. In his paper, our world gets turned into a wasteland as the world's water is turned to room temperature ice. Throw a little Ice-nine into the water and it all turns into Ice-nine. Water turning to ice is bad because we need liquid water for life. Oceans, lakes and rivers turn into solid ice. More ice skating. No plants. Eventually we all die from a permanent winter holiday.

Learn this word: Nuclear

> *Nuclear is used to describe things at the level of atoms. More often though, nuclear is used to describe nasty radiation from atomic bombs, leaky atomic power plants, and fancy wrist watches that glow in the dark. The average person pronounces this word incorrectly as nookUlar, or worse, nukulerar. The best way to remember how to pronounce nuclear is as*

---

66 http://en.wikipedia.org/wiki/Ice-9

nook-lee-are. Think of an atomic blast creating new clear glass: new-clear. The word will just trip off your tongue like a very cunning linguist. The best choice is to fall back to football and punt with 'nuke' which is pronounced: newk. Another punting of nuclear is The Football. This is the briefcase that holds the nuclear launch codes for the President of the United States.

You might think Ice-nine is the ravings of an intellectual. Well, it is, but there is also something called Polywater. Polywater was discovered by Russians.[67] Not quite a seed crystal, but it would have the same effect. Caution: Do not add pollywogs to Polywater.

Polywater freezes at minus 40°C and boils at 150°C. Most ice would disappear, and snow would probably never be seen again. It's like anti-Ice-9. Once summer hits for the first time, icecaps will melt and will never return. Opposite of seed crystals, but a cool way for the world to end.

Polywater is gooey. Imagine motor oil in place of water running through your veins. When all the water in the world turns to Polywater, it'll be like living in lime Jello-world.

There are other possibilities for these runaway chemical reactions. We could get Slime-9 or Skittles-9 too. The possibilities are endless. What happens when a candy scientist invents Gummi Bear-9?

Mayonnaise and Potato Salad

Here at Boys Books we share a common nightmare. We live in fear of potato salad. Why? Because potato salad is made with mayonnaise. Mayonnaise is *evil*.

Mayonnaise starts with raw egg. Then we add oil and mix. That's it. Raw egg and oil. No heating. No cooking. Evil!

Now add a picnic on a hot summer's day. Are you starting to feel a little afraid of potato salad? No? Give us a moment and

---

[67] The Career Consequences of a Mistaken Research Project: The Case of Polywater and Better not mention the polywater

you too will be as repulsed as we are by the white death we call mayonnaise.

Potato salad is always found sitting in the sun without a lid. Just add a sprinkling of bird poop and airborne bacteria. Your brother also picks his nose and flicks boogers with unerring accuracy. Scientists who study mayonnaise have calculated that the average moment that potato salad becomes toxic is five minutes after it is placed on a picnic table.

Interesting fact: Flies really love to walk on warm potato salad.

Ever see vultures circling picnickers in the park? It's the anticipation of a death by potato salad.

The food safety police recommend that you keep potato salad be kept in an air tight container at a temperature similar to your refrigerator. Sadly the last member of the food police died in 1978 from tainted mayonnaise at a family picnic.

Within 25 minutes of a bowl of potato salad being put on a picnic table, its mayonnaise goes from putrid brown to gangrenous yellow-green. This is the natural color of potato salad, so you can't tell its gone bad. Aunt May has a coughing fit in the general direction of the bowl. Your second cousin, Lenny, dips in a spoon that a stray dog licked. The vultures start circling lower. Then, just as the bacteria reaches critical mass, somebody yells, "Hey, there's still potato salad! We need to eat it before it goes bad!"

The screaming you are hearing is your own. We are sorry we had to put you through that. Your gag reflex will calm down in a few minutes.

How could the world end because of mayonnaise? There aren't that many picnics, are there? It isn't quantity, but the quality of mayonnaise that ends the world.

The trouble starts three weeks before the 4th of July. That's the worst time because there's a skyrocketing demand for mayonnaise. A truck hauling nuclear waste from a hospital (glow in the dark Band-Aids from irradiated cancer patients), crashes into another truck containing 5,000 bottles of mayo. The accident happens near an ill-kept pig farm and within minutes, millions of flies are walking all over the glowing condiment of death. Global warming enables the bacteria contaminating the mayonnaise to grow ten times faster than normal. Al Gore is right, global warming will kill us.

Monsters are created from nuclear radiation, as Godzilla can attest. Mayonnaise with little dirty fly footprints, irradiated with fissionable materials from bloody Band-Aids and warmed by our carbon emissions is a lot worse. The puddle will begin to grow into a giant blob that eventually covers the entire surface of the Earth. It doesn't kill anyone outright, but the smell is awful. Scientists have calculated that the stench is so stomach turning that the Moon will be pulled out of its orbit. When the waves stop crashing against the world's beached, millions of irate surfers burn the world to the ground.

Burgercide

We love meat. We use drugs to make the cows healthier and fatter. We've fed them ground up bits of themselves because it's a sin to waste protein. Eventually cows are contaminated by dozens of toxins and diseases, but we keep on eating because the flavor is improved by special additives that are also slowly killing us.

Eventually ninety percent of us get a bit of cow madness. You might say, "Not everyone eats meat." You are right. However, we do all poop. As these toxins build up, we put some of the excess through our poopy shoots into the ecosystem. Cow patties and people doo are used as fertilizer all over the world. Organic produce will get most of the toxin because organic farmers use poop for fertilizer. Guess who eats organically grown fruits and vegetable? That's right, vegetarians!

We don't just feed ourselves meat, we also feed it to other animals, like our pets and livestock. Rover gets kitchen scraps and pigs are fed kitchen waste. Each contains the beef which has the poison. Mittens and the kittens are dumpster diving when you let them out at night too. Our deaths are guaranteed when our loving pets lick our face after licking their unmentionables.

Flying Fireballs of Bovines

Cows produce vast quantities of methane. Methane is a greenhouse gas *and* combustible. What could go wrong? Add food additives, genetic engineering, drugs, greed, and stupidity for a world-ending bovine blast.

Cows fart methane and methane causes global warming. Scientists are creating methane-free cattle feed to solve the problem. We get meat, no cow farts, and fewer summer days in December. Sounds good, but no leap in science goes unpunished. There is always a downside.

We have calculated that the beginning of the end will all start with a new type of cattle feed. Imagine a cattle feed that is a mixture of lead, Thalidomide, Mentos, Diet Coke, and Pop Rocks. Put it all in a cow and things could go very, very, very wrong.

The cattle feed will be from China. The Chinese were born with the greedy gene. They seem to make odd decisions about ingredients and have a propensity to substitute ingredients with lead or other nasty things that are cheaper.

We have already seen evidence in baby formula, dog food, toys with lead paint, and even the simple staple of Chinese cooking, the glass noodle, was a victim. Glass noodles (also called cellophane noodles) are made from mung beans which are not expensive, but corn starch is much cheaper. Corn starch makes faux glass noodles that are unfortunately white, rather than clear, so the chemical geniuses added a bit of the Chinese all-purpose additive: lead. Now imagine again what they'll do with anti-fart cattle feed.

We won't say the Chinese are going to put lead in cattle feed. Well, yes, we did say that. Lead seems to squeeze out a little more profit. It's only a matter of time before we see a spectacular and unexpected result.

When cows are given dodgy Chinese feed, we won't know the long term effects until we get mugged by a heifer in a dark alley. When China starts mixing cattle feed with the dead bodies of bird flu-infected chickens, we get fowl hamburgers!

The mixture of cattle feed and secret ingredients and special spices triggers a massive, silent but deadly, gas. This gas could linger for a long time and build to high levels. Perhaps, like plastic explosives, its harmless until the right conditions are reached for a proper detonation. A little triggering boom and you get a chain reaction that spreads all across the globe.

Ballistic cattle missiles will fill the sky. Their stinky super farts won't kill everyone. The true death will come when a few these

Jersey missiles are spotted arcing over the Polar cap by the Chinese. China will launch all their missiles and we all start glowing in the dark. This will of course be an accident. China would never think of destroying the United States. Where else would they dispose of their lead? We all die from a terrible miss steak. Yes, that last pun was a cowtastrophe.

Our New Bovine Overlords

Gary Larson is turning in his grave. After decades of drawing cartoons of intelligent cows, a new feed formula from China gives cattle an IQ of 185. The first hints are from the thousands of farmers who had their credit cards stolen. The cattle were found to be ordering parts to create robot hands to build weapons of human subjugation.

Cattle are vegetarians, so we won't be their dinner. Instead, we are forced into labor on vast alfalfa farms and rocket factories. That's right, alfalfa and rockets. They have massive brains, but they are suckers for nursery rhymes about cows jumping over the moon.

Life with our Lactating Overlords is tolerable but there are new problems. Every time you hear one talk, you laugh so hard that milk comes out your nose. You'll be immediately arrested and put to death because human consumption of cow's milk is udderly forbidden.

Eventually we are found to be redundant by an a-cow-tant. We move into the woods and jungles of the world and forget how to speak. We stay savages for hundreds of years until a time-traveling astronaut who looks like Charlton Heston comes to Earth.Charlton will befriend a Jersey Cow that sounds like Roddy McDowall.

You Might Want to Know

Gary Larson, at the time of this writing, is not dead. Given the long lead time from prediction to production of world-ending scenarios, we expect him to be safely turning in his grave before the cows come home.

Demonic Dairy

You know that cows are possessed by demons when cows start growing horns. You might say that cows have horns, so what's the big deal? Not all cows have horns, so growing them will be suspicious – so will their barbed and pointy tails. The red, glowing eyes will seem a little odd too. When the cow patties start smelling like brimstone, it's a sign of the end-times.

Why would cows become demonic? We'd blame this on the Jewish God. All those Hasidic Kosher laws. You may not be aware, but the Old Testament has page after page about how to slaughter, butcher, and cook a cow.

Can you imagine a religious tome written to bake your butt? The Devil has the perfect carrot to whisper rebellion in a cow's tagged and numbered ear. Very fierce fighters are created from subjugation that is less embarrassing than being forced to lactate 24/7. The world is about to get lactose intolerant.

Their Fowl Brethren

Imagine your anger if you were forced into a daily abortion. Yes, we are talking chickens. Every day we force millions of chickens to give up their unborn children. Imagine the revenge of 16,000,000,000 chickens. The world won't go to Hell in a hand basket, it'll be an egg carton.

Chickens are dumb right now, so something is going to happen to give them a little more smarts and lasers that shoot out their cloaca. The world will end in fowl ways. There will be a fowl smell in the air and fowl words will be spoken in anger. We will all witness a world that becomes clucked beyond all recognition.

If Pigs Could Fly

The world will end when pigs fly. That will be the first sign. The causes are the usual suspects of genetic manipulation. A pig on the wing sounds cute, but it is pure swine-o-cide!

Swine flew is worse than swine flu. The domesticated hog will go from food source to bringer of pain, misery and disease. Political pork will require a pilot license. The new menace of the air will be unstoppable (you can't shoot them because a hog falling from a 1,000 feet will make a crater).

The saying, when pigs fly, will go from adynaton—a figure of speech so hyperbolic that it describes an impossibility—to a daily prediction in the local weather forecast.

The piggy spawned from demonic conjuring will be the worst. Imagine squadrons of emancipated porkers with red glowing eyes and black wings. These porcine avians of evil will bomb us with their caustic poop and pee mixed with more diseases than your average Parisian sewer. The consistency and stench of their weapons will make you wish you were born into a family of third-generation devout Christian vegetarians.

The odiferous effluence of a common pig farm will be multiplied with the addition of brimstone, rotten flesh, disease, tape worms, and trichinosis-laden projectile diarrhea. Imagine this squirty pig poo raining on you from a squadron of flying piggy harpies. *Just threw up a little....*

There is only one reasonable defense: Umbrellas. Windproof golf umbrellas will be the most sought after accessory on the planet. Umbrellas are better than hazmat suits for a walk in the park. Don't have any breakfast before you venture out, it will only come back up when the piggy rain comes down.

Dog Farts

Have you ever owned a dog? You know how toxic a dog fart can be! They are usually silent, so there is no hope of warning. One moment you are you are watching TV and the next you are inhaling the bouquet of ode de kibble with a subtle overtone of roadkill squirrel. Dog farts are already deadly, so any unnatural kibble additives (probably from China) will add just enough to become a slow acting poison.

Slow-acting poisons are the worst because you don't know you are dead until it's too late. You can't hold your breath. You can't put on a gas mask. There is no warning that you need an antidote. You'll gag on a dog fart one day and then three years later, you become as sick as a dog in the morning and die by lunch.

Not a pet owner? Sorry, you are still dead. Your neighbors own pets and dog farts carry quite a distance. Dog farts neither rise nor fall to the ground. These presents from Fluffy's pink little sphincter, magically float at the height of the human nostril.

With millions of owners walking their dogs through the neighborhoods of the world, there is no escape. The cloud of dog farts will get thinker and thicker. Eventually we all begin to die as the poison shuts down our organs (organs like hearts and livers, not Hammond or Casio).

Societies without dogs will die as well. The third world is who makes our squeaky dog toys. They'll all starve when we stop buying rawhide chews and rubber bones.

When scientists figure out that Chinese dog food cause the problem, there will also be a war. War means things catch fire. When China burns, so will all the tainted dog food. A cloud of poisons from the baked dog food will then kell whatever remains of humanity. It's a doggone bad way to die. This scenario is appropriately called, The Dogs of War, or for the brave punster, The Pet Peeve.

The last person in the world will die on a dog day afternoon.

You Might Want to Know

> *Don't confuse the "slow-acting" in "slow-acting poisons" with slow-acting actors. Although a slow talker like the Duke is entertaining, he is usually not associated with death by poison.*

Experiment: Playing God

How would you end the world? Build a diorama of the death and destruction and enter it in the school science fair. If you are home schooled, send your diorama to Fox News.

Questions

- ✓ How did you choose your apocalyptic scenario? Did your parents help?

- ✓ What was the reaction of the judges (or the news anchors) to the mutilated bodies?
- ✓ Do you like your new psychologist?

True Believers: How to Know if You are One

True Believer Syndrome[68] was first coined as a mental dysfunction in M. Lamar Keene's 1976 book called *The Psychic Mafia*. The syndrome refers to people who continue to cling to their beliefs in the paranormal, even when it has been proven to be wrong or faked. When you say you are psychic, then bend a spoon, then prove it was all fake, people still think you are a spoon-bending psychic.

Our favorite quote about true believers is from James Randi, the famous magician and debunker: "*No amount of evidence, no matter how good it is or how much there is of it, is ever going to persuade the true believer to the contrary.*"[69]

When you believe in the end of the world, no amount of evidence is going to sway you from that belief — especially when it's certainly not true. The best way to describe it is like Bugs Bunny and Daffy Duck having an argument about rabbit season.

Imagine the world has been magically changed and that all bad stuff is just an illusion. Anyone that says different is gullible, uneducated and has a chip in their brains and is getting instructions from the CIA. By Randi's logic you now have to believe that the world the world will not end. Because reading this paragraph has brought you to your senses, please send us 20% of the money you'll save in therapy and antidepressants.

Cognitive Dissonance

Cognitive dissonance is an uncomfortable feeling caused by believing two contradictory ideas or beliefs simultaneously. The dissonance happens when you believe in one thing, like God will protect you from a hurricane and then a hurricane kills you. Your last thought is, how could God protect me and yet I am dying....

---

68 http://en.wikipedia.org/wiki/True-believer_syndrome

69 ABC News, "The Power of Belief: How Our Beliefs Can Impact Our Minds"

When you believe God is ending the world next Tuesday, but the church still has a list of hymns to sing and announcements for the church bake sale the following Sunday, you might feel these things are contradictory. This is cognitive dissonance. This feeling gets as itchy as a mosquito bite when things stop making sense.

Cognitive dissonance only starts to give you a hint that you are a true believer after the old poop has failed to hit the fan. No poop, no fan, no dissonance.

You Might Want to Know

> *Several times in this book, we used the phrase "old poop" rather than more accurate profanity like coprolite (fossilized poop). Please understand, we can't use the naughty version as Mom may be reading this book. Hi, Mom!*

Cognitive dissonance causes unfortunate creativity when two contradictory realities collide. Imagine the world is going to end again at 2:22 A.M. on February 22, 2022, during the next great alignment of the Great Turtle. Your Great Turtle Guru says you'll all hitch a ride on a Betelgeuse rescue ship. Good thing too because a massive turtle turd will soon destroy the Earth.

2:22 A.M. on February 22, 2022 comes and goes with no hitchhiking with aliens and the turtle turd fails to destroy the Earth. Things are a bit worse because you sold your car, house, boat, and jet ski to get into the Grand Turtle Cult and your hot wife has left you for the Great Turtle Guru.

There you are, no end of the world, no alien rescue, no turtle turds, no hot wife and no worldly possessions. You finally start to realize that there are no aliens, no free ride to Betelgeuse, and your stuff is owned by a sixty-year-old con man who's sleeping with your hot wife. Do you get smart and leave the Grand Turtle cult? Sorry, no…

The first thing your brain says is, "You look like an idiot!" The second thing your brain says is, "I can't look like an idiot!" Then you start getting creative. "The alien gave the Grand Turtle an enema and saved the Earth from being destroyed by a planet-sized turtle turd?" Yep, that's much more believable than the credulities of being stupid. "Heck, all that sacrifice saved the planet!"

See the problem? Suddenly you are making stuff up to avoid looking stupid, and that means more turtle church in your future and still no hot wife.

So, with your cognitive dissonance in play, you head to the airport to give out flowers for donations to ensure they don't foreclose on your Guru's mansion and keep super unleaded in your Guru's Bentley.

You are not alone. There are still hundreds of little cults all over the world that continue worshiping after their world didn't end. One of the big ones, as you perhaps will remember, had that war at Armageddon prediction. Remember it was supposed to happen during the lifetime of old John of Patmos. How many people came to their senses after 2,000 years of disappointment?

Ah, the power of cognitive dissonance! We will do anything to keep from looking stupid. Even when that means we stick with stupid beliefs. Yep, we're stupid!

Critical Thinking

Critical Thinking is how you evaluate something to see if it is true. Critical Thinking[70] is a process that helps you find out what is true or stinks like monkey poo on a sunny day. Examining the source of the evidence, the correctness of the logic, the believability, motivations and other factors examined to estimate of how true something is.

Learn This Word

> ***Truthiness***: *Truthiness is the opposite of critical thinking. Truthiness is a word conceived by Steven Colbert. Truthiness is a fact based on an emotional appeal or "gut feelings" rather than messy evidence. Simply, truthiness is a belief as truth.*

---

70 http://en.wikipedia.org/wiki/Critical_thinking

When it comes down to personal opinion, feelings, guilt, unsubstantiated statements, the truthiness is in the air. Of course, this is impossible to argue against. Truthiness is like kryptonite to critical thinking. How do you convince someone that their gut is an idiot?

The only defense against truthiness is to train a person in critical thinking. Critical thinking isn't easy to learn for someone already convinced about a subject. You need common ground and the sense to avoid an argument. A belief is a hard thing to change, so set your expectations low.

What is critical thinking? How about a little poetry first?

> *I keep six honest serving-men*
> *(They taught me all I knew);*
> *Their names are What and Why and When*
> *And How and Where and Who.*
>
> *~ Rudyard Kipling, "The Elephant's Child"*

Rudy is referring to the six Ws[71] (there are actually five but "how" gets an honorable mention for effort). Critical thinkers use these to cover all the core questions to confirm a statement's truth.

Critical thinking is nothing more than asking these questions and checking the facts. We need to examine motivation of the sources, emotional language, and of course, logic versus logical fallacies. Sound complicated? Yes, that's why there aren't that many critical thinkers in this world. School systems had to pull it from their curriculums to improve tests scores (that's the absolute truthiness).

We won't get into training you on critical thinking, but we will give you a couple key pieces of advice. Never get angry, always check your own facts, and always use humor.

Why are Smart People in Cults?

Brains don't give you immunity to the magnetic attraction of a religious cult. Smart people like doctors, scientists, Republicans (well mostly smart people) join cults every day.

---

[71] http://en.wikipedia.org/wiki/Five_Ws

How is it that someone that went to medical school became a member of a cult in the middle of no-place Waco, Texas?

Learn This Word

> ***Cult**: You may have heard of cults before, like the Branch Davidian's in Waco, or your average end-of-the-world church, or very wacky cults with poison snakes or aliens. Cults are everywhere The media defines a cult as a group that lives in an isolated compound that won't grant media interviews. Cults are found in every religion that prevents you from questioning the your beliefs (i.e. all). There are severe penalties like banishment, excommunication, death, or no ticket to either a cool afterlife or a premium cabin on an alien spaceship.*

Faith is not really about suspending intelligence or applying the scientific method. It's about dodgy evidence and saying yes too many times. Saying, 'yes' is how cults get their members. Let's look at an example. Your cult leader sermon goes like this:

> **Cult Leader:** *The sky is blue! God made it that way because it's a pretty color.*
>
> **Analysis:** *You can't argue with that. Even if you are a scientist. It's a pretty shade of blue, and you can't empirically prove that God wasn't color blind. Okay, true so far.*
>
> **Cult Leader:** *I was looking at the pretty blue sky yesterday, praying to God for guidance.*
>
> **Analysis:** *Easy to believe. It was sunny yesterday, and by definition a cult leader would be praying. Yes, there is much truthiness in this the sermon.*
>
> **Cult Leader**: *As I was praying, a cold wind blew and a raven let out a caw of warning.*
>
> **Analysis:** *Easy to believe again. This guy even used the proper term "caw"'for the noise a*

raven might make. More truth, or at least easily believable bird calls.

Cult Leader: *I looked into the Sun and saw how God would end the world in a blazing fire.*

Analysis: *Okay, this rings true enough. Gotta be careful about burning your retinas, but I have to believe what he saw. It was his experience, not mine. Why did they lock the door and then give us juice and coffee? I really need to pee.*

Cult Leader: *I then saw how God would save us, the chosen people.*

Analysis: *Yes! I want to be a member of the chosen! The theme is consistent. I like that he used the words "we" and "chosen people" in the same statement. I must be on the exclusive list. These people were so nice and I've never felt so much love. It must be true, for me to feel so special. If I say I am ready to join now, can I go potty?*

Cult Leader: *The way to salvation is to donate our worldly goods to our church to build an altar. We won't need our wealth or possessions when we are taken to Heaven. We would all live here until the end, which is soon.*

Analysis: *Yes, but you are starting to scare me. All my possessions? Oh, guess it's okay, the end is near. Building the altar seems like a good way to show my commitment. As for staying here until the end, again I feel special being part of the club.*

Cult Leader: *Are you ready for your special place in Heaven?*

Analysis: *Well, you can't argue with that. Sign me up! Can I pee now?*

As you see, the logic has few holes. The convert is persuaded to say yes to everything. A personal experience with God is easy to accept when you have a shred of belief and a small bladder. The rest tumbles like dominoes.

Experiment: Create a Cult

Cults are fun! Create a cult that believes the world will end next week. All cult members must surrender all their possessions to you, The Unquestionable Leader.

The ideal converts are down on their luck (emotionally, not financially because you need the cash), possibly depressed, and friendless because they are socially inept. Be friendly, hug people often, and lock the liquor cabinet.

On the appointed day and hour of your predicted doom, record the reactions of your cult followers. You get more points for each member who still believes in your cult the next day.

Note: There is no reason to give any money back to the followers after the experiment. Should they ask for their cash, remind them about the school of hard knocks or something about a fool his money and a trial separation of the two.

Questions

- ✓ Does it help to say that an angel or alien will protect cult members when they join?
- ✓ How did you get your cult members to deny logic?
- ✓ What did you do with your cult members' possessions?
- ✓ Where you able to get your psychologist to join the cult?

Life in the Enclave

When most of the world is destroyed or civilization collapses, there will be enclaves. Enclaves are like little castles or those fancy fenced-in communities. The goal is to limit the inhabitants to a certain type of people and keep out the riffraff.

When our civilization has collapsed, enclaves become little pockets of civilization. Not every enclave will be a success. Little pockets usually fill with lint and old pieces of moldy candy and enclaves are no better. We need to choose wisely and find an enclave that will help us survive.

Enclaves fall into different types that will greatly affect your lifestyle and color your choices for joining such a mini-society that suits your needs.

Learn This Word

> ***Enclave:*** *Enclaves are protected communities. They are similar to a neighborhood or town, except for a twenty-foot fence and guard towers.*

Evil Overlord

You might think that having a psychotic, narcissist, evil overlord is a bad thing. Evil helps the enclave to survive, though sometimes at the expense of its members and the odd innocent bystander. The fewer morals your leader has, the more wealth and food you'll have. If you are okay with torture, mental abuse, have a need to satisfy every whim of your leader, you might do well with an evil overlord.

Evil is great! You steal from everyone. You have slaves work for you on penalty of death. Even better, you have Roman-like battles to the death for your entertainment. As a member of the evil overlord's court, the benefits roll downhill. Sometimes literally as scraps, but that's better than nothing.

Don't be the number-two man to an overlord. Evil overlords are always expecting you to kill them with a sharp knife in the back. A hint of power envy and you'll find yourself in a pit trying to make friends with a hungry lion.

A great job is bootlicker. As the overlord's boot licker you'll be closer to the juicy scraps. All the food tastes like bootblack and leather, but that's the cost you pay for survival.

The best job is doctor, or when things are a little crazy, witch doctor. Be sure to keep your leader's acid reflux in control and you'll live a long life.

Military Rule

The military enclave is a fairly good life. There's work and sacrifice, with good food. In general, with a general, there is comfort and good grub at the end of a long day of soldiering and pushing around civilians.

Beware of this style of enclave when you are not a proper jar head. The rules are very strict and you only learn these basics in a boot camp. Living in military society is irritating for civilians.

When joining a prospective military enclave, try to get a quick interview with the leader first. Ask who his heroes are. If they mention relatively unknown military commanders or Presidents, like Kennedy or Obama, he might be okay. Should the leader mention their respect of the rule of Mussolini, Genghis Kahn, or the beloved Emelda Marcos, think about quietly sneaking out the back door on the next moonless night.

Leaving a military enclave is not simple. The best excuse to give is that you left a few personal possessions outside, like a stamp collection or your foot fetish porn. Don't say anything about caches of food or weapons, as they will be more than happy to provide armed escort which limits your escape strategy. We'd get out of sight and make noises like a hell hound is ripping out our throat. No reason to chase you down when you are in bite-sized pieces.

Religious Sect

Like the idea of a charismatic leader who is always working to get you into Heaven? A religious sect is a good choice. These are similar to military compounds without all the sergeant types yelling about your haircut.

Beware of psychotic charismatics. When your leader is always talking to someone who isn't there, your world can get a little too interesting. Life might be going well one day and then the great leader burns all your food and clothes the next.

Religious sects can be similar to a military enclave. Unlike a military enclave, the religious are not great military strategists. They are always whipping out a religious text or getting advice from voices. Such books and voices wont help you stay alive, especially when you are the chosen martyr. Martyr translates into battling a 12 foot demon with a Bible in one hand and a piece of string in the other. Martyr is sacrifice and you don't want to be a sacrifice.

Honor Society

Honor societies include knights, cowboys, and others that live and die on their reputation. Each with their own quirks or rituals. The underlying idea is that your word is your bond.

The military and ex-military gone professional soldier of fortune might start such an enclave. Unlike military enclaves, the atmosphere is a little more relaxed and you don't need to keep your boots shined.

Honor societies are based on the my-word-is-my-bond philosophy. Seems good, but these enclave can be dangerous as even minor arguments end in a duel to the death with someone that likes the smell of gun oil and fresh blood. The good news is your death will be quick and painless.

Keeping your mouth shut, say at the communal meal, will prevent a dual to the death with sporks or whatever is relatively sharp and easily accessed, like a sharp elbow through your cranium.

You Might Want to Know

An old tradition of honor is that you should always let the lady go first. This ritual of honor is based on the snake problem in Ireland. Before Saint Patrick banished the slippery vermin, knights and others would open doors and usher the woman through the door first, "Because there might be snakes."

Intellectuals

When disaster strikes and civilization is less civil, the best place to live will be with the smarties. Not the deliciously sour candy–don't be a wise guy. There is clean water and creative weapons that work against the undead too.

Intellectual enclaves won't be nirvana, but fairly comfortable and reasonably safe from the effects of disaster, evil, and horrors of a civilization taking the long road to Hell when demonic giraffe are roaming the streets looking for small children to eat.

It's not all test tubes and Bunsen burners. Intellectual enclaves could be excessively optimistic peace nicks and thus very dangerous and incompetent. Putting peace ahead of survival sucks the smart right out of a lab-coated scientist. They will walk right up to a zombie waving a white flag, a drafted peace treaty, and a fruit basket. They will gladly open the front gate for anyone, even when their eyes glow red and there is a bit of human ear stuck between their teeth. Of course, they will walk away (or rather run screaming like a little girl) when the zombie tries to make a meal of their lower intestines.

There could be a wrong mix of scientists too. You need someone that can build a killer robot or cure zombie diseases or at least repel the demon hoards with an air freshener. Sadly you'll probably get astronomers, geologists, or rocket scientists that specialize in pooping in space. Check out the resumes before joining!

Learn This Word

> ***Incompetence:*** *Incompetence is not, as many believe, a sign of stupidity. There are legions of smart, but incompetent people. Intelligence is knowing what we know and what we don't know. Incompetence is when we don't know what we don't know.*

Intellectual enclaves also love experiments. They think that Hell spawn is just an ordinary "disease." Seems a little silly that a disease makes skin turn red, horns to grow and have an unhealthy appetite for human flesh. Breathing brimstone is just a genetic mutation, right? Let's whip up a little recombinant DNA and Mr Beelzebub will be right as rain.

Scientists are great at capturing demons. Demons are certainly not rocket scientists, so they are easily lured into a trap properly baited with a virgin geek. The scientists then take the slathering demon home to the enclave for experimentation. The inevitable happens. Suddenly you are up to your pocket protectors in hungry spawn of Hell spawn (like guppies, all demons are pregnant).

Scientists are also the first to be bitten and infected by a zombie. Before you know what's happened, you're sitting around the campfire and Dr. Poindexter starts gnawing on your ankle.

You Might Want to Know

Zombies are not pets!

Fantasy Societies

Imagine all the World of Warcraft players in the world. They live and breath fantasy in this world and want to bring it with them in the next. The Dungeons and Dragons players get to play in real dungeons and real dragons! The guys that like to dress up as knights and get the poop kicked out of them get to smell some real medieval poop.

The first thought that pops into the heads of the fantasy fanatics is, "Yikes, this stuff is real!" The second thing that pops into their heads, after a change of underwear, is, "Cool, now I get to do this for real!" At that point they start looking for last Halloween's Warrior Elf King costume and start calling their buddies. Weapons will be replica swords from The Hobbit or made of rubber.

Themed societies are like the fable "The Ant and the Grasshopper." The supply of Hot Pockets, microwave popcorn, Ho Hos, Twinkie's, and Dr. Pepper will run out a week after the 7-Eleven stores are destroyed. At best, there will be a few seeds from a marijuana stash, but nothing we'd create a salad from. Sadly, a marijuana crop will fail too. They lack a basic understanding of horticulture and farming is less important than roll playing.

Experiment: Themed Post-Apocalyptic Society

Have a favorite TV show like *Buffy*, *90210*, *Care Bears*, *Star Trek*, or *SpongeBob SquarePants*? Loved the book *Lord of the Flies* or are really into anything with elves and hobbits? Take advantage of your cult-like following of a genre and turn it into a cult-like post-apocalyptic society.

Things to do:

- ✓ Design your enclave with themed buildings. How about Barbie's doll house, or doors that have that Trek swoosh sound?
- ✓ Develop a set of rules to govern your society.
- ✓ Write laws on how the leader is chosen. Be careful to choose rules that automatically make you the leader, high priest, or dungeon master.
- ✓ Design costumes so that you can tell your cult members from others.
- ✓ Create designs of vehicles like those in the Road Warrior movies that follow your theme.
- ✓ Take your ideas to a science fiction and fantasy or comic convention and see how many followers you can recruit.

Questions

- ✓ Even a polite enclave of Care Bears needs to protect itself, so how would you make your weapons look cute?
- ✓ What society would you be at constant war with? For example, the SpongeBob enclave will be at war with Mr. Clean enclave (think about it for a second and you will understand the problem).

Leaving Your End-of-the-World Cult

Apocalyptic cults are everywhere. You may know someone in these cults or you are a member or you want to help someone escape. How do you escape or help someone escape? Here is some advise our lawyers heartily recommend you use only in case of an entertainment emergency:

The Mental Gymnastics of Denial

We are a product of our education, our social interactions, and our mental proclivities. We don't need proof to believe. We just need to believe. Once you have a belief, it sticks like gum on your shoe.

Use the scientific method to prove or disprove any physical phenomena. However, you can't use the scientific method to disprove a faith-based belief. If we could disprove belief, the first reasonably smart scientist would have unplugged the world's religions long ago. Religion is a psychological quirk of humans that doesn't have a dependable off switch. Even if there are no gods, we want to believe in them.

So, talking about religion and science in the same breath or respecting each other's views is silly. Believing that belief can be changed by logic is akin to believing the nature of gravity could suddenly reverse direction.

Chip away at reality (real or imagined) and fantasy becomes a fact. Allow for a possibility and the possibility becomes more believable.

How do deprogrammers fix cult members? Forget about a dialogue between science and religion. It's the silliness that we refuse to see. Expose the silliness. Attack its weakest link, the silliest!

Deprogramming is mental torture. Facts are the deprogrammer's sharpest weapon. Facts annoy the faithful and gives them mental pain. The deprogrammer treats beliefs like a bully. They send belief to fact check prison where the belief drops the soap in the shower.

One absurdity at a time, the deprogrammer creates a world that replaces beliefs with facts. The subject's belief-based personality is slowly destroyed with puns, heckling, and bad jokes. The subject's reality becomes so painful, they laugh at themselves. Interesting fact: The best deprogrammers are failed comedians.

Can you get the Pope into a room for days at a time and badger him until he questions and abandon his beliefs? Sure, but then you get arrested. Tell him a joke and maybe he'll wear his pope hat when he goes to the bathroom. There is no guarantee. The mind can be very stubborn, even when it wants to be changed.

The hardest cult to escape is a cult as sugary sweet as the Methodist Church. They don't scream fire and brimstone. They don't have lynchings. Methodists don't even like automatic weapons. A run-of-the-mill Methodist church is the worst of cults because it doesn't seem like a cult. We believe it was Heinlein who said, "There is nothing as harmless as a congregation of Methodists."

We don't mean to demonize the Methodists. There is a Methodist to our madness! Methodists are at the root of a conspiracy that causes the high prices of Viagra. We don't know why, but they're *up* to something.

What to Do When the World Does Not End

The odds are enormously good that the world will not end. Name any doomsayer or look at any end of the world prediction of the past and you will see a failure to execute a timely end of the world. We're still here!

All your preparations for the end of the world are wasted. Especially when you were preparing for a specific date, like 2012. When nothing happens, then what?

We are not saying you should not prepare for the end of the world. You never know when some idiot gets it right this time. We are merely cautioning that you should be prepared to be disappointed.

After a failed apocalypse, you're going to need to get rid of all the survival equipment and get ready for just another day at the office. You need to mentally prepare yourself for the not-end-of-the-world. It doesn't hurt to have a therapist on speed-dial too.

Do-It-Yourself Deprogramming

Want to stop believing in the end of the world? It's not as simple as leaving your religion. You need to be your own deprogrammer.[72]

How Did This Happen to You? Your brain is wired to believe in supernatural stuff.[73] It gets even worse when you are stressed by deaths, disaster, addictions, job loss, and Fox News. You'll believe in anything for the promise of relief.

So you were suckered in, but how did you go from a sane person to really falling for this nonsense?

You now have hard-won beliefs. You brain is a very frugal and efficient machine. It does not like to change its mind, because that takes energy. That's why you keep going back to Starbucks. Once you believe their coffee tastes good, why go through the effort of comparing it to all other coffee shops?

Learn This Word

> ***Guerilla:*** *is the diminutive of the Spanish word guerra which means "war," so guerilla means "little war." Diminutive means "smaller version" in this case and is another word to learn, sorry. When you say, "guerilla warfare," you are being redundant. Guerilla warfare — yeah we are being redundant because it sounds better — has nothing to do with Planet of the Apes. That would be gorilla warfare.*

Deprogramming is nasty business. Destroying a faith requires guerilla warfare of the mind. It's a hard thing to deny, so deprogramming becomes an uncivil war. There is no proof that what the cult taught you isn't real. Your only hope is to use silliness.

---

72 Java programmers call this decompiling.

73 http://tinyurl.com/bfdfkq

Here is a checklist for self-deprogramming. Put it on your fridge to remind you every time you get a snack.

Deprograming Checklist

- ✓ Get rapport with yourself. Make friends. Give yourself a hug. Share cookies and milk.
- ✓ Don't sleep. Tired people are easier to persuade when they are idiots.
- ✓ Pain is a great motivator. Self torture is not easy, but threatening yourself with pain is not enough.
- ✓ Drink two pots of coffee, but don't allow yourself to piddle until you accept that a belief in your cult might be wrong. Nothing's better than a full bladder to get someone to change their belief.
- ✓ Read books about cults and mind control. This will help you understand how cults control their flock and your place in it.
- ✓ Seek out advice from an atheist. They have been living without a god for a while, and can show you the ropes. Avoid crazy atheists. An Agnostic or Methodist will also do in a pinch. Episcopalian would be better. They believe nothing.
- ✓ Look for things that annoy you about your cult. Got a gripe? The food they serve in the cult cafeteria is too bland and you are getting tired of the water boarding baptism every afternoon. Maybe they don't recycle? Add up your complaints and see if it's time to seek greener pastures.
- ✓ Cults don't let you think. There is no free will in a cult. We have fought for hundreds of years for freedom — why throw that away? Don't let The Man tell you what to do, even when he does have a collection of automatic weapons.
- ✓ Think like an agnostic. Accept that if any of the gods are real, you'll find out when you die or the world ends, whichever comes first.
- ✓ Don't do the crazy stuff! If people are starring, that's your clue that it is crazy.

- ✓ Assume that if you are not pure, you are going to see Hell. Accept this and live a full life and worry about Hell when you get there.

Experiment: Post Cult Blues

Time to leave your cult. Follow the instructions in this chapter and hit the road.

Questions

- ✓ Were you cult's leader? Was it easier to leave because you knew it was a sham?
- ✓ Why did you join the cult?
- ✓ Are your friends in the cult happy that you left?
- ✓ Is your therapist happy you have left the cult or unhappy because your therapist joined the cult?

Behind the Doomsayers

In our research, we came across a great article on the web:

http://www.wcg.org/lit/Bible/Rev/apocalyptic.htm

What its author, Paul Kroll, said was fairly profound. Quite simply, the doomsayer is trying to explain our sad and pathetic lives and give us a shovel to dig our way out. Oh, and we get to punish the people making our lives pathetic and sad.

Think about all the bad things that happen to the wonderful people in the world (those that think like us). Disease, crime, poverty, starvation, wars, rumors of wars, book authors (except us), and just plain mean folks are making it hard for the rest of us. The bullies of the world escape punishment daily. Where's our hug? Where is that corn-based sweet, oh sweet, revenge?

The doomsayer has the ultimate solution: Kill everyone. Only the perfect people go to Heaven. Doomsayers hope the world is wiped clean, but they are generally okay with a few faithful surviving in their well-stocked bomb shelters. Generally everybody dies. Overall, no more bad people!

The Book of Revelation is a great read when you look at as a revenge fantasy. It doesn't matter when or exactly how the prophecies come true. All that matters is that the doomsayers enemies are tortured and the victims, especially the doomsayer, are rewarded.

The meek shall inherit the Earth and then we get revenge! That's what doomsaying is all about. It's just revenge. Nothing more.

Nature Protects Bullies

The problem with the world is that it's not fair. No matter what. At some point in your life, you are going to step in a pile of poo. Even if things are all beer and skittles, bullies are getting more beer and skittles.

If you have ever been bullied, you know there is nothing better than belief in an old-fashioned apocalypse. Apocalypse tilts the scales of justice and has no loopholes. We also get our share of beer and skittles.

Revenge is the MacGuffin[74] of doomsaying. A MacGuffin is something in a book, play, or movie that everyone is chasing. It is like the Maltese falcon, or the pot of gold. For the doomsayer, its revenge against the bully.

Apocalyptic scenarios are quite satisfying. There is nothing better than seeing a rich bastard die a horrible death. It's that one last bloody nose. The bully gets punished!

The apocalypse is also final. What better reason would a god have for destroying mankind than to stop evil "evermore" (as that raven says) and to take revenge as well?

No second act. No sequels. No more babies, so no more innocents. No more Paris Hilton or Adolph Hitler. Just the devout. Of course, the end solves those question about who is right.

Even if you bet on the wrong religion, you are going to feel good about the world ending. At least you will know who the right god was. You can be damned to purgatory with a smile on your face. Too bad your bullies will be there too.

Science and Doomsayers

Scientists love a good game of test tube told you so. Scientists are doomsayers too. The same psychology of sacrifice and revenge works for scientists. Even though they have lab coats with pocket protectors, they are fighting against similar evils.

Scientists are fighting tooth nail and calculator to get grant money. They fight off politicians trying to fund religion over science. Scientists have a few metric tons of enemies they want to go away. Scientists wouldn't mind having a bit of revenge.

Why do you think scientists are always thinking about death from space?

---

74 http://en.wikipedia.org/wiki/MacGuffin

Starting Over

The whole point of a god destroying its creation is because it has failed. Look at the Judeo-Christian mess. God keeps trying to make his creation run right by killing and more killing, threats upon threats, and set of rules longer than your arm. Man will never be perfect. Time to eliminate the problem by destroying it completely.

Looking at it from a supernatural point of view, if your creation is constantly getting out of control, time to flush this version and start over. Doomsayers understand this. That's why they aren't worried about fixing the world. It's obvious that the one thing their god goofed on was creating man and man has got to go.

The Cure to Cognitive Dissonance

Doomsayers and their followers don't like to be wrong. Their gods are too busy to end the world. Why not make your doomsaying a self-fulfilling prophecy?

Recall our lesson on Cognitive Dissonance. People feel bad when their predictions don't come true. When their faith is misplaced, they feel like idiots. The smart doomsayer knows they are wrong and plans to be correct, even when their god is a little less than dependable.

That's why the real wackos are so dangerous. They don't want justice. They don't want to strike a blow against the infidel. It isn't the reward of vestal virgins that gets them excited. The true payoff is not looking like an idiot.

Did You the eVite for the End-Times?

If you known when the world is going to end, please just send out an eVite to everyone so we can get ready. Please update your Facebook status too.

The End Beckons

It's good to laugh at delusional people. We need to end of the worlders to laugh too. We need to avoid a man-made apocalypse because that's the one thing that isn't funny.

We hope that you have laughed far more than made you cry. It has been a pleasure to have had such an intelligent and good looking reader as yourself. Really!

Hope to see you in Heaven, Hell, Purgatory, on the pirate ship, orbiting in the tea pot, at the throne of the flying spaghetti monster, or in the pasture when we are reincarnated as dairy cows of another planet.

Learn This Word

> ***Reincarnation:*** *Reincarnation is often called the "do over." You didn't get something right in your last life, so you get another chance. This is a belief in many Eastern religions. The key component is that you are either rewarded for your mistakes or rewarded for your goodness. This is also called Karma. If in your past life you were not tortured, you get tortured in the next. When you have reached the karma you come back as a cow.... Some confuse reincarnation with Buddhism, but pure Buddhists believe death is the end of life and no "do over."*

Experiment: The Quality of Revenge

They say revenge is best served cold. Why not find out. Are people happier if their enemies are served piping hot on brimstone? Are people happier when they smite at a normal room temperature on Earth? Give the following survey to friends, family and as many total strangers as possible.

Hello, I am giving this survey so that I can learn about the world. Please answer all the questions and be truthful. Answer as quickly as possible.

1. What is your religion?
   b) Christian
   c) Muslim
   d) Jewish
   e) Buddhist
   f) Agnostic
   g) Atheist
   h) Other
2. Imagine that everyone rich got the money because they killed someone. How should they be punished?
   a) Executed by lethal injection
   b) Life in prison
   c) Sent to Hell for the ultimate punishment
   d) They are tortured during the apocalypse
   e) None of the above because you plan to punishing the evildoer yourself
3. Imagine a rich person killed someone and only you know. What would you do?
   a) Kill them the same way their victims died
   b) Steal all their money
   c) God will send them to Hell for the ultimate punishment, so do nothing
   d) Call the law for proper punishment
   e) Do nothing, because it is survival of the fittest
4. Rich people are rich because?
   a) They are evil
   b) They got lucky
   c) They are more intelligent
   d) They are aliens
   e) They probably killed someone

5. Rich people are?
   a) Evil
   b) Human
   c) Alien
   d) All of the above

6. Because this test is anonymous, please use the space below to write your name, address, social security number, and major credit card for our records.

____

____

____

____

____

Questions

- ✓ Is there a correlation between the subject's religion and the other answers?
- ✓ Did people seem happy when they answered the second question?
- ✓ Are you rich now from credit and identity theft and does that make you want to be sent to hell?

The End of the End

We are glad you've enjoyed this book. We are sorry about the mess in your pants and the odd looks from strangers as you giggled like a maniac. We are woefully sorry about the psychologist bills, legal fees, and excommunication caused by performing the experiments. We warned you!

We intend for you to laugh, and yes, even feel great mental and physical pain from the punography. We had a message too: Armageddon, doomsaying, and society's preoccupation with the end of the world is human nature. We also wish there was less of it.

You Might Want to Know

> *According to the great science fiction author, Spider Robinson, kicking furniture is the most sincere form of applause for the punster. Much better than* ***pun****ching the offender in the nose.*

Are you a little calmer because you read this book? That was our secret plan. Laughing at the apocalypse will help you forget about the stinky lump in the back of your pants.

Selling fear should be criminal just like yelling fire in a theater. Selling to those with fear? Maybe that's okay.

Humor might cure the doomsayer or their followers, but perhaps taking their money is a quicker cure. Don't be dishonest, just be helpful, entertaining, and expensive.

Don't try to be their psyhologist. Psychology is best left to the psychologist. You also don't have malpractice insurance.

Imagined horrors are the least useful capacity of our human minds. Such imaginings cause stress, irrational behavior, violence, insanity and, of course, organized religion.

Do you want to know how to stop a suicide bomber? Make him laugh at himself, his religion, and his cause.

You Might Want to Know

> *We used the masculine to refer to these terrorists out of convenience — we hate doing the he/she thing. Not that all suicide bombers are men; it's an equal opportunity world. Just that if we used "it" we would be talking about suicide bombing aliens.*

Want to stop a politician from making laws that prevent you from wearing shoes on airplanes? Make him laugh at the idea. Know a wacky cult member? The only way to get him to see the light is to make him laugh at himself.

Follow skeptical etiquette,[75] because you don't want to have people ticked at you. Don't jump in their face and call them stupid. The key is a friendly dialogue. Questions are better than the questioning of their assumptions.

Rolling on the floor laughing is the best cure for doomsayers. Silly beliefs are cured by making people laugh so hard that milk comes squirting out their nose.

You Might Want to Know

> *Don't laugh at people with silly beliefs, as this only gives them more justification for their beliefs. Same goes for suicide bombers who just might press the button for your ill-timed giggling. Laugh with them, not at them.*

I want to say this clearly so there is no mistake:

Humor can stop war, terrorism, cults, and fear of the impossible.

Laughter could save the world. Now it's your turn. Let's add so much humor to the world that it can't be ignored. Imagine a terrorist watching your YouTube video just before he is scheduled to strap on a suicide vest. We want him to realize how backslapping funny it is that he ever believed in such nonsense.

---

[75] http://twistedphysics.typepad.com/cocktail_party_physics/2009/01/skeptic-etiquette.html

Celebrating Chaos and Destruction

Each month at Boys Books we will choose the best of the following categories. We don't care where you host the content, but you need to mention Boys Books and this book with a link to the book's website for a valid entry. Go to http://cluck.com/eotw/ to fill out a form to enter the contest officially.

What's in it for you? Besides a possible Pulitzer Prize, you might also get your submission published in our next book, blog, or video (we are investing in a 3D hologram mind control theater). We can't pay, but we will credit you for your effort by telling the world your name (we will resect your need for anonymity or use your web ID or C.B. handle if you prefer). Nothing better than getting to the end of a book or movie and seeing your name in print. Put it on your resume!

Use your imagination, don't plagiarize, be original and please be silly.

We want to poke fun at the people who are trying to scare us. Take a swipe at these fear mongers, charlatans, politicians, potentates, and the senseless media that will do anything to make a buck or take advantage of true innocents. They have been trying to get us to switch religions, throw away our rights, hide in caves, and generally live looking over our shoulders for supernatural beings.

Don't forget the real terrorists, either. The doomsayers. They are preachers, cult devotees, the media, your mother, and your neighbor. They want to make us so scared that we will just lay down and do whatever they say. Stop living in fear and toss these yahoos into the flaming vats of mayonnaise hell.

One thing is true. We are sheep. Our brains are wired to follow instructions from authorities. Make something seem true and it's true. Fight back with parody. Parody is the only tool we have to fight the evil incarnate sheep herders.

Now your turn. Poking fun at this nonsense. We all win when the doomsayers start squirting milk out their noses.

Here are a few ideas to get you started:

Web Video

We love video! It's how we will document the end of days. Why wait? Start now! Create your video and be a part of documenting the future.

Any video that promotes violence against any person, religion, or race will be ignored. We are looking for good clean fun, great acting, gratuitous special effects, and wicked credits at the end.

Daniel, Jib, and Becky celebrate the apocalypse with a friendly tiger. Note the chain.

Photo and Photo Essay Contest

Writing and video not your cup of arsenic tea? Why not a photo or even a photo essay?

Sorry to use the word essay in a sentence. People are scared silly of the word 'essay' because of draconian English teachers. The word essay worse than torture, demonic possession, dentists, and *Dancing with the Stars*. Probably made you put a little yellow stuff in your pants … unless you read in the porcelain library.

A photo essay is just a story with pictures. See, not so bad. Go clean yourself up. We'll wait.

Best Products for the End-of-the-World Contest

End of the world products is a unique contest. Conceive of products and packaging, and submit a marketing plan. This should not be work, but a labor of love. It's good fun, but you may get recognized by a marketing mogul or entrepreneur!

We recommend summaries because you are never really too sure how close the end is. Strike quickly or miss the last boat to Hell.

Here are a few hints to help your submissions shine:

- ✓ Images of the product and packaging: What does the product look like? How will people see it at Wal-Mart?
- ✓ Marketing plan:
    1. How are you selling your product?
    2. Who is your target customer?
    3. What specific end of the world scenario that best sells your product?
- ✓ Advertising mockups and videos: Be creative!

Artist's Interpretation

We are looking for everything from drawings and paintings to sculptures and performance art. Unless it's small, just take pictures of the big stuff. Send us the small stuff, when it can be mailed without breaking any postal laws.All entries will be considered, none will be returned, even if you do provide return postage.

We may sell the art submitted, minus commission fees, and the balance will go to charity (unless hung on the wall or put to the fire to save on heating costs). We will reserve the right to use images, videos and digital representations of the art for the website, books, and videos. Remember, we have to make a living. We'll give you credit if you say in advance how you want to be credited, otherwise credits will be anonymous.

Guest Appearances

This book was a labor of love, but we need help to make it a real success through old fashioned promotion. We need to be on every TV show, talk show, and podcast. You are our Hollywood, Bollywood, or Dollywood agent. We can't pay you, but we will acknowledge your help.

Daniel Brookshier will represent us during all appearances. He looks a little like Cary Grant, especially from behind and when you squint.

John Stewart, Hear Me Mock

Are you John Stewart's personal assistant, monkey boy, or other lackey? Slip this book to him. Tell him not to read it. That always works. *The Daily Show* will be the best of all marketing to get this book into as many hands as possible for a proper book burning.

You may have guessed, Stewart isn't our first choice. Colbert would be the bee's kneecaps. He did invent "truthiness." We assume that John Stewart's personal assistant, monkey boy, or other lackey is a mole. Being blind and loving dirt, this minion will give our book to Colbert.

Your Radio, Our Doomsaying

What's better than inviting an expert on your radio show? Things are especially scary on the radio. Especially call-in shows, because there are some really wacky people out there with phones.

Call-in radio gets rather fun with the subject is the end of the world. Imagine all the new-agers, fanatic Christians, and Republicans who will call into your show. Most of them will be totally clueless that this is all for fun.

If you do believe in the end of the world, please invite us on your show too. Mock us! We dare you!

Interviews

We love reporters. Not in a carnal way, but we do have a fondness for people that bleed ink. You can't beat[76] the written word.

We'll do any sort of interview with just about anyone. Think we are godless idiots and want to expose us? Cool! Love our humor and want a laugh? You are our people!

Want to be part of the effort to punk the masses with another wacky end of the world author? We are one with the universe!

Why not lure us to a country where what we write is blasphemy? Sorry, no. We avoid those places. We might loose our heads.

Format for Interviews

If you have never interviewed a book writer before, here is a little help on what to do.

Start with asking about what the book is about. This way we get the book plug out of the way really quick.

Ask why we wrote this book and what haunting moments in our childhood caused us to write on such a bizarre subject. Then it's time to have some fun! Here are a few subjects to cover:

- ✓ What is the best dog to own for the zombie apocalypse?
- ✓ How will the Republicans (or Fox News) cause the end of the world?
- ✓ What's the next date predicted by doomsayers for the end of the world?
- ✓ How can you make money from the end of the world?

---

[76] The written word is fast. Writers can sneak up behind you and give you a word wedgie during a game of Scrabble. Cross word attacks happen every week in most newspapers.

- ✓ What are the best religions to join to protect your soul?
- ✓ How do you feel about blasphemy? Any fatwas against you?
- ✓ What are your favorite end-of-the-word scenarios?
- ✓ You seem to have a vendetta against the History Channel. What did they ever do to you?
- ✓ Last question, what will you do when the world ends?

These are just suggestions. Make up your own questions, we are easy.

Legit news organizations with an audience a little bigger than 5 – yes, even CNN – call us! We're happy to do a phone/Skype or other medium for the interview. We'll also meet in person if there is a no-guns-on-premises rule. We'll travel to you after you pay the expenses and an appearance fee.

Tell us about yourself and your audience. We like to know whom we are talking to. This also prevents us from accidentally getting kidnapped or tortured by true believers.

The End of the End of the End

Here is the last Bible quote. It is probably the most true statement in the Bible, even when you are Atheist:

"It is better to take refuge in the LORD than to trust in man." – Psalm 118:8

If Murphy was Christian, this would be Murphy's First Law. Humankind is the problem. We have these big sloppy brains that are geared for survival. Survival skills not going to save you from an electric bus and won't help you separate fact from fiction unless you can work a calculator. All mankind's ability for poetry, art, and old fashioned thinking helps us believe in some really insane nonsense.

You might trust in the Lord (or any god of your choosing), but you can't trust man's imagination one little bit.

Religion is from some guy down the street; in other words, from a member of humankind. Until some god writes the law in fifty-foot stone letters while the world watches, it is a good bet that some fakery, imagination, and mental health issues are involved.

One of our favorite examples of mankind's ability to fool itself was the Halloween radio broadcast of *War of the Worlds*. People who tuned in at the beginning heard a great story of aliens. Those who tuned in late thought that aliens were on their doorstep.If you don't know something fake, its real. Happens all the time to Fox News reporters.

It's easy to believe in the end of the world. We need to be careful not to fall into this very human failing. Best to assume that if it is real, you are already dead. Why worry? Why panic? Just act like nothing is happening and you'll stop that urge to run naked in the streets. That way you won't look like a total idiot when, just like it always has, the world keeps on ticking. The only thing you should fear is Mayonnaise in your potato salad on a hot summer day.

Beware of fake science too. Just because someone claims to have the facts, is not a reason to believe them. Check their prison records or their history of false claims. Are they married to their first cousin and live in a trailer park? Most claims of apocalypse are from nuts and we have a nut allergy.

Yes, the world will end. It may happen today, tomorrow, or in a million years. You will die. Either today, tomorrow, or when you get mentioned in the local paper for reaching the ripe old age of one hundred — unless you get your head frozen like Walt Disney (remember to wear a hat).

Death by natural cause is billions of times more likely than being killed by something that ends the world. It isn't worth your time to think about the end of the world unless you are telling a good joke about a lawyer, a Catholic priest and a Rabi.

The *Boys Book of Armageddon* is about having fun with the end of the world. Spread the word: The end is nigh and it is time to laugh at anyone that says so!

Teachers Guide

As a convenience to teachers, we have published this teachers[77] guide. Here are the three basic principals covered in every chapter:

- ✓ Fear mongering is bad.
- ✓ Proof is in the pudding.
- ✓ Think for yourself.

The answers to the experiment questions are 'yes', except for number 33 which is 'b.' We have not numbered the questions, and they are in a random order to prevent cheating. Teachers should not be worried about cheating. Just remind your students of the eternal punishment available from most religions.

Head to the Boys Books classroom on Google at the following address:

https://sites.google.com/site/boysbookofarmageddon/

The Last Experiment: History Channel Email Campaign

A great amount of doom-based programming is from the History Channel. We don't think it is worthy of an organization that is supposed to be teaching children honest history.

The History Channel has some cool stuff. Presenting everything from dinosaurs to great leaders, they educate their

[77] Be a great teacher and read, *The Myth of Laziness* by Mel Levine M.D.

viewers. Unfortunately the channel plays the fear card to get ratings. The programming certainly isn't history.

Write an email to the History Channel and let them know. Make sure you Cc their advertisers too. Post comments on various social media sites like Twitter (use the Twitter hash tag #boysbooks so we can spot you) and Facebook that are frequented by the advertisers. Send a copy of the email to letters@cluck.com and be sure to go to the book's website to give us permission to publish what you wrote.

Here are a few things to cover: Opinion, hearsay, speculation, hyperbole, and belief are not history. You shouldn't quote scientists out of context. Speculative fiction isn't history. Predicting the future isn't history, even when the historical figure is historical. Nostradamus was a charlatan and a bad poet. When covering founders of churches, the History Channel should be required to include criminal records, infidelities, and outright abuse of power by these church leaders. Until the History Channel has truly discovered and has physical and verifiable evidence for Bigfoot, Nazi UFOs, the Ark of the Covenant, Loch Ness Monster, aliens, proof of ancient aliens (more than rocks and bad art), Atlantis, ghosts, gods, or angels, then they absolutely don't exist.

Request the History Channel to do documentaries on critical thinking, logical inquiry, and fact-based journalism. For good measure, have the History Channel change its name to the Pseudoscience Channel or Fox News.

Questions

- ✓ Do people agree with your opinions of the History Cannel?
- ✓ Are advertisers upset that you are upset?
- ✓ Do crazies that believe in the History Channel respond to your comments?
- ✓ Does your psychologist feel better now that you don't sound as crazy as the History Channel?

The Last Page

Yes, you have reached the end of the end. Don't let that frighten you. There is more to come. Look for the *Boys Book of Pseudoscience*, coming soon!

About the Author

Daniel Brookshier is the founder of Boys Books Publishing who's core principal is: *Making Fun of Making Fun of Everything*™

Daniel Brookshier has never seen an end of the world, but he thinks it would be a hoot.

Does he believe in any one of the endings? When asked, he says, "I'd like to be surprised."

Why write a book like this? Daniel replies, "I have a biblical Old Testament first name. Second, I needed some quick cash for entertainment expenses."

Is the author qualified to write this book? When asked, Daniel's thoughtful response was, "You need a license to write a book?"

This Page Accidentally Left Less Than Blank

19274341R00185

Made in the USA
Lexington, KY
12 December 2012